Object Relations and
Psychothera

Dedication

This book is dedicated to Peggy, Ingegärd and Nils

Object Relations and Integrative Psychotherapy

Tradition and Innovation in Theory and Practice

Edited by

INGER SÄFVESTAD NOLAN M PSYCH SC

and

PATRICK NOLAN CQSW, Dip PSYCHOTHERAPY

W
WHURR PUBLISHERS
LONDON AND PHILADELPHIA

© 2002 Whurr Publishers Ltd
First published 2002
by Whurr Publishers Ltd
19b Compton Terrace, London N1 2UN England and
325 Chestnut Street, Philadelphia PA 19106 USA

Reprinted 2003 and 2005

British Library Cataloguing in Publication Data

A catalogue record for this book
is available from the British Library.

ISBN 1 86156 338 8

Contents

Chapter 13   186

The strengths and limitations of a psychodynamic perspective in
organizational consultancy
  Eric Miller

Chapter 14   199

Tribal processes in psychotherapy: the stand off between
psychoanalytic and systemic schools
  Sebastian Kraemer

Index   215

Acknowledgements

Many people have helped us in bringing this book to completion. We would like to acknowledge the hard work of the contributors in writing their chapters. We wish to say a special thank you to Michael Kearney for his personal support, good advice and the interest he has shown at the various stages of writing this book. There are many other people whose help has been invaluable: Maggie Butler, Michael Nelson, Christopher Simms and Rob Weatherill. We would also like to acknowledge the support of Phil Kearney, Dave O'Brien, Tommy Nilsson, Hjördis Nilsson-Ahlin, and our fellow trainer Catrin Carter for the many stimulating discussions about integrative issues while running training programmes together.

We are grateful to our publishers for their patience and personal support throughout.

Permissions

The kind permission of the following publishers to reproduce material under 'fair dealing' arrangements is gratefully acknowledged:

1. A much revised version of 'What Narrative?' published in Renos Papadopoulos and John Byng-Hall (eds) (1997) *Multiple Voices – A Richer Story: Contributions to Systemic Family Psychotherapy from the Tavistock Clinic*. London: Duckworth. Reproduced with permission.
2 Figure 5.1: A. Ryle (ed.) (1995) *Cognitive Analytic Therapy; Developments in Theory and Practice*. Chichester, J. Wiley & Sons. Reproduced with permission.

List of contributors

Editors

Inger Säfvestad Nolan, M Psych Sc, has been working for the last 14 years as a psychotherapist, supervisor and teacher at the Irish Institute for Integrated Psychotherapy in Dublin. She has worked for over 30 years in Sweden and Ireland as a psychologist with consultancy, family therapy, individual counselling and psychotherapy. She is certified in clinical psychology, and as a psychotherapist. She has written articles about children starting nursery school, dreams and about art in psychotherapy.

Patrick Nolan, CQSW, Dip Psychotherapy, has trained in integrative and body oriented psychotherapy, psychosynthesis and psychoanalytic psychotherapy and is currently completing an MSc in Psychotherapy at University College Dublin. Following a career in social work, he has worked as a psychotherapist supervisor and trainer for over twenty years. He is certified as a psychotherapist. He has written about integrative psychotherapy, and about the body in psychotherapy.

Contributors

Fierman Bennink-Bolt, LLB, MSocSc (psychotherapy), was a member of the Legal Service of the European Commission in Brussels. He then worked in the Jellinek Clinic in Amsterdam. He currently works as a CAT therapist, supervisor and trainer in Ireland and the UK.

Margareta Brodén, PhD, is a psychotherapist and clinical psychologist. She has been a pioneer in Scandinavia in developing a treatment model for early intervention in the mother–infant relationship, at Viktoriagården in Malmö, Sweden. This model is described in her first book *Mother and Child in No-Man's Land*.

Jane Gooen-Piels, PhD, received her PhD in Clinical Psychology from Adelphi University. She is a Research Fellow at Memorial Sloan-Kettering Cancer Centre.

Mavis Henley, BSc (Soc), PGCE, Dip Ed, Dip Alcohol Studies, Dip in Group Psychotherapy, has a postgraduate diploma in alcohol studies and has worked with people with alcohol problems for many years. She trained in group analytic psychotherapy at the University of Sheffield and is registered with the UKCP.

Sebastian Kraemer, FRCP, FRCPsych, has been a Consultant Child and Adolescent Psychiatrist at the Tavistock Clinic and at the Whittington Hospital, London since 1980. His principal interests and publications are in parent and family therapy, paediatric liaison, the training of child and adolescent psychiatrists, the origins and roles of fatherhood and the fragility of the developing male.

Mikael Leiman, PhD, Docent, University of Joensuu, Finland, has a special interest in activity theory and in the semiotic understanding of the psychotherapy process. He is also a practising psychotherapist and trainer in Cognitive Analytic Therapy. He is the author of several books and articles, most recently in the areas of semiotic mediation in early development and in psychotherapeutic discourse.

Gertrud Mander, PhD (Berlin), FPC, UKCP, Fellow of BACP, is a long-time supervisor and trainer for the Westminster Pastoral Foundation, London. She is a former Course Organiser of the WPF Diploma in Psychodynamic Supervision, and is in private practice as a psychoanalytic psychotherapist and supervisor. She is the author of many papers on supervision and psychotherapy, and of *A Psychodynamic Approach to Brief Therapy*. She is a translator of John Bowlby (into German) and George Groddeck (into English).

Deirdre Mannion, BA, M Psych Sc, Dip Integrated Psychotherapy, is an integrative psychotherapist, currently maintaining a private practice in Dublin. She has over 20 years experience in training psychotherapists and other related disciplines to work therapeutically with sexual abuse issues. She is the author of several articles and co-author of *Surviving Sexual Abuse*.

Eric Miller, MA, PhD, Dip Ed (Hon), joined the Tavistock Institute, London in 1958 (Director, Group Relations Programme, 1969–97. Core Faculty, Advanced Organisational Consultation Programme). His main field was organizational research and consultancy, combining systemic and psychodynamic perspectives, and he worked with a wide variety of organizations in the United Kingdom and internationally. He published widely in the area of organizational consultancy over the last forty years.

Lennart Ramberg, MD, is a child and adolescent psychiatrist, psychoanalyst, family therapist and body oriented psychotherapist. He has a private practice in Stockholm, where he is a teacher and supervisor. He is a training analyst in the Swedish Psychoanalytic Association and a member of the board of the Swedish institute for body oriented psychotherapy. He

has published several books and articles in the area of personality development, individuation and 'the symbolizing self'.

Hilde Rapp, MA Oxon, BA Hons, Dip Ed, Dip Psych, Dip Supervis, is chair of
the Counselling and Psychotherapy Central Awarding Body, chair of the
Training Standards Committee of the Universities Psychotherapy and
Counselling Association. She is a consultant in training, psychotherapy,
supervision and organizational development. She is also a writer and
lecturer.

Anthony Ryle, DM FRC Psych, qualified in 1949 and worked in general
practice, in the University Health Service and as a consultant psychotherapist in the National Health Service. His development of CAT over the past
25 years is documented in numerous papers and four books. He is a Senior
Research Fellow (Kings College London) and Hon. Consultant
Psychotherapist at Guy's Hospital, London.

Paul Sepping, MD, FRCPsych, BA (Hons), BSc (Hons) is a group analyst and
consultant child psychiatrist, recently retired from public practice, who is
completing a PhD on storytelling in the analytical psychotherapies at the
Dept of Psychoanalytic Studies, University of Essex. He has written about
narrative and interpretation.

William B. Stiles, PhD (UCLA), is a professor of Psychology at Miami
University in Oxford, Ohio, USA. He is the author of *Describing Talk: A
Taxonomy of Verbal Response Modes*, Past President of the Society for
Psychotherapy Research, and currently North American Editor of the
journal *Psychotherapy Research*.

George Stricker, PhD, is Distinguished Research Professor of Psychology in
the Derner Institute, Adelphi University. He received a PhD in Clinical
Psychology at the University of Rochester and an honorary PsyD from the
Illinois School of Professional Psychology, Meadows Campus. He has
published widely, most recently in the area of psychotherapy integration,
and *Scientific Practice of Professional Psychology*.

Arlene Vetere, PhD, Dip Clin Psychol, AFBPsS, AcSS, works in The Tavistock
Centre, London and University of East London. She is a principal lecturer
and organizing tutor on the Doctorate in Systemic Psychotherapy,
Tavistock Centre and UEL. She is a Chartered Consultant Clinical
Psychologist and a Family Therapist registered with UKCP. She has
published books and articles in the area of family therapy, and presented
numerous papers at conferences.

Björn Wrangsjö, MD, PhD, is a child and adolescent psychiatrist, psychoanalyst, family therapist and body oriented psychotherapist. He is a member
of the board of the Swedish institute for body oriented psychotherapy
(Downing) and the director of the Institute for training in child and
adolescent psychiatry in Stockholm. He has edited and written several
books and articles in the area of clinical psychology and psychotherapy.

CHAPTER 1

Tradition and innovation in theory and practice: an orientation

INGER SÄFVESTAD-NOLAN AND PATRICK NOLAN

The value and truth of ideas is dependent on the context from which they emerge. Over the last hundred years innovations within psychotherapy have been based on existing ideas and traditional practices, as the profession has moved through recurring periods of challenge and change.

This book explores how an object relations-integrative perspective may combine in-depth psychodynamic principles and theories with the flexibility afforded by an integrative framework. Object relations theory is rooted in a psychoanalytic tradition which views the individual as essentially social and holds that their need for others is primary. Integrative psychotherapy attempts to combine the theories and/or techniques of two or more therapeutic approaches.

We believe that this volume will be useful for graduates, undergraduates and trainee psychotherapists as well as social workers, psychologists, psychotherapists and counsellors who are interested in broadening their understanding of different therapeutic approaches and integrative endeavours.

The contributors to this book consist of an international group of practitioners and theoreticians who draw on the knowledge of object relations and other therapeutic orientations as well as innovations of the integrative movement. Some of the contributors grapple directly with integrative questions, while others examine ways of working with specific client groups or methods, where integrative ideas enrich their work.

The first six chapters present historical and theoretical perspectives on object relations and integrative psychotherapy. They also examine some of the methodological issues and dilemmas involved in attempting to integrate different therapeutic approaches. Outcomes from current research about the effectiveness of psychotherapy together with findings and implications for psychotherapy of infant research are examined.

Chapters 7–11 contain a cross-section of clinical applications with particular themes in relation to different client groups, methods and theoretical orientations. In the final three chapters the perspective is broadened to include supervision and organizational work, concluding with a discussion of the human and historical factors which may militate against integrative efforts.

We will now describe some of the broad overarching themes, which are woven throughout the different sections of this book.

An object relations-integrative model of psychotherapy

As editors our primary orientation is towards the psychoanalytic and object relations tradition. However, given that there are no fixed truths in the relatively young field of psychotherapy, we place a value on dialogue and openness to learning from other therapeutic perspectives. We believe that fixed ideological positions can limit the creativity of practitioners as illustrated by Casement's statement that 'Dogmatic certainty will always constrict an analyst's capacity to think imaginatively about the patient' (Casement, 1990, p. 6).

Object relations theorists believe that the basic structure of a person's internal world is to a great extent formed within the first few years of life and is created through relating. The person's need to relate to others is placed at the centre of what it is to be human. Thus, the relationship, with its internal and external aspects is the central factor in both the theory and practice of psychotherapy.

Models of integrative psychotherapy are based on the assumption that no one form of psychotherapy is adequate for all clients or clinical situations. These models look for integrative and common factors, which transcend different orientations. This is done in an attempt to provide a more comprehensive understanding of the client, and to draw on a wide range of methods, therapeutic stances and ways of relating to work with the particular client. George Stricker and Jane Gooen-Piels (Chapter 3) present four levels of psychotherapy integration, which include theoretical integration, integrating 'common factors', technical eclecticism and assimilative integration. Assimilative integration is an overarching model, as it includes elements of the other three levels. The object relations-integrative approach espoused by the editors corresponds to this type of model.

Patrick Nolan (Chapter 2) outlines an object relations-integrative approach, which attempts to recognize the uniqueness of each client. He gives a brief history of, and outlines some of the central concepts of, object relations theory and practice. Through examining therapeutic concepts such as 'potential space', 'the therapeutic relationship', 'the organic nature of therapy', assessment and frames, he raises comparative and integrative questions to show how different approaches can be enriched by and can learn from each other.

Based on their thorough investigation of research methods and findings, Stricker and Gooen-Piels propose that the therapeutic relationship is a more important factor for therapeutic success than either methods or theories. They report current research findings, which support the strategy of combining cognitive, behavioural and object relation therapies, depending on what therapeutic style or frame the client is most able to use at a particular point in their life.

A solid theoretical base: sources of knowledge and conceptual clarity

The vocabulary of a given school of psychotherapy, and the way in which a person's problems are described theoretically as well as clinically, expresses a particular view of human beings. This view is sometimes linked to the socio-cultural context from which a term originates. For example, psychodynamic therapists have been criticized for describing clients by inferred qualities derived from a pathological realm of knowledge.

Margareta Brodén (Chapter 6) challenges the idea of describing a normal infant in psychiatric terms, and discusses 'the theoretical child' as opposed to 'the observed child'. She investigates this by outlining a historical overview of how 'the body of knowledge', in relation to understanding infant development, has evolved since Freud.

Hilde Rapp (Chapter 4) demonstrates how this dilemma of sources of knowledge can be examined through a conceptual analysis, including a historical account of background concepts. She highlights the importance of using relevant populations for underpinning a theory, by analysing aspects of Klein's theory of human development. Apart from this, Rapp presents examples of conceptual analysis through examining different uses of the term 'internalization', as well as exploring the elements of the concept 'projective identification'.

When integrating different theories, it is necessary to pay close attention to the description and definition of concepts. In this regard, Mikael Leiman and William Stiles (Chapter 5) examine the compatibility between descriptions of certain therapeutic concepts in more depth. They argue that problems and dilemmas, which are expressed in a dialogic form, highlighting the relational aspect of behaviour, may not be compatible with descriptions in terms of a sequence of behaviours. The latter lacks the relational aspect taking one person, rather than two, into account. They discuss these issues using the Cognitive Analytic Therapy (CAT) model as an example, supported by the theory of 'tool-mediated activity' proposed by Bakhtin and Vygotsky.

Basic assumptions about development

The assumptions and belief systems of practitioners inform their practice and their view of a client's capacity to change. Whatever the therapeutic approach, we believe that any in-depth therapeutic model requires a relational perspective as well as a solid developmental theory. This is based on our assumption that the individual has both an innate sense of self and an inborn need to relate.

Brodén outlines the current view of development based on contemporary infant research. These findings highlight that the child is more active and has more social competence than was previously thought. The newborn baby has an innate capacity to try to influence their carers to respond adequately, and has proven to be able to differentiate perceptually between 'self' and 'other'. Brodén outlines some of the implications, which she considers such findings have for the practice of psychotherapy and concludes that the emotionally charged authentic meeting between therapist and client is the central factor in therapy.

An integrative-object relations perspective on clinical themes: interpretations, frames and therapeutic 'holding'

Working therapeutically on a symbolic level by using narratives is practised in different models of psychotherapy. The value of an object relations understanding of narratives is illustrated through Paul Sepping's (Chapter 7) account of long-term work with children. He discusses how his young clients use the transference to the therapeutic setting and the therapist as an 'object' from his past. Sometimes Sepping offers a possible meaning for the narrative, in relation to the child's family situation, while at other times he keeps the therapeutic work on the symbolic level.

Thus, Sepping's chapter raises the issue of whether interpretations are always necessary in working with children. This touches on questions faced by every psychotherapist in relation to how cure or healing happens. As editors, we hold that the use of interpretations as with other therapeutic methods depends on the particular clinical situation.

Lennart Ramberg and Björn Wrangsjö (Chapter 11) refer to current brain research, which explains and confirms the notion of the body–mind unity. From this perspective, empathy is seen as being based on a person's capacity research as well as from the increasing body of knowledge from modern philosophical, socio-cultural, medical and other scientific perspectives.

References

Beutler LE, Mahoney MJ, Norcross JC et al. (1987) Training integrative/eclectic psychotherapists. Journal of Integrative and Eclectic Psychotherapy 11.
Casement P (1990) Further Learning from the Patient. London: Routledge.

CHAPTER 2

Object relations as a context for an integrative approach to psychotherapy

PATRICK NOLAN

> It is not possible to be original except on the basis of tradition ... the interplay
> between originality and the acceptance of tradition as the basis for inventiveness
> seems to me to be just one more example, and a very exciting one, of the interplay
> between separateness and union. (Winnicott, 1971, p. 117)

Each person and every therapeutic journey is unique. This means that
although theories are essential to practice, no theoretical construct can fully
capture the mystery of the person or the essence of psychotherapy. Clinical
practice does not fit neatly with theoretical orthodoxy, so whatever the
training and orientation of a therapist may be, each psychotherapy is
different. Moreover, each moment of therapy involves a distinct human
encounter between the particular client and therapist so its nature and direction cannot be fully predicted.

Bearing this in mind, I will describe how a flexible object relations
perspective may be used as a context for an integrative approach. My interest
in this integrative model has developed through training in humanistic,
integrative and psychoanalytic psychotherapy and through my work as a
psychotherapist, supervisor and trainer over the last 20 years. I believe that
the flexibility afforded through combining the in-depth knowledge of object
relations with the wide-ranging perspective of an integrative approach
enhances the possibility of matching the treatment to the particular client.

I will begin by outlining a brief history and some concepts of object
relations. This will be followed by exploring some aspects of psychotherapy
where a crossfertilization between different schools may be considered.

Freud and the evolution of object relations theory

Object relations theory stemmed from Freud's (1961) idea that the ego and
the superego were formed through object relations, which are internalized.[1]

8

His understanding of object relations remained within both an instinctual and a 'one-person' intrapersonal framework rather than an interpersonal or 'two-person' psychology. For Freud, the word 'object' referred to the target at which a drive is aimed for instinctual satisfaction. The object relations theorists have kept this impersonal term even though its meaning has changed as a more interpersonal understanding of psychoanalysis has developed.

Freud emphasized the progressive emergence of instinctual energies in bodily zones such as the mouth, the anus and the genitals and viewed the oedipal stage as being central. He also argued that human beings were primarily pleasure-seeking and that innate biological drives shaped the personality.

Despite the perception of Freud as being detached and intellectual in his clinical work, he had at times a flexible and personal way of engaging with his patients. Alix Strachey recounted how, during her analysis with Freud, he had after a significant interpretation fetched a cigar saying 'such insights need celebrating' (Khan, 1973, p. 370). Also, he seemed to adopt an open attitude both to the therapeutic stance and to technique: 'I do not venture to deny that another physician differently constituted, might find himself driven to adopt a different attitude' (Freud, 1958a, p. 111). Later, he went on to add, 'I think I am well advised to call these rules recommendations and not to claim any unconditional acceptance for them' (Freud, 1958b, p. 123). He accepted that technique would in time have to be 'modified in certain ways' (Freud, 1957, p. 145). In contrast to this picture of Freud, many of his more ardent followers were more dogmatic.

Ferenczi's view of psychoanalysis as a social phenomenon

Sandor Ferenczi,[2] one of Freud's closest colleagues, could be regarded as being the father of object relations. He viewed psychoanalysis as a 'social phenomenon' in which environmental as well as intrapsychic factors were regarded as important (Ferenczi, 1980a). He highlighted the importance of the mother–child relationship and the traumatic effect of maternal deprivation.

Apart from reframing psychoanalysis within a more interpersonal context, Ferenczi was a clinical innovator. He found that the classical way of working outlined by Freud was ineffective with many patients. In spite of compliance with the 'fundamental rule of free association'[3] suggested by Freud and in spite of deep insights into unconscious complexes, many patients could not get beyond 'dead points' in the analysis (ibid., p. 102). Because of this, he experimented with psychoanalytic technique. In recommending a more empathic, active, interpersonal and responsive therapeutic approach, he heralded a two-person psychology. It was around 1918 that he developed his 'active technique' (1980a), in which he experimented with different methods. For example, while working with a hysterical patient, he suggested that she lie without crossing her legs. This led to intense physical and emotional reactions resulting in her being able to recall repressed memories and some important traumatic reasons for her illness (ibid., pp.189–97).

Following the tradition of Ferenczi, object relations[4] theories evolved in Britain in the 1940s through the work of Fairbairn, Klein, Winnicott and their followers and has been one of the more radical innovations within the psychoanalytic movement.

The relationship as a central factor in object relations theory

Object relations theories emphasize the first three years of life, 'the pre-oedipal period', in which satisfying early human relationships pave the way for optimal development both physically and psychologically. The internal objects are formed through experiences with significant persons and situations. Object relationships refer to both internal and external aspects of the person, which affect each other. This point is articulated well by Mitchell: 'the interpersonal and the intrapsychic realms create, interpenetrate and transform each other in a subtle and complex manner' (Mitchell, 1988, p. 99).

Object relations theorists like Ferenczi, place more emphasis on social and environmental influences. In contrast to Freud, they hold that the relationship, rather than biological drives, is the central factor in human development.

Fairbairn maintained that the 'libido is essentially object-seeking', and that people were primarily driven to establish satisfactory relationships rather than being primarily pleasure-seeking (Fairbairn, 1986, p. 82). He was the first object relations theorist to challenge Freud's drive theory in a fundamental way.[5] So, if the self is essentially social, it follows that not only do relationships make us human, but it is through relating that we are motivated, develop, mature, and derive meaning in life.

From an object relations perspective, personality formation and the development of the self are related primarily to the child's experience in relationship with his or her mother.[6] Fairbairn suggests that the child needs to be 'treated as a person in his own right', to feel loved and to feel that 'his love and his need to relate is accepted' by his mother (ibid., p. 17). Winnicott (1965) suggests that the parent's role is to provide a 'facilitating environment' in which the 'good-enough mother', through her empathy and intuition, does not impinge but adapts and responds sufficiently to the child to facilitate the growth of the infant by making herself available as a 'usable object'. In this way, the environment can both respond to and allow for the individuality and capacities of each person, enabling him or her to grow and progress.

Progression towards mature dependence

The development of the child is seen as beginning in total dependence and being based on a secure attachment (Bowlby, 1969) to the parent as the infant progresses towards mature dependence (Fairbairn, 1986; Winnicott, 1990). The self develops through stages based on changing relationship needs. Winnicott's (1987) term 'transitional phenomena' refers to objects such as rags, blankets or the cooing sound which the child uses in managing its fears in the process of separating from its mother. Transitional objects open up the world of play for the child. He called the intermediate world between the inner and outer realities where play takes place 'potential space' (ibid.).

Transitional objects provide security as the child moves from an experience of omnipotence in the phase of absolute dependence, towards the phase of relative dependence in which the child begins to see its mother as separate and develops a greater capacity to tolerate frustration. This period of parental 'de-adapting' normally involves a good-natured dethroning of the child. Thus, it is necessary that the mother gradually 'fails' in relation to the level of caring that she provides (Winnicott, 1989). This disillusionment or loss of paradise corresponds to Freud's (1964) 'reality principle' or Lacan's (1977) 'paternal metaphor' in which the child accommodates to the reality of limits and rules and to the fact of other people existing in the external world.

Mahler (Mahler, Pine and Bergman, 1975) and object relations theorists such as Winnicott believed that the infant progresses from a state of symbiosis or fusion towards a differentiated state which acknowledges the separateness of the other.

Anxiety and the development of defence mechanisms and symptoms

Object relations therapy tries to address the primitive anxieties which form the underbelly of all defence mechanisms, neurotic and psychotic symptoms and psychosomatic illnesses. Rycroft (1995, p. 8) defines anxiety as 'the response to some as yet unrecognised factor, either in the environment or by the stirrings of unconscious, repressed forces in the self'. Bowlby (1969) described the phases of 'protest, despair and detachment' in relation to the child's anxiety at being separated from its mother. Winnicott (1990) believed that all psychopathology springs from an inadequate facilitating environment, which arrests the maturational process of the child and can lead to the development of a 'false self'. He believed that these early traumas related to 'impingements from the environment', when the child is in a stage of absolute dependence (Winnicott, 1987). Winnicott (1990) described the infant's experience of 'unthinkable anxieties'. These 'primitive agonies' can be experienced internally as going to pieces, falling apart, falling forever, having no relation to the body, having no orientation and experiencing complete isolation because there is no means of communication.

Fairbairn (1986) proposed that the most basic wound for the child is not to feel loved or not to have his or her love accepted. Bollas (1989) suggests that all pathology is an expression of some block in the inborn need to elaborate the self. Because of environmental failures,[7] as well as innate dispositions, the child's progress towards maturity will be interrupted or frozen and he or she will defend himself or herself in different ways.

Klein (1930) wrote of the infant's sadistic fantasies towards its mother and described primitive anxieties evoked by the child's dread of its mother's retaliation. This fear may lead to projective identification (see below) and to psychotic and paranoid processes, resulting in defence mechanisms such as splitting of people or objects into extremes of 'entirely good' or 'entirely bad'.

Bion (1962, 1970) described how the infant projects its 'unthinkable anxieties' into the mother. If all goes well, she can, in a state of calm receptiveness which he called 'reverie', take in the infant's feelings and terrors and give them meaning, thus providing the child with the bedrock for thinking. If the mother is unable to 'contain' and 'detoxify' these experiences, and even punishes the child for expressing distress, the infant may be left with a feeling of 'nameless dread'.

Picking up on these primitive pre-verbal feelings forms a major part of the countertransference work. Ogden describes projective identification as a process 'in which feeling states corresponding to the unconscious fantasies of one person (the projector) are engendered in and processed by another person (the recipient), that is, the way in which one person makes use of another person to experience and contain aspects of himself' (1982, p. 1).

Clients may only be able to let the therapist know about their unmanageable experience in a non-verbal way. One example is of Frank, a client who was tormented by primitive levels of anxiety. He experienced even short silences in therapy as persecutory, which resulted in an unbearable level of tension and anxiety in the therapy room. While in this state, he often blamed and rejected me. The impact of these encounters forced me to experience in a raw and direct way the unbearable hopelessness and fear which he had to endure, when he was regularly criticized and dumped on by his mother. It was essential that I was able to handle these difficult episodes in a mindful and receptive way, which helped him to understand rather than add to the distress of his original traumatic experiences.

From an object relations perspective, the therapeutic setting is intended to provide adequate holding and support to allow the individual to regress sufficiently to experience the deeper traumas and anxieties described above. Winnicott (1987) views this kind of regression as a healing process, which enables the person to progress and mature.

Part of the task of psychotherapy is to help clients to regulate their experiences and develop flexible ways of defending themselves. This capacity for self-regulation is necessary to be able to deal with the stresses of life and to function in relationships. If a person is unable to defend him or herself against anxiety in a balanced way, the person may be flooded by raw and intense feelings (mostly unconscious) and this may, in extreme cases, lead to psychotic episodes, depression or suicide and psychosomatic symptoms (Nolan, 1993).

The capable and relating infant striving towards maturity and self-realization

The picture painted by contemporary infant research is of an alive, vibrant infant who is actively engaged in a mutual relationship with its mother from the start (Stern, 1985). The child is born with a sense of self and a range of affects and capacities which mature rapidly (Tomkins, 1962, 1963), as well as being other-oriented from birth. Innate motor, perceptive and affective patterns of the baby are seen as being more holistic (see Brodén, Chapter 6 of this volume) than had previously been understood.

These findings seem to concur with Winnicott's notion that the infant has an innate programming for a maturation process and a striving towards self-realization. Bollas calls this tendency an urge to articulate the true self or to elaborate the potential of the personality, which he calls the 'destiny drive' (Bollas, 1989). The findings also endorse the attachment theories of Bowlby, as well as Fairbairn's assertion that the child seeks relationships from the beginning.

The infant research referred to by Brodén (Chapter 6 of this book) refutes Mahler's view of symbiosis as well as the notion of absolute dependence, and instead asserts that the infant relates to another person as different to them from the beginning.

The task of the parent is to be sensitive enough to the cues of the child to be able to respond to its needs. This picture of the mother and infant being engrossed in a mutual and evolving participation in which they tune into each other seems to correspond to an intersubjective (see below) approach to psychotherapy. Unlike the interpersonal schools,[8] the model which I advocate combines an interpersonal approach to psychotherapy with an emphasis on intrapsychic and developmental aspects of clients.

Through examining different therapeutic concepts, I will now proceed to raise some comparative and integrative questions about the value of linking object relations with other therapeutic approaches.

Object relations and other therapeutic approaches – an integrative endeavour

Object relations can, despite significant differences from other approaches, be compatible with most other therapies and can be used within different therapeutic contexts, if applied with a flexible and non-dogmatic attitude. Already object relations has been used together with family therapy (Slipp, 1988), couple and brief therapy (Savege Scharff and Scharff, 1998), interpersonal psychoanalysis (Mitchell, 1988), self psychology (St Clair, 1986), group dynamics (Bion, 1961) and work within the medical profession (Balint, 1954), to name but a few.

For over fifty years, there has been a tradition of attempting to integrate behavioural and psychoanalytic theories (Arkowitz and Messer, 1984; Dollard and Miller, 1950; Wachtel, 1977). This integrative tradition, while maintaining a cognitive bias, broadened in the 1980s (SEPI)[9] to include a wider group of psychotherapeutic approaches such as systemic and existential approaches. The human potential movement, which began in America in the 1960s, is another distinct integrative tradition. This approach draws from such diverse streams of thought as Maslow's (1971) idea of 'self actualization'; existential philosophy; Rogers's (1951) 'person-centred approach'; Reich's emphasis on the body; mysticism; Lewin's group dynamics; neo-Freudian and Jungian analysis.

In proposing an integrative approach, Norcross (Norcross and Arkowitz, 1992) argues that no one theory has a monopoly on truth and that no one approach is clinically adequate for all problems, patients and situations. There are several models of eclectic and integrative psychotherapies, which look for the integrative and common factors that transcend different orientations (Stricker, Chapter 3 in this volume).

In practice, many psychotherapists draw from and are influenced by a variety of therapeutic orientations in working with their clients. I believe that any serious attempt at integration should build on a common and compatible ground in relation to the philosophy, values, theory, strategies and techniques of the different approaches.

Each therapist will approach the question of integrating theories or techniques in their own individual way. However, in my opinion practitioners could integrate in a more solid, less haphazard and chaotic manner by bearing the following elements in mind in any integrative endeavour: the primacy of the therapeutic relationship and the intersubjective nature of psychotherapy; the organic nature of therapy and the importance of following the client; the importance of assessment, the therapeutic frames, the therapeutic setting and the therapeutic space; a developmental and intrapsychic understanding of clients; clarity in relation to varying one's stance as a therapist.

I will now outline an object relations-integrative approach, which includes the above elements. Attending to and developing these factors would, I believe, add a more reflective, meaningful and in-depth relational perspective to any therapeutic approach.

Assessment – the fit between therapeutic practice and clients

The question of assessment and particularly that of diagnosing clients reveals important differences between schools of psychotherapy. Psychoanalytic models consider that a clear assessment period is essential and some psychoanalytic approaches use the DSM IV[10] psychiatric categories in diagnosing patients. In contrast, humanistic and existential approaches tend to resist any kind of formal diagnosis in a wish to avoid a reductive labelling which they would view as being dehumanizing. Despite this, I believe that in practice these approaches also use diagnostic categories, even if this is done in a more descriptive way. For instance, gestalt therapy (Perls et al., 1974) outlines people's ways of interrupting contact through projection, introjection, retroflection and confluence.

Although assessment is ongoing, it is particularly important in the initial stage of therapy. Based on information gleaned from the client's life as well as from one's experience of the person in the room, experienced therapists can arrive at informed hunches as to whether the person is suited to therapy and whether there is a sufficient fit between the therapist and client. Practitioners can also ascertain what approach and level of therapy may be appropriate.

An assessment interview may indicate that the client may be more suited to the non-intrusive, receptive and more aloof atmosphere of a psychoanalytic approach. This may offer a deeper quality of holding, listening and recognition, enabling the person to talk in a more uninhibited and meaningful way. On the other hand, a client whose parents were constantly depressed or absent, may experience the 'privation' or lack of responsiveness of a psychoanalytic way of working as an intolerable abandonment, and may need a more engaging and interactive form of therapy.

Clients with a psychiatric history, or who may be suicidal or psychologically fragile (see case vignette of John below), may require a supportive or ego-building type of therapy as they may be unable to tolerate the anxiety evoked by a more in-depth approach.

By paying close attention to the client, through self-examination and with the support of supervision, the therapist continually assesses the changing needs of each client. Some clients may need different therapeutic approaches at different stages in their life or within a particular therapy. For example, a client in crisis with a debilitating depression may initially only be ready for a short-term goal-oriented therapy. At a later stage she or he may be willing to enter a long-term therapy to look at deeper and more complex issues. Another client may need to be listened to in a climate of safety in the earlier stages of therapy. As he or she develops a stronger sense of self and is able to trust more, their tolerance for a more active involvement from the therapist may increase. This more active stance may involve more confronting inter-pretations within a psychoanalytic psychotherapy, or more active interven-tions in a body-oriented psychotherapy. This is illustrated in my work with John.

> John was a 28-year-old man from a family in which both his mother and father were alcoholic and depressed. Throughout his childhood, his parents were regularly committed to psychiatric hospital. During these periods, John and his siblings were either fostered or put in care. The recurring episodes of abandon-ment, chaos and lack of safety left him with a deep sense of insecurity, terror, anxiety and paranoia. Like his parents, he was depressed and was plagued by psychosomatic symptoms. In the early stages of therapy, I tried to provide a safe non-intrusive atmosphere to help him to contain and tolerate his pervasive sense of terror. In the second year of therapy, as his trust in me deepened, it became possible for him to begin to recall, experience and share the traumas, which he had lived through in his childhood. Gradually, I was able to work more actively on a verbal level with these fears, as they were re-experienced in the relationship with me. During this period it was possible for me to offer more robust interpreta-tions which led to significant insights. At a later stage, as John developed a stronger sense of himself, it was possible to work with more active techniques. For example, attending to the body through breathing, movement, particular body tensions and embodied images helped to further deepen his sense of trust in me. This focus also helped John to both access a deeper level of experience within as well as developing a stronger sense of himself both within the therapeutic relation-ship and in the world outside.

The initial assessment revealed John's fragility and pointed to the need to start with a predominantly listening and containing approach. The ongoing assessment highlighted how John's internal psychological flexibility and strength increased as the therapy progressed. The work with John illustrates my attempt to create sufficient space for him to form the therapeutic relation-ship, which he needed. In principle, the therapist's ability to maintain such a holding environment provides a sense of safety which enables the client to face and struggle with their deeper desires, memories, fears, fantasies and anxieties.

The concepts of 'potential space' and 'intersubjectivity'

I will now briefly outline Winnicott's concept of 'potential space' and examine how it has been developed in Ogden's notion of intersubjectivity (Winnicott, 1975; Ogden 1982). Linked to his concept of transitional phenomena described earlier, Winnicott's potential space refers to the intermediate experiencing which lies between fantasy and reality, and includes the areas of play and creativity as well as social and cultural experience. The therapeutic space is a specific example of potential space, unique because the work is aimed at enhancing its potential for insight, healing and development.

For Winnicott, play was an essential aspect of psychotherapy which he viewed as being done in 'the overlap of two play areas, that of the patient and that of the therapist. If the therapist cannot play, then he is not suitable for the work. If the patient cannot play, then something needs to be done to enable the patient to become able to play, after which psychotherapy may begin' (Winnicott, 1971, p. 63).

The concept of 'potential space' has many similarities to Ainsworth et al.'s (1978) notion of the child's experience of a 'secure base', which develops within the first few years of life. When the child is securely attached to a parent, the sense of having a secure base from which he or she can explore and play confidently will develop. This stimulates curiosity and playfulness, which the child uses in learning about the world. Ainsworth et al. found that children play less if they are insecurely attached to their parents.

Winnicott (1971) recommends that the therapist should avoid imposing meaning prematurely on the therapeutic or potential space. Rather, it should be 'formless', so that clients may through creative play fill it with their own personal tone, shape, colour and emotions and so come to make their own personal meaning of it.

In this sense, the therapeutic setting is used to create an emotional and psychological space within both the therapist and the client as well as between them. In this way, clients can use the therapeutic setting, the person of the therapist and the various interventions in relation to the past, the present and the future to explore their potential and their capacities in an effort to forge new ways of being, relating and meaning.

This intersubjective space or field between the therapist and client corresponds to Ogden's (1994) 'analytic third' and to Freud's (1958a) 'evenly suspended attention' in which the therapist suspends 'his personal inclinations, prejudices and theoretical assumptions' (Laplanche and Pontalis, 1988, p. 43). It has also much in common with Winnicott's (1987) 'primary maternal preoccupation', in which the mother has a heightened sense of attunement and sensitivity to her baby, and with Bion's 'reverie'.

The intersubjective field includes the combined interplay of the subjectivities of the client and the therapist. It is an invisible yet palpable field between the therapist and the client, which is continuously changing throughout the course of the therapy.

Ogden's description of the analytic third (1994) highlights the particular quality of each therapist and client in a dynamic field, which is both separate from them yet uniquely formed within their intersubjective milieu. The third is a creation of the analyst and analysand, while at the same time the analysand and the analyst are created by the analytic third. Following Winnicott's assertion that 'there is no such thing as an infant', Ogden wrote that 'there is no such thing as an analysand apart from the relationship with the analyst, and no such thing as an analyst apart from the relationship with the analysand' (p. 63).

The organic nature of therapy

Psychotherapy, and particularly the longer term,[11] in-depth approaches can be viewed as an attempt to facilitate an organic process. This means trusting that in the right therapeutic climate clients will change. This may involve a client's significant insights, or an ability to act differently in the outside world, or perhaps feeling more reconciled in relation to the death of a parent. Thus, like a wise midwife, the therapist can create the context and conditions for progress but will not try to make it happen before the client is ready. This involves an attitude of being receptive, attuning, and waiting in a state of creative ignorance. Such waiting for an as yet unknown, unarticulated, background level of the therapeutic situation means being able to tolerate the tension between the known and the unknown (Bion, 1975). This requires an ability to allow the patient to be separate, alone and unknown to the therapist.

Bion (1967) recommends that therapists should learn to work without letting memory, desire or understanding intrude too much. This state of reverie implies putting aside theories as one is affected by, and attempting to understand, one's clients. It involves a mental state akin to an 'act of faith' (Bion, 1967) as one keeps one's mind open to receive an accurate understanding of the dynamic in the therapeutic relationship. This understanding is not just 'knowing about', but involves a deeper sense of struggling, living and being the psychic reality.

These ideas of Bion's are echoed in Bollas's (1987) notion of the 'unthought known'. This is 'a form of knowledge that has not yet been mentally realised, it has not become known via dreams or fantasy, and yet it may permeate a person's being, and is articulated through assumptions about the nature of being and relating' (p. 213).

In a similar way, Boyesen (1982) in her concept of 'ripeness' recommends that body psychotherapists work with their client's capacity for healing by waiting for the 'stimulus from within the organism' to emerge in its own time. From a body oriented perspective, psychological and body processes are understood as being parallel and as having a reciprocal effect on one another. The body speaks a language that antedates and is as important as verbal expression. By paying attention to the language of the body as expressed through movement, pose, posture, attitude and gesture, it is possible to complement work on a verbal level. Also, attending to somatic and psychological countertransference experiences is essential in helping therapists to understand what may be happening in the therapeutic relationship (Nolan, 2001). Paying attention to bodily cues at the 'right moment' may open pathways to significant experiences.

My work with Damien illustrates these points.

> Damien's mother died suddenly when he was 12. He did not attend her funeral and the reality of her death had been denied in his family. He had a distant, vacant and detached presence and his breathing was almost immobile with little movement on the exhalation. Throughout the therapy, Damien always seemed lost and bereft and although he was committed to therapy, it was not possible to explore his detached way of being in any significant or meaningful way. In the third year of therapy, when Damien seemed more open in a particular session, I brought his attention to his breath and the corresponding unyielding quality of his jaw and chest. This led to a sudden outburst of deep crying. Because the timing was right, he could allow himself to express feelings of grief that he had been unable to experience in the 24 years since his mother's death. This catharsis lead to previously unavailable memories, which he could talk about later in a more connected way.

Attuning to Damien on a body and emotional level enabled me to find the right timing to allow the opening described above. I did not know what effect my intervention would have, but I sensed that it would be significant. This example illustrates that the waiting and not knowing which Bion describes can apply to different levels of experience including the body.

Countertransference – intersubjectivity, empathy and vegetative identification

In the main, psychoanalytic literature has depicted countertransference as either an obstacle or a valuable tool in working with patients. For the most part, Freud (1957) adopted a narrow perspective, which viewed countertransference as being a manifestation of the analyst's pathology. He believed that these reactions interfered with the treatment of patients, and told analysts to have more analysis in an effort to overcome their countertransference reactions.

A broader view was adopted by object relations theorists, who recognized the reciprocal nature of the analyst's and the patient's subjectivities. According to Balint (1965), '. . . the analytic situation is the result of an interplay between the patient's transference and the analyst's countertransference' (p. 206). He viewed the countertransference as including the totality of the analyst's feelings, attitudes and behaviours towards the patient. Heimann (1950) made a distinction between analysts' non-pathological reactions and their neurotic transference to their patients. She proposed that analysts use their emotional responses as a key to understanding their patients' often hidden communications. Heimann (1960, p. 10) suggests that the analyst 'needs a freely roused emotional sensibility so as to perceive and follow closely his patient's emotional movements and unconscious'. Winnicott (1975) discusses the place of hatred in the countertransference and recommended that analysts work towards being at home with their feelings of hatred.

King (1978) called the emotional responsiveness in psychoanalysts 'the analyst's affective response'. In a similar vein, Sandler's (1976) concept of 'role responsiveness' refers to an unconscious receptivity in the analyst to equally unconscious cues from the patient for the analyst to behave in particular ways which correspond to experiences or people in the patient's early life. This unintentional re-enactment creates the stage for a very real working through of early traumas. Bollas (1987) views countertransference as a receptive intuitive state in which the analyst maintains a 'countertransference readiness' to receive news from within (p. 202). He too believed that the analyst is compelled to experience aspects of the patient's early life in the countertransference through his emotional, internal response to the patient.

This more inclusive view of countertransference helps in adapting to the individuality of each client. Monitoring and metabolizing the impact which the client has on the therapist has a containing effect, and helps in learning about the inner and outer world of the client. This way of reaching the client is illustrated by Bollas's (1987) statement that 'in order to find the patient we must look for him within ourselves' (p. 202).

The theme of mutuality in psychotherapy is also stressed in interpersonal schools which base their approach on the assumption that '. . . transference and countertransference together form an intersubjective system of mutual influence' (Stolorow et al., 1987, p. 42).

This emphasis on the therapist's personal experience is highlighted in humanistic approaches like gestalt and person-centred therapy. It is also emphasized in body oriented psychotherapy through Reich's (1971) concept of 'vegetative identification' in which therapists gain information about their clients' processes through being aware of how their own bodies resonate to the many subtle tensions and emotional states in their clients.

The balance between adapting and structuring in psychotherapy

In all therapeutic work, there is an interplay between adapting to the client on the one hand and focusing on clear therapeutic boundaries on the other. Psychoanalysis stresses the importance of the therapeutic frames more than other therapies, because of the longer term holding it provides. Cognitive and behavioural therapies tend to be more goal-oriented, directive and structured. Humanistic and client-centred therapies tend to be more fluid and adapting, and to focus less on frames and structure.

Therapeutic frames involve matters such as clarifying arrangements around the frequency of sessions, settling the fee, payment for cancellations and other practicalities related to the therapeutic contract. The clarity of these agreements is intended to provide stability, security and structure and so protect the therapeutic space. It is important for the therapist to pay attention to how the client deals with these agreements, as this may reveal significant information about the client's inner world. It may also symbolize how he or she relates generally and is able to adapt in the world. The frames may help in focusing a person who is avoiding important issues by either attending late or missing appointments. The limits of the therapeutic space and the relationship may provide a sense of safety for a person who feels overwhelmed by internal impulses, chaotic feelings or the impact of the therapist. This is illustrated through my work with Diane.

> As a result of severe sexual abuse throughout her childhood, Diane felt constantly flooded and tormented by perverse and violent sexual fantasies. In talking about these internalized images and memories, she re-created an erotic, raw and unsafe atmosphere in the room as she vividly relived the memories of her abuse. At times, she had difficulty in distinguishing inner and outer reality. In her torment, Diane was out of control and could fly into uncontrollable verbal outbursts in the therapy sessions and in her relationships. Apart from the damage caused to her relationships, she was frightened by her behaviour and it eroded her self-esteem. She needed my help to develop a greater ability to control both her addiction to the tormenting images and her behaviour in her life in the world outside. I firmly and gently prohibited her from lashing out physically and interrupted her destructive emotional eruptions in the therapy room. In this way it was possible to help her to experience a more adult and self-contained sense of herself, and gradually to develop a more stable life.

The work with Diane illustrates the importance of a firm psychological holding for her. My persistence in helping her to stay in the here and now in an ordinary, matter of fact way enabled her, over time, to disengage from the anguish of her inner life and to engage in a more adult way with the outer world. The holding function of these frames corresponds to the 'reality principle' described earlier in this chapter.

Ethical rules such as confidentiality[12] and the prohibition of any form of sexual contact between the therapist and client create clear limits in therapy. Apart from these, important limits may also be established by the ways in which the therapist will not facilitate or adapt to the client. This could involve the therapist warning an alcoholic client that he or she will terminate therapy if the client starts drinking again. It could also entail a refusal to receive phone calls or text messages from a client outside the therapy hour.

The manner in which therapists introduce structures reflects their theoretical assumptions, their belief system and the person of the therapist. Psychotherapists who place too much emphasis on adapting may (like an over-attentive mother) co-create a too fused or even smothering environment with the client. This one-sided approach may keep a client in an overly dependent or interminably regressed state, or may avoid evoking and encountering difficult emotions such as aggression, hate or disappointment within the relationship. On the other hand, therapists who over-emphasize the importance of structure and rules may (like a too-harsh or depriving father) overlook the client's need for more encouragement and flexibility in the relationship.

The therapeutic encounter viewed from different therapeutic perspectives

The relationship between the therapist and the client is the central factor in psychotherapy, and other aspects of therapy such as technique and theoretical orientation are secondary to it (Stricker, Chapter 3 in this volume). Although there are significant differences, the working alliance, which provides the basis for the client and therapist to work together, is common to all therapies.

Depending on the school of therapy, different aspects of the relationship may be emphasized. For instance, psychoanalytic orientations tend to pay more attention to the transference–countertransference relationship, in which the client's unconscious fantasies, wishes and fears are transferred and experienced within the therapeutic relationship, enabling these to be experienced fully in the here and now and understood. These schools recommend a balance between concern, understanding and empathy (Kohut, 1971) and tend to be more depriving because of their neutral stance which is designed to allow space for the analytic work.

In contrast, Carl Rogers (Rogers, 1951) espoused 'unconditional positive regard', 'empathy' and 'congruence' in the here and now relationship, and rejected the use of transference as a clinical concept (Rogers, 1990). In a similar vein, existential and gestalt therapists believe that healing happens through an authentic meeting or genuine relationship in the here and now.

The therapeutic space could be regarded as providing the 'container' in which the individual can come into Being (Kearney, 1986). Psychotherapists often have to 'stay with' clients as they experience loss, emptiness and confusion without recourse to an obvious solution, for example, following the death of a spouse. In a Rogerian or psychoanalytical practice, this experience of emptiness might be recognized though a supportive presence or through an interpretation. A transpersonal therapist might look for the meaning of the crisis. In systemic therapy, the therapist often does not stay with the emptiness in a mirroring way. Instead he/she may explore in an active way how these experiences of emptiness differ between family members, and how they affect people (Tomm, 1984).

Psychotherapists have to develop a feel for knowing when to work in the past or the present with clients. Working in the 'here and now' is a central aspect of any therapeutic approach and may help the client to find new ways of relating. However, I believe that to focus solely on this aspect of the relationship underestimates and dismisses the power of the repetitive nature of early traumas. On the other hand 'the repetition[13] in the analysis can be worse than the original trauma' (Ferenczi, 1980a, p. 268). This may happen in a psychoanalytic setting where the psychoanalyst is too neutral, depriving and distant.

In my opinion, the humanistic approaches may benefit from incorporating an understanding of both the developmental aspects of the person and the symbolic meaning of the relationship together with the emphasis on the here and now relationship.

Unlike humanistic psychotherapies (Lowen, 1971; Perls et al., 1974), psychoanalysts have for the most part eschewed working with the body. I believe that psychodynamic approaches could be enriched by embracing a more inclusive perspective of the here and now encounter by allowing the body, feelings, imagination and intuition and thus a wider range of experience, to be more centre stage in therapy, as in the example of John above.

An inclusive approach to psychotherapy

The object relations-integrative approach espoused in this chapter recognizes that communication, experience and interaction take place within a cultural context and on many intersubjective levels. Also, the psychotherapist and the patient are involved in a mutual evoking of different aspects of each other on the level of thinking, feeling, imagination, sensory and motor experience both on a conscious and unconscious level.

Research in neuroscience (Ramberg and Wrangsjö, Chapter 11 in this volume), which views the mind–body as seamlessly interwoven, corresponds to a unified view of the person. This perspective has many parallels with Reich's idea of 'functional identity' of body and mind which transcends the dichotomy between the two, understanding them as manifestations of the same energetic process.

Psychotherapy is both a practice based on a theory of knowledge and an intuitive art. The theoretical concepts and principles provide the therapist with a framework so that they do not have to rely only on their hunches and immediate responses to the present clinical encounter. Thus, an inevitable tension for the therapist is to use theoretical knowledge to elucidate rather than to stifle their practice.

A healthy scepticism enables therapists to question and challenge ideas from their own particular orientation, and so prevent theory from becoming a fixed dogma of unquestioned truth. Thus, rather than being blinkered and shackled by theoretical tradition therapists could become innovative in ways which are informed by both research and developments in other fields and schools of psychotherapy.

Notes

[1] 'Internalization is the process by which objects in the external world acquire permanent mental representation, that is by which precepts are converted into images forming part of our mental furniture and structure' (Rycroft, 1995).

[2] Ferenczi had a major influence on the object relations schools in England and on the neo-Freudian movement in North America. This influence is due in part to the fact that he analysed Melanie Klein and Michael Balint in England, and Clara Thompson in the United States.

[3] The fundamental rule of free association involves the patients saying whatever comes into their mind without censoring it.

[4] Fairbairn, Klein and Winnicott were later joined by the analysts Bowlby, Balint, Rosenfeldt, Guntrip, Sunderland and Bollas of the independent group and by Kleinians Bion, Segal, Spillius and Joseph. An American form of object relations has developed in the last 25 years through the work of Kernberg (1976) and of Greenberg and Mitchell (1998).

[5] While Fairbairn rejected Freud's drive theory, other object relations theorists such as Klein, Winnicott and Balint did not.

[6] In my opinion, object relations theorists do not give sufficient attention to the role of the father or to the more paternal function of the therapist in psychotherapy.

[7] The development of psychopathology is multifaceted and it is important not simply to blame the mother. The so-called 'failure of the mother' could also be related to the innate difficulties of the child or the child's projection on to the mother of its own hate or envy which makes it difficult to feel the mother's love.

[8] The interpersonal approach to psychoanalysis was developed around 1930 by Sullivan. He and his followers asserted that people are inherently relational. They, like many humanistic and existential schools, tend to neglect the developmental aspects of people's lives.

[9] The Society for the Exploration of Psychotherapy Integration formed around 1980 in America. The ideas espoused by this grouping are published in the *Journal of Psychotherapy Integration*.

[10] *The Diagnostic and Statistical Manual of Mental Disorders* (DSM-IV) is published by the American Psychiatric Association.

[11] Large-scale research (Seligman, 1995) with 7,000 respondents noted that long-term therapy was invariably more effective than short-term therapy. These findings also demonstrated that those who actively sought out therapy did better than passive recipients.

[12] Confidentiality provides one of the cornerstones of psychotherapy and has been seriously infringed in recent years through demands from solicitors and insurance companies. Legally, there is insufficient recognition of the importance of confidentiality for this profession, and consequently there has been insufficient protection for psychotherapists and their clients in this regard. It is essential that the psychotherapy profession take steps to protect itself against such infringements.

[13] 'Repetition-compulsion' is a '. . . term used by Freud to describe what he believed to be an innate tendency to revert to earlier conditions and used ... to explain the general phenomena of resistance to change' (Rycroft, 1995, p. 156).

References

Ainsworth M, Blehar MC, Waters E, Wall S (1978) Patterns of Attachment: A Psychological Study of the Strange Situation. Hillsdale, NJ: Lawrence Erlbaum Associates.

Arkowitz H, Messer SB (eds) (1984) Psychoanalytic Therapy and Behaviour Therapy. New York: Plenum.

Balint M (1954) Training general practitioners in psychotherapy. British Medical Journal 1: 115–31.

Balint M (1965) Primary Love and Psychoanalytic Technique. London: Tavistock Publications.

Bion WR (1961) Experiences In Groups. London: Tavistock Publications.

Bion WR (1962, 1970) A theory of thinking. Int. J. Psycho-Anal. 43: 306–10.

Bion WR (1967) Notes on memory and desire. Psychoanalytic Forum 2: 271–80.

Bion WR (1975) Brazilian Lectures 2. Rio de Janeiro: Imago Edirora.

Bion WR (1984) Transformations. London: Karnac Books.

Bollas C (1987) The Shadow of the Object. London: Free Association Books.

Bollas C (1989) The Destiny Drive. London: Free Association Press.

Bowlby J (1969) Attachment and Loss. London: Hogarth.

Boyesen G (1982) The primary personality. Journal of Biodynamic Psychology. Biodynamic Psychology Publications, London 3: 3–8. Washington DC: American Psychological Association, 200–33.

Damasio ANR (1994) Descartes Error. New York: Avon Books.

Damasio ANR (1999) The Feeling of What Happens. London: Heinemann.

Dollard L, Miller NE (1950) Personality and Psychotherapy: An Analysis in Terms of Learning, Thinking and Culture. New York: McGraw-Hill.

Elderman GM (1992) Bright Air, Brilliant Fire. New York: Basic Books.

Fairbairn FW (1986) Psychoanalytic Studies of the Personality. London: Tavistock.

Ferenczi S (1980a) Further Contributions to the Theory and Technique of Psychoanalysis. London: Maresfield Library.

Ferenczi S (1980b) Final Contributions to the Theory and Technique of Psychoanalysis. London: Maresfield Library.

French TM (1933) The relations between psychoanalysis and the experimental work of Pavlov. American Journal of Psychiatry 9: 1165-1203.

Freud S (1957) The Future Prospects of Psychoanalytic Therapy. Standard Edition 11: 141-51. London: Hogarth Press.

Freud S (1958a) Recommendations to Physicians Practising Psycho-analysis. Standard Edition 12: 111-20. London: Hogarth Press.

Freud S (1958b) On Beginning the Treatment. Standard Edition 12: 123-44. London: Hogarth Press.

Freud S (1961) The Ego and the Id. Standard Edition 19: 3-66. London: Hogarth Press.

Freud S (1964) An Outline of Psychoanalysis. Standard Edition 23: 139-208. London: Hogarth Press.

Greenberg JR, Mitchell SA (1998) Object Relations in Psychoanalytic Theory. Cambridge, MA: Harvard University Press.

Heimann P (1950) On countertransference-transference. International Journal of Psychoanalysis 31: 81-4.

Heimann P (1960) Countertransference-transference. British Journal of Medical Psychoanalysis 33: 9-15.

Kearney R (1986) Modern Movements in European Philosophy. Manchester: Manchester University Press.

Kernberg O (1976) Object Relations Theory and Clinical Psychoanalysis. New York: Aronson.

Khan M (1973) Obituary: Mrs Alix Strachey (1892-1973). International Journal of Psycho-Analysis 54: 370.

King P (1978) Affective responses of the analyst to the patient's communication. International Journal of Psychoanalysis 59: 329-34.

Klein M (1930) The importance of symbol formation in the development of the ego. International Journal of Psychoanalysis 11: 24-39.

Kohut H (1971) The Analysis of the Self. New York: International Universities Press.

Lacan J (1977) Ecrits, A Selection. London: Tavistock.

Laplanche J, Pontalis JB (1988) The Language of Psychoanalysis. London: Karnac Books.

Lowen A (1971) The Language of the Body. London: First Colier Books.

Mahler M, Pine F, Bergman A (1975) The Psychological Birth of the Human Infant. London: Hutchinson.

Maslow A (1971) The Further Reaches of Human Nature. Harmondsworth: Penguin.

Mitchell SA (1988) Relational Concepts in Psychoanalysis: An Integration. Cambridge, MA: Harvard University Press.

Nolan P (1993) An integrative approach to psychotherapy. In E Boyne (ed) Psychotherapy in Ireland. Dublin: Columba Press.

Nolan P (2001) Body and mind in psychoanalysis. Irish Forum for Psychoanalytic Psychotherapy 6(1): 64-73.

Norcross JC, Arkowitz H (1992) The evolution and current status of psychotherapy integration. In W Dryden (ed) Integrative and Eclectic Therapy. Milton-Keynes: Open University Press.

Ogden T (1982) Projective Identification and Psychotherapeutic Technique. New York: Aronson.

Ogden T (1994) Subjects of Analysis. New York: Jason Aronson Inc.

Perls F, Hefferline R, Goodman P (1974) Gestalt Therapy. Harmondsworth: Penguin.

Reich W (1950) Character Analysis. London: Vision.

Reich W (1971) The Function of the Orgasm. New York: Meridian.

Rogers C (1951) Client Centred Therapy. Boston: Houghton Mifflin.

Rogers C (1990) The Carl Rogers Reader. Kirschenbaum H (ed). London: Constable.

Rycroft C (1995) A Critical Dictionary of Psychoanalysis. London: Penguin.

St Clair M (1986) Object Relations and Self Psychology: An Introduction. Monterey, CA: Brooks/Cole.

Sandler J (1976) Countertransference and role-responsiveness. International Review of Psychoanalysis 3: 43–7.

Savege Scharff J, Scharff DE (1998) Object Relations Individual Therapy. London: Karnac Books.

Seligman MEP (1995) The effectiveness of psychotherapy. The Consumer Reports Study. American Psychologist 50: 965–74.

Slipp S (1988) The Teaching and Practice of Object Relations Family Therapy. New York: Basic Books.

Stern D (1985) The Interpersonal World of the Infant. New York: Basic Books.

Stolorow RD, Brandchaft B, Atwood GE (1987) Psychoanlaytic Treatment: An Intersubjective Approach. New Jersey: Analytic Press.

Sullivan H (1954) The Interpersonal Theory of Psychiatry. New York: Norton.

Tomkins S (1962) Affect Imagery and Consciousness: Vol. 1 The Positive Affects. New York: Springer.

Tomkins S (1963) Affect Imagery and Consciousness: Vol. II The Negative Affects. New York: Springer.

Tomm K (1984) One perspective on the Milan systemic approach. Journal of Marital and Family Therapy 10: 253–71.

Wachtel PL (1977) Psychoanalysis and Behaviour Therapy: Towards an Integration. New York: Basic Books.

Winnicott DW (1965, 1990) The Maturational Process and the Facilitating Environment. London: Karnac Books.

Winnicott DW (1971) Playing and Reality. New York: Basic Books.

Winnicott DW (1975, 1987) Through Paediatrics to Psychoanalysis. London: Hogarth.

Winnicott DW (1989) Psychoanalytic Explorations. London: Karnac Books.

CHAPTER 3

Integrative and object relations focused approaches to psychotherapy: theoretical concerns and outcome research

GEORGE STRICKER AND JANE GOOEN-PIELS

We have been asked to address the area of research related to object relations as a component within integrative approaches to psychotherapy. Although attention to integration was present in the writings of Freud (1905/53), and can be seen in the 1930s in the works of French (1933) and Rosenzweig (1936), the history of the psychotherapy integration movement did not really experience an upsurge until the 1970s with the watershed work of Paul Wachtel (1977) and his presentation of *Psychoanalysis and Behavioral Therapy*. We can think of psychotherapy integration, therefore, as having a long gestational period with its birth occurring in the early 1970s. Keeping within the developmental metaphor, psychotherapy integration has experienced its infancy, teenage years, and young adulthood, and has been acquiring its basic foundation skills and shaping its identity. The place of direct research in this exploratory and developmental period has been relatively limited, although some developing integrative models have been formed on the basis of existing psychotherapy research. However, there has been a recent call for this period of initial exploration and rapprochement to give way to the introduction of a more systematic period of assessment (Lampropoulos, 2001). With the existent research being somewhat limited, we will approach this chapter with the goal of presenting research that exists on those integrative psychotherapies that incorporate an object relations approach and have also acquired a more substantial identity in the field of psychotherapy integration. We will also outline the diverse research needs that are required to substantiate these approaches.

Many areas must be taken into account when addressing research regarding object relations and integrative approaches to psychotherapy, including research paradigms, problems within them, and the component schools and resulting integrative approaches. We will begin with a brief overview of two categories of research methods on psychotherapy, and problems that exist along with them, in order to have a context in which to consider the research on the integrative approaches we will discuss. Then, we will provide a short synopsis of the main tenets of object relations theory, as this area is covered in Chapter 2 of this volume, so that its role in the integrative psychotherapy approaches presented is recognized and understood. We will also describe psychotherapy integration to aid in the understanding of the integrative approaches discussed. Once we have looked at the parts preceding the integration of schools of therapy, we will present those methods of psychotherapy integration that use an object relations approach. The next part of our chapter will discuss research that has been conducted on the methods of psychotherapy that incorporate an object relations approach, and what is required of future research to help substantiate and develop integrative psychotherapies incorporating object relational approaches.

Psychotherapy research

Outcome research

The goal of psychotherapy research is to explore whether psychotherapy has a cause and effect relationship with positive change in a patient, and once that is established, to examine what it is about psychotherapy that is specifically responsible for that change (see Russell and Orlinsky, 1996, for review of history of psychotherapy research). The two methodologies that correspond to these areas of enquiry are outcome and process, respectively. Outcome answers the question: did psychotherapy cause a change in the targeted problem? Process answers the question: how did psychotherapy accomplish that end?

Under the rubric of outcome research are two arenas in which to explore the impact of psychotherapy: efficacy and effectiveness. Efficacy means that a psychotherapeutic intervention has been demonstrated to be of benefit to a patient population via controlled research. Efficacy studies use randomized clinical trials to test hypotheses. This type of research is an adaptation of the experimental method in which participants are randomly assigned to the treatment under investigation or to a comparison condition. The basis of using a random assignment method is that, if participants are placed into groups by chance, then any prior differences that might affect outcomes will cancel each other out. Therefore, if a change occurs between the two groups, it will be causally attributable to the difference in treatment (Haaga and Stiles, 2000). However, we can only conclude the existence of a cause-and-effect relationship, but we do not know the specific factors that are involved in the change (Borkovec and Castonguay, 1998).

Guidelines were developed by the Task Force on Promotion and Dissemination of Psychological Procedures (1995) to help clarify research standards by which a treatment could be considered efficacious. A hallmark feature of efficacy research is treatment manualization. Therapists are given specific training in a treatment approach via the manual, and expected to adhere tightly to it. The use of manualized treatments ensures that the treatment variables being studied are those that occurred during treatment. Additionally, efficacy studies usually recruit a narrowly defined patient sample, often limited to patients with circumscribed symptoms. The goal of the use of tight controls is to provide a situation where, to the degree possible, treatment efficacy can be purely tested.

Most often, efficacy research addresses the question of whether a treatment was helpful in symptom reduction. Although this type of research is important for establishing whether or not a treatment can affect change in a patient's symptoms or problem areas, once this is achieved, the question that follows is what happens in the world outside the laboratory? Is the treatment condition that has been found to be efficacious in the experimental condition effective in a natural setting? This question points to the issue of generalizability. Efficacy studies are very helpful in examining if psychotherapy can affect change beyond confounding variables of history, maturation, repeated testing, regression to the mean, selection bias, and other threats to internal validity. However, two facets of efficacy research limit its generalizability: the tight controls that are in place and the homogeneity of the sample. Control is provided by manualization, randomization of assignment, and careful inclusion criteria that limit participants to a specific group on which to test an intervention. The subsequent sample does not represent most patients who present in the clinical setting. Efficacy research, therefore, can only answer whether an intervention is beneficial when applied within a controlled condition. It tells us little about how effective psychotherapy will be in a natural, clinical setting. To answer this important question, effectiveness research is employed.

A psychotherapy intervention is labelled effective if it has been shown to be of benefit in the clinical setting. Patients in effectiveness research are not randomized to a treatment group, but are typically studied in single case or pre-post test designs of single-group comparisons. This type of research addresses the 'ecological validity' (Lambert, 2001) of a treatment intervention. It does this, however, at the expense of removing the tight controls present in a randomized clinical trial. Therefore, whereas efficacy research is vulnerable to threats to external validity (i.e. are the results generalizable?), effectiveness research is vulnerable to threats to internal validity (e.g. history, maturation, repeated testing, regression to the mean, selection bias). However, used in tandem with efficacy research, effectiveness research can test generalizability.

It is important to know if therapy is useful in affecting change toward the improvement of a patient's problems, be it in an experimental or natural setting. However, once this information is attained, it becomes even more meaningful to know what it was about the treatment that was responsible for patient improvement. That is, what occurred within the process of the treatment that caused the treatment's outcome? This question is answered under the scope of process research, which is a natural outgrowth of outcome research.

Process research

Process research examines the mechanisms of change within therapeutic treatment. This strategy focuses on how treatment unfolds, the experience of the treatment by the patient, the contribution of the therapist to the treatment, issues regarding patient–therapist relationships, and how change is influenced by them (Kazdin, 1995). (For a review of psychotherapy process research see Luborsky, Barber and Crits-Cristoph, 1990; Orlinsky and Howard, 1986.)

The fundamental methodological issues in the practice of process research are the formulation and interrelation of variables (Marmar, 1990). There are numerous challenges that arise in defining the variables that represent the theorized model of change process. Specifically, two disparate approaches have been taken: discrete approaches that yield easily quantifiable variables, and more abstract approaches that deal with complex variables (Marmar, 1990).

Discrete occurrences within the therapeutic session may include those that are a function of interaction between therapist and patient, such as gazes, silences, text content, and quantity. What the therapist did can also be evaluated (Goldfried and Wolfe, 1996). In this pursuit, the therapist is perceived as the hypothesized agent of change. The more abstract variables of process of change are included in the realm of the dynamic interaction between therapist and patient, including, for example, issues of alliance, transference, and countertransference, to name but a few, and in the individual experience of the patient, including gains in insight, self-esteem, and sense of identity.

Garfield (1990) proposes four areas within which variations in the meaning process are exemplified. These areas include the question of observational perspective, the focus on treatment process versus change process, the analysis of temporal and causal sequences, and the use of multiple levels of description. Achievement of this process exploration can be examined through questionnaire survey, audio and video methods.

Issues of assessment

Assessment in outcome and process research each presents its own set of difficulties. There are also specific difficulties that arise when examining psychodynamic psychotherapies, such as object relations, which is the focus of our discussion. We will not cover the entire range of difficulties inherent in each approach, but will highlight aspects of assessment that are of paramount concern in psychotherapy research.

In first approaching an outcome research design, the choice of selecting an assessment aimed at efficacy or effectiveness must be made. If the tight controls of efficacy research are chosen, then the question of how effective the treatment will be in a clinical setting, with patients who do not meet specific inclusion criteria, remains outstanding. However, if effectiveness research is selected, although it can be determined if a change occurred in conjunction with the treatment in a natural setting, that change can be attributed to factors other than the treatment. Therefore, the question of the intervention's usefulness is open to speculation. The choice of which limitation to select is guided by the questions one seeks to answer first.

Time presents as a limiting variable in efficacy research. It is difficult to evaluate longer-term approaches in comparison to a control group because of ethical considerations regarding denying treatment to people in need of care. Therefore, treatment comparison designs must be implemented. However, treatment benefit is then determined in comparison to another treatment, which could be equally helpful, and the issue of whether the treatment is better than no treatment at all remains unanswered. If it is possible to design a study with a no treatment group, the confound of selection bias emerges. A difference in treatment outcome between the experimental and control group, therefore, could be attributed to inherent differences in the samples, if there is no random assignment, or to people dropping out of the control group.

Specific problems emerge when assessing object relations based treatments and related outcomes. Often, the goals of treatment are aimed at characterological and emotional issues. Operationalizing dependent variables in these domains is problematic. Measures have been developed that quantify static experiences of anxiety and depression, but how does one quantify insight or integration of internal structures? Furthermore, it is impossible directly to measure unconscious factors, such as internal representations or other intrapsychic structures. Derivatives of these facets can be measured, but then these derived operations are vulnerable to interpretation, speculation and doubt.

In pure-form research, manualization is possible, although even in these types of designs questions arise around manual adherence and issues of generalizability to a clinical population where patients are multisymptomatic. Object relations therapy and integrative treatments that incorporate an object relational psychodynamic orientation are not conducive to manualization. These approaches require interventions in response to individual needs. Manuals are inherently inflexible, and they need to be for purposes of controlled research, to maintain validity, and to secure an understanding of what actually occurred in the treatment process.

Object relations theory

Object relations theory is a broad school in which varying theorists posit intrapsychic consequences of early interactions with the primary caregiver (for an extensive discussion of object relations theory, see Chapters 2 and 6 of this volume). Central to the theory of object relations is the role of internalized objects and internalized object relations (Wolitzky and Eagle, 1997) Throughout life, these internalizations become patterns for interactions with others; the individual will project onto others and other situations aspects of the internalized other.

Wolitzky and Eagle (1997) provide a synopsis of object relational goals in psychotherapy treatment. Interpretations generally focus on early infant–mother interactions and on relationships with internalized objects. There is an emphasis on the therapeutic relationship, through which the goal is to repair early negative object relationships, and subsequently, negative internalized objects.

Psychotherapy integration

Psychotherapy integration attempts to cross the boundaries of discrete schools of psychotherapy so as to develop approaches to psychotherapy that incorporate facets of therapies that have been found to be of benefit to patients. Its inception can be traced back to the 1930s and 1940s when Freudian psychoanalytic concepts were put into the terms of learning theorists (Gold, 1993; see Arkowitz, 1997, for extensive discussion of the history of psychotherapy integration). However, since that time a great deal of growth has occurred in the field, with great expansion beginning in the early 1970s.

Norcross and Newman (1992) present interacting variables that encouraged the growth of psychotherapy integration. They cite the emergence of numerous separate psychotherapies, including the appearance of shorter-term, focused psychotherapies, as well as the failure of any single intervention to demonstrate remarkably superior efficacy. They also discuss the inability of any single theory to explain and predict pathology, personality, and behaviour change, as well as the emergence of common factors in all psychotherapies. On a more practical note, they note the pressure that has resulted from economic concerns and the failure of third-party payers to underwrite traditional, long-term psychotherapies.

There are three major forms of psychotherapy integration: theoretical integration; common factors approach; and technical eclecticism. These forms are distinguishable from each other based on the 'hypothesised point at which the component therapies meet and meld with each other' (Stricker and Gold, 1996, p. 49).

Theoretical integration attempts to integrate two or more traditional theoretical approaches to personality or psychopathology with the goal of developing a new theory that presents new perspectives and guides practice (Stricker and Gold, 1996). Stricker and Gold (1996) note that 'at times, the clinical efforts suggested within a theoretically integrated system substantially may resemble the choice of techniques of a technically eclectic model. The essential differences may lie in the belief systems and conceptual explanations that precede the clinical strategies selected by the respective therapists' (p. 50).

The common factors approach posits that a set of factors are included in all effective psychotherapies and account for the curative component of therapeutic success. The goal of the common factors approach is to identify these factors and integrate them into the therapeutic approach. The search for common factors results from the repeated finding that most therapies are found to be equally effective (Wampold et al., 1997; Westen, 2000). Findings that one approach is superior to another tend to dissipate when investigator allegiance is controlled (Westen, 2000). Weinberger (1995) summarizes the five common factors that have been found to be empirically related to therapeutic change: the therapeutic relationship; expectations of therapeutic success; confronting the problem; providing an experience of mastery; and the attribution of success to internal factors.

Technical eclecticism systematically applies techniques and interventions that are based on existing theories of psychotherapy or are culled from research findings. In this way, the foundation of technical eclecticism is empirical in contrast to theoretical (Goldfried and Newman, 1992). Techniques and interventions are tailored to meet specific patient needs, with new interventions added on a case-by-case basis. Technical eclecticism in the integrative framework is differentiated from an eclectic approach, in that theory informs the choice of techniques and interventions in the former. Beutler, Consoli and Williams (1995) note how technical eclecticism is distinguished from its two integration counterparts: 'Technical eclecticism is distinguished from theoretical integration by its focus on clinical operations rather than on theory and from the common factors approach by its focus on the distinguishing and specific procedures' (p. 275).

Psychotherapy integration approaches that incorporate object relations theory

The psychotherapy integration movement is, in many respects, still in an early developmental phase. In congruence with its youthful status, research endeavours related to specific approaches are somewhat limited. We will limit the approaches we address to those approaches that have established themselves in the forefront of psychotherapy integration and that clearly incorporate an object relations component. The approaches we will address fall under the domain of theoretical integration, including (a) cyclical psychodynamics (Wachtel 1977, 1997); (b) assimilative psychodynamic psychotherapy (Gold and Stricker, 2001; Messer, 1992; Stricker and Gold, 1996); and (c) Cognitive Analytic Therapy (Ryle, 1990, 1995; Ryle and Low, 1993). Once these approaches have been described, we will focus on research that has been conducted in relation to them and on related research issues.

(a) Cyclical psychodynamics

Cyclical psychodynamics was developed by Wachtel (1977) and was first presented in his book *Psychoanalysis and Behaviour Therapy: Toward an Integration*. This work has been described as a watershed in the psychotherapy integration movement (Gold, 1993), and maintains its status as 'the most comprehensive and successful attempt to integrate behavioural and psychodynamic approaches and one of the most influential books in the entire field of psychotherapy integration' (Arkowitz, 1997, p. 233).

Wachtel's (1977, 1997) theory of cyclical psychodynamics originates from the idea that approaches of psychodynamic and behavioural therapy to both therapy and personality are more compatible than generally recognized, and that clinical work with patients as well as our understanding of human behaviour would be greatly enriched if concepts and observations from the two orientations were integrated into one approach.

When Wachtel presented his theory in 1977, it was originally introduced as being developed in part from interpersonal psychotherapy and a behavioural approach (1977). However, in keeping with the evolving nature of psychotherapy integration, Wachtel, in his appended version of *Psychoanalysis and Behaviour Therapy*, newly titled *Psychoanalysis and Behaviour Therapy and the Relational World* (1997), notes that, 'In the present theoretical climate, it may be less confusing to depict cyclical psychodynamics as a relational theory than as an interpersonal theory' (p. 346). He is not neglecting the interpersonal formulations espoused in the original edition. He notes, however, that unlike some interpretations of interpersonal theory that eschew intrapsychic phenomena and adhere to overt relational-pattern issues, cyclical psychodynamics holds the importance of fantasies, unconscious motivations, conflicts, affect states, and representations of self and other as integral to the model (Wachtel, 1997).

Wachtel incorporates the role of early childhood experience, the resulting unconscious processes, and the influences of interpersonal interactions later in life. These are formulated within the psychodynamic traditions of object relations and interpersonal psychotherapies, supplemented by the active intervention techniques, attention to the environment in which behaviour occurs, goals a patient brings to treatment, and importance of empirical evidence that are integral to behaviour therapies (Arkowitz, 1997).

The main concepts of cyclical psychodynamics are unconscious wishes and motives, which are referred to as the contextual unconscious, the vicious circle, and the ironic vision of neurotic conflict and behaviour (Gold and Wachtel, 1993). The vicious circle corresponds to the reconfirmation of intrapsychic structures of self and others developed through early childhood experiences and maintained through later life interpersonal interactions. Early experiences, with their resultant character structure, affect the person's manner of perceiving, thinking, feeling, and behaving, and lead to interpersonal relationships that confirm these expectations. This leads to an ironic vision of neurotic conflict and behaviour, which reflects the notion that, although a person may seek new experience, he or she is unsuccessful because he or she unintentionally enters into repetitions of past traumatic experiences and maladaptive relationships.

Assessment within this paradigm includes the patient's patterns of interactions, distortions of character and relatedness, and points of anxiety (Wachtel, 1977). Treatment uses psychodynamic exploration and active interventions that are behaviourally oriented, as well as interventions from other models, including gestalt and family therapy (Gold and Wachtel, 1993). Mechanisms of change include inquiry, exposure, insight, and gradualism. Inquiry, such as is used in a pure form psychodynamic treatment, is a large part of the therapeutic work and a source of change in itself (Wachtel, 1977). Reinforcement and new behavioural consequences are incorporated into the model, as are attention to skills deficits and to the therapeutic relationship (Gold and Wachtel, 1993).

The therapist is at the hub of patient change, integral to questioning, interpreting, assigning active interventions, and offering feedback related to behaviour. Exploration of the transference is a major source of growth. Transference is understood as ways of thinking and representations of self and other that originate in the past, as well as accurate perceptions of the therapist's behaviours or attitudes (Gold and Wachtel, 1993).

(b) An assimilative, psychodynamic approach

Assimilative integration can be seen as a type of theoretical integration or of technical eclecticism, and has also been suggested as a fourth overarching model of psychotherapy integration (along with theoretical integration, technical eclecticism, and common factors; Lazarus and Messer, 1991; Messer, 1992). This mode of integration posits that one superordinate theoretical framework is maintained while attitudes, perspectives, or techniques are incorporated from auxiliary therapies (Messer, 2001a). This approach invokes a contextual phenomenon, as it is theorized that techniques imported into the superordinate theory take on a different meaning in the new context compared to the meaning they had within the context of their original theoretical orientation. Assimilative integration differs from theoretical integration in that, in the former, one superceding theoretical position is maintained and techniques from other theoretical approaches are incorporated into it, whereas in the latter, two or more traditional theoretical orientations are merged into a novel orientation that proposes a unique understanding of personality, psychopathology, and psychological change. Assimilative integration differs from technical eclecticism in that the former uses selective importation of techniques from other theoretical orientations that 'fit comfortably into the larger theoretical context' (Lazarus and Messer, 1991, p. 153), whereas the latter uses techniques that have been empirically proven to work regardless of theoretical compatibility.

Stricker and Gold (1996) developed an assimilative approach using psychodynamic theory as the main theoretical foundation. Their psychodynamic approach involves an object relations orientation towards intrapsychic life that is occupied by representations of self and other. These theorists, however, perceive influences on intrapsychic life as multi-determined, including interpersonal, cognitive, and emotional variables. Their approach incorporates a 'three-tier' model of personality structure and change (Gold and Stricker, 1993; Stricker and Gold, 1996). Tier 1 refers to overt behaviour, tier 2 corresponds to conscious cognition, affect, perception and sensation, and tier 3 reflects unconscious mental processes, motives, conflicts, images and representations of significant others. Change is believed to occur in a circular fashion reflecting movement between the three tiers. They argue that 'insight can be the cause of change, the result of new experiences and ways of adaptation, or a moderator variable that intervenes in the effects of other change processes' (Stricker and Gold, 1996, p. 51). Overt behaviour, conscious ideation and emotion can be addressed from any of the three tiers. However, work in these areas will be most effective when there is a complete understanding of the meaning of the behaviour or thought. It is also more effective when interventions are selected and presented in ways that are nonthreatening to the patient, and the patient, therefore, is able to accept them and experience them as not only benign but helpful.

There are gaps in development of 'character disordered' individuals that manifest in impairment in tiers 1 and 2, behaviour, cognition, affect and interpersonal relations. When working on these issues, pathology must be addressed at all three tiers. An advantage of working from a cognitive and behavioural level, in addition to the psychodynamic, is that patients who are not ready to address problems through the psychodynamic tier can angle at their problems from the less threatening cognitive and behavioural tiers. The psychodynamic tier is not to be ignored, however, because it provides the depth underneath the cognitive and behavioural components. For example, cognitions and behaviours have deeper meanings than their surface manifestation, which are often unknown to both the patient and the therapist. A patient may, for example, have certain beliefs or act out certain behaviours because of unconscious representations that are tied to one's sense of self. Exploration of these phenomena from a psychodynamically oriented perspective is necessary to appreciate fully the patient's needs in these matters. From there, active methods can be introduced in ways that will seem most benign and helpful to the patient (Gold and Stricker, 1993).

Object relations are central to this model, as unconscious meaning and representations are seen as integral to an ongoing interpersonal, experiential web. The interpersonal and experiential matrix is influenced by unconscious preconceptions, conflicts, and desires that serve the function of reproducing and reinforcing those maladaptive meanings, conflicts, and images. Integrating a three-tier approach enables the therapist to address difficult unconscious conflicts and meanings that are often impervious to direct interventions on more conscious levels of experience (Gold, 1996).

It goes beyond work that is focused only on the transference by providing alternative routes to problems that are multi-determined, with the goal of arriving at underlying meaning and understanding, in the service of change, from this different route.

(c) Cognitive Analytic Therapy (CAT)

Cognitive Analytic Therapy (CAT) is a time-limited, integrative therapy based on cognitive psychology and object relations developed by Ryle (1990, 1995; Ryle and Low, 1993). (Because CAT is covered extensively in Chapter 9 of this volume, we will provide only a brief description of it here.) CAT makes use of cognitive-behavioural methods and transference in conjunction with tools specific to CAT to help promote self understanding in the service of patient change (Ryle and Low, 1993).

Three main patterns patients enact that are responsible for maintaining maladaptive processes include traps, dilemmas, and snags (Ryle, 1979). Traps are negative beliefs or assumptions that promote ways of behaving or inter-acting that result in consequences that appear to confirm the original negative belief or assumption. A trap is inherently circular in nature. Dilemmas involve the distorted perception that there are only two options available for action in response to certain beliefs. Perceiving only two options is a gross narrowing of the field of options, which then often results in maladaptive behaviour. Snags represent a behavioural response to the assess-ment that others will react negatively to one's expressed thoughts or behav-iours. A person, therefore, may take an inappropriate course of action based on conscious or unconscious motivation because of the appraisal that the course of action is not allowed.

Object relations theory was incorporated into the model, in restated cognitive terms, which became known as the Procedural Sequence Object Relations Model (Margison, 2000). How a person's schemes or procedures for interpersonal relating and for structuring the self develop and are maintained are integral to the theory. Within this aspect of the model, the bases for appraisals are understood as being developed from the early proce-dures developed in infancy that were used to predict how one's actions would affect the resulting action of the other (Ryle and Low, 1993).

Research on cyclical psychodynamics, assimilative psychodynamic approach and Cognitive Analytic Therapy

There is a great deal of psychotherapy outcome research that has been conducted to date (see Lambert and Bergin, 1994). However, research directly evaluating the efficacy and effectiveness of the integrative approaches outlined above is limited. In fact, Cognitive Analytic Therapy is the only approach that has had research conducted on it to date, and that research is quite limited. Research does exist, however, that provides evidence for the effectiveness of these integrative techniques. This research preceded and coincided with the development of these approaches and was used by theorists to aid in the therapeutic formations. It is not our goal to tackle the impossible task of explicating the history of psychotherapy research toward the end of examining the development of these integrative techniques. What we will do, however, is to focus on research that provides evidence supporting the effectiveness of these approaches.

All three of the approaches described in the previous section share some common attributes. They all incorporate an object relations approach to personality, as well as cognitive and behavioural components. These approaches postulate that beliefs, cognitions, and intrapsychic structures of representations of self and other influence affect, behaviour, and perceptions in an interactive manner. In fact, all three approaches invoke a circular system of reinforcement of cognitions, behaviours, and affects that originate in an intrapsychic orientation to self and other. Because they all incorporate a relational perspective, insight and corrective emotional experiences, facilitated in conjunction with an empathic relationship with the therapist, are inherent features that are needed to produce change (Alexander and French, 1946; Gold, 1996).

We will begin our discussion of research in these areas by looking at studies supporting these approaches' component parts. All three approaches are based on cognitive, behavioural and psychodynamic approaches. We look first for research to answer the question, is there support for the efficacy and effectiveness of the therapies from which the integrative techniques are derived? The second area of research that we will address is evidence that supports integrating single-school approaches, their concomitant techniques, and how integrative techniques benefit patient matching. Next, we will present research that relates to the central personality component of the therapeutic approaches, intrapsychic representations of self and other, and the notion that intrapsychic structures influence beliefs that affect behaviours that reinforce beliefs in an interactive web. Lastly, we will discuss research that supports the role of the therapeutic relationship within the change process.

Research supporting the efficacy and effectiveness of pure-form therapies

There is a large body of research that largely supports the efficacy of cognitive and behavioural treatments, and the validity and effectiveness of psychodynamic approaches. We will not address this extensive literature, but will refer the reader to existing reviews for cognitive and behavioural treatments (Dobson, Bachs-Dermott and Dozois, 2000) and psychodynamic approaches (see Henry, Strupp, Schacht and Gaston, 1994; Strupp, 1993; Strupp and Binder, 1984; Weiss and Sampson, 1986).

Research supporting the benefits of integrating therapeutic approaches and techniques

The first Sheffield Psychotherapy Project (Shapiro and Firth, 1987) examined the efficacy of combining existing approaches. The goal of this research was to compare a cognitive-behavioural therapy with a psychodynamic approach. The study design was such that participants received both forms of therapy back to back; participants received either cognitive-behavioural treatment and then psychodynamic, or vice-versa. Results indicated an order effect. At the three month follow-up, participants who had received psychodynamic therapy followed by cognitive-behavioural showed greater symptom improvement. These gains were maintained at a two-year follow-up (Shapiro and Firth-Cozens, 1990). Furthermore, participants reported a difference in experience of treatment based upon sequence of presentation, with those participants receiving the psychodynamic treatment first reporting a smoother process than those participants in the cognitive-behavioural-psychodynamic sequence (Barkham, Shapiro and Firth-Cozens, 1989). Participants in the latter group also tended to deteriorate more frequently in the second phase of the treatment.

Research on Klerman, Weissman, Rounsaville and Chevron's (1984) integrative interpersonal psychotherapy (IPT) for the treatment of depression and Ryle's (1990) Cognitive Analytic Therapy have demonstrated greater efficacy compared to other pure-form treatment interventions. The former approach incorporates interpersonal, cognitive, and behavioural psychotherapies. Two efficacy studies have been conducted on this treatment. Results of the first study (Weissman et al., 1979, as cited in Klerman and Weissman, 1993) found IPT to be as effective as medication, and, combined with medication, superior to either IPT or medication alone. In the second study (Elkin et al., 1989, as cited in Klerman and Weissman, 1993), in which IPT was compared to cognitive therapy, medication, and a placebo-clinical management group, severely depressed patients had better outcome in the IPT and medication groups than placebo, and IPT was found to be superior to the cognitive intervention. Short- and long-term versions of Cognitive Analytic Therapy have been found to be more effective than interpretive or behaviourally oriented approaches (Ryle, 1990).

Integrating treatments enables the clinician to match technique to patient needs. Research on prescriptive matching and eclectic psychotherapy elucidates the benefits of integrating techniques from pure-form schools of psychotherapy. Elkin et al. (as cited by Glass, Victor and Arnkoff, 1993) evaluated predilection for treatment in data from the National Institute of Mental Health's Treatment of Depression Collaborative Research Program in which cognitive-behavioural therapy, interpersonal therapy and medication plus clinical management were compared in the treatment of patients with depression. Patients were assigned to treatment based on their explanation for their problems and what they thought treatment should provide them. Patients whose assigned treatment matched their predilection were less likely to drop out of treatment and showed better therapeutic alliance.

Beutler and Clarkin's (1990; Beutler and Harwood, 2000) prescriptive psychotherapy supports the benefit of matching patients with treatments based upon inherent patient variables and how they influence treatment issues. Within this model patients are evaluated and then treatment is matched as indicated. Decisions involve four variables: patient predisposing variables, including diagnosis, personality and coping styles; treatment context; relationship variables; and tailoring strategies and techniques. Results of research on this approach found that behavioural and cognitive procedures were beneficial to patients with an externalizing coping style. Those who were higher on internalizing showed more progress in insight-oriented or self-directed therapy. Patients high on reactance did better in self-directed treatment where there was less authoritative intervention (Beutler et al., 1991).

The transtheoretical approach of Prochaska and DiClemente (1992) is based on the notion that patients present at different places in their readiness to undergo change. This approach presents an opportunity to implement interventions that meet where patients are in their process of change. Research results of a variety of studies have supported this model (see Prochaska and DiClemente, 1992).

Preliminary research supports the inherent advantage of integrative techniques abilities to accommodate specific sequencing of interventions as well as to respond to inherent patient attributes that call for individualized therapeutic approaches. Because cyclical psychodynamics, assimilative psychodynamic psychotherapy and Cognitive Analytic Therapy integrate theory and technique from cognitive, behavioural and object relations theories, they are able to respond to the varying needs individuals present in treatment. The object relational stance helps to create a holding environment and strong therapeutic alliance in which other techniques can be implemented. As the results of the first Sheffield Study suggest, establishing a relationship in which to work on patient issues may be beneficial in affecting and maintaining change (Glass, Victor and Arnkoff, 1993). Furthermore, research results on patient matching support the effectiveness of these integrative approaches, as their premise is to match patients at the level where the patient is able to allow access, be it emotionally, behaviourally or cognitively.

Research supporting internal representations and the circular theory of personality maintenance

Object relations posits a system of internal representations that influence perception and behaviour. Although there can be no direct evidence for the presence of these internalizations, Priel and Besser (2001) point to empirical research that, through the study of derivatives, has examined this concept. They note the study of internalizations of primary object relation patterns via representations of primary figures in an individual's life (Blatt, Brenneis, Schimek and Glick, 1976), as well as changes in these internalizations following long-term treatment (Blatt, Stayner, Auerbach and Beherends, 1996).

Research on personality and expectancy effects and self-fulfilling prophecy supports the cyclical mechanism that incorporates internal representations, beliefs, affects and behaviours, as theorized by the integrative approaches described above. Such research includes preliminary work on Andrews' (1993) Active Self Model of personality and psychotherapy. This model purports that feedback and feedforward relationships exist among behaviour, affect, cognition and interpersonal relations. Movements among these facets are all in the service of expressing and reinforcing intrapsychic representations of self and other.

Other evidence that supports the view that behaviour, affect, cognition, interpersonal relations and intrapsychic factors reciprocally shape each other can be found in research on expectancy effects and self-fulfilling prophecy (Wachtel, 1997). We will limit our presentation of this research to highlight relevant points (for reviews see Jussim and Eccles, 1995; Snyder, 1984). Sherman, Judd and Park (1989) demonstrated that people tend to see what they expect to see, and that they remember information that confirms what their expectations of others are. There is also evidence that people induce in others the behaviours that they expect from them (Blanck, 1993; Jussim, 1986; Snyder, 1991). Smith, Jussim and Eccles (1999) found that self-fulfilling prophecies created by a perceiver's expectations are maintained over time. In terms of the integrative theories discussed, this research supports the notion that people have cognitions about themselves and others that are based on their internal representations that influence their functioning at affective, behavioural and interpersonal levels. They believe certain things about themselves and others and expect to see what they believe. When they do see that behaviour, based on expectancy effects, they behave in a certain way. This behaviour then reinforces what they believed they would see, and once again their internal representations are confirmed.

Research that supports the role of the therapeutic relationship within the change process

The processes of all three approaches presented reveal an emphasis on the therapeutic relationship as an agent of change. Sexton and Whiston's (1994) review of psychotherapy research concludes that the therapeutic relationship contributes more to treatment success than therapeutic techniques, therapeutic procedures, patient characteristics, and therapist characteristics. Luborsky, Crits-Cristoph, Mintz and Auerbach (1988) found the most significant factor related to successful outcome was the nature of the relationship between the patient and the therapist. Gelso and Johnson (1983) studied the therapeutic relationship in short- and long-term therapies. They found that the stronger the real relationship, the more effective the therapy. These researchers suggest that, as the relationship deepens and develops over time, transference distortions are able to be resolved and patients are able to develop more realistic representations of self and other. Orlinsky and Howard (1986) found a strong relationship between the quality of the therapeutic relationship and positive patient outcome in 80 per cent of the studies they reviewed.

The research described above is evidence for the value of combining cognitive, behavioural, and object relations therapies in an integrative approach, as do the three approaches that we have described. Research on each of these individual approaches is required to examine the unique benefits they each contribute. Of the three approaches described, Cognitive Analytic Therapy has been the only one to be subject directly to research procedures.

Research on Cognitive Analytic Therapy

Although Cognitive Analytic Therapy has been the subject of more direct research, compared to cyclical psychodynamics and assimilative psychodynamic approaches, outcome research on this therapy is still limited. However, case studies and research to date support the effectiveness of this therapeutic approach.

A study conducted by Brockman, Poynton, Ryle and Watson (1987) compared CAT to a more pure form of psychoanalytic therapy. Outcome revealed that patients treated with CAT demonstrated greater cognitive change on a grid measure of self-attitudes. Patients with anorexia-nervosa participated in a pilot study (Ryle, 1995) of CAT compared to an educational therapy. Patients in the CAT group reported greater subjective improvement. In a single-arm, pre-post assessment study (Ryle and Golynkina, 2000), 27 patients with borderline personality disorder (BPD) participated in CAT. Outcome demonstrated that 14 of the patients no longer met the BPD criteria following treatment. This result was maintained at 18 months follow-up. A pilot study evaluating the impact of CAT on patients with BPD was conducted with five patients (Wildgoose, Clarke and Waller, 2001). At a nine-month follow-up, all five patients presented with a reduction in severity of BPD. Three participants showed significant decreases in level of personality fragmentation.

Treatment superiority

Treatment superiority at this point is not a useful construct because there are too many unanswered questions, leaving a shortage of information from which to draw this conclusion. Research to date demonstrates no significant differences between treatments in terms of treatment efficacy (see Wampold et al., 1997). Even if research did show a treatment superiority in effect on outcome, how useful is this information? On the face of it, the answer to the question of how a treatment compares to another in alleviating a targeted problem provides important information. However, research directed at answering that question leaves us unable to conclude that the results are from the specified intervention (Wampold, 1997). As Messer (2001b) points out, factors common to all therapies may be responsible for the outcome. Therefore, we would not know for certain why a treatment intervention resulted in a superior outcome over another.

The means to evaluating treatment superiority can only come from examining the elements that are believed to be the catalysts for change in the treatment. Once this understanding is acquired, we can know why a treatment works. Even then, the issue will not be treatment superiority, but which treatment is best for whom.

Future research directions

As indicated by the dearth of direct research on the integrative therapies discussed herein, there is yet a great deal of research required to empirically substantiate these therapies' efficacy and effectiveness. More importantly, we need to explore these treatment paradigms to help increase our understanding of the mechanisms by which people change.

Current efficacy research seeks to simplify the research context so as to magnify treatment effects. In so doing, it limits its ability to address complex therapeutic issues. Integrative therapies are complex by nature. The study of them requires expansion of the currently narrow approach.

Research goals for the integrative techniques discussed must be determined with the overall goal of psychotherapy integration kept in mind. This goal is 'not to construct a comprehensive, multidimensional, and unitary approach to treatment, but to choose therapeutic interventions according to the responses of the patient and the goals of the treatment, based on a superordinate understanding of the process of treatment and the evidence provided by research and clinical experience' (Stricker, 1994, p. 1). To achieve the goals of psychotherapy integration, therefore, a 'superordinate' understanding of treatment process must be acquired. This understanding thus becomes of paramount research concern.

Research directed at understanding treatment process requires a conceptual web of interrelations. This web involves investigation of treatment interventions, patient responses to those interventions, and the impact of the therapist within that matrix. Furthermore, it cannot be assumed that, because an intervention was found to have a certain meaning in its pure-form approach, it will have the same meaning in the integrated approach. Messer and Warren (1995) point out that supplementing a technical strategy within an existing or new treatment paradigm may change the meaning to the patient. Therefore, although techniques have been found to be efficacious or effective in their pure-form environment, research is required to examine the influence of the new theoretical context on the imported technique. To examine the plethora of variables in an interrelated manner is a nearly impossible task. Therefore, the research machine must be broken down into discrete bites while maintaining a conceptual web of variable relationships.

Research has demonstrated the efficacy of pure-form therapies. As we have shown, research has also supported the benefit of integrated treatments. There is only limited research comparing integrative techniques to pure-form therapies. Studies must be conducted to examine if integrative techniques are in fact more beneficial than pure-form techniques. This research could be conducted in an efficacy study. However, it also would be important to test clinical effectiveness, because an integrative approach may be equal to a pure-form therapy when patient symptoms are narrow and much control is exerted, but integration may be superior in a natural setting where patients often exemplify multiple problems.

Within the study of effectiveness, treatments must be examined to understand what intervention was useful toward the desired goal. Process research needs to be undertaken to mine this area. Process must then be examined in relation to outcome, with outcome conceptualized not solely in terms of symptom reduction, although that is a desirable end, but also in terms of processes reflective of personal growth and development.

How patient predispositions influence appropriate intervention must be further explored. It is this area that will aid in the development of treatment matching, which is a central goal of integrative techniques.

The relational approach these therapeutic stances incorporate calls for more study regarding the role of the therapist and therapist–patient interaction on patient change. Because integrative psychotherapy is aimed at shaping treatments to individual needs, research in this area does not fit neatly into a group design, nor does it ready itself to the current standard of manualization. Research ends, therefore, call for an expanded perspective of research guides, including the integration in methodology of process and outcome research, as well as a move beyond quantitative data toward qualitative assessment.

References

Alexander F, French T (1946) Psychoanalytic Theory. New York: Ronald Press.

Andrews JDW (1993) The active self model: a paradigm for psychotherapy integration. In G Stricker, JR Gold (eds) Comprehensive Handbook of Psychotherapy Integration (165–86). New York: Plenum Press.

Arkowitz H (1997) Integrative theories of therapy. In PL Wachtel, SB Messer (eds) Theories of Psychotherapy: Origins and Evolution (227–88). Washington, DC: American Psychological Association.

Barkham M, Shapiro DA, Firth-Cozens J (1989) Personal questionnaire changes in prescriptive vs. exploratory psychotherapy. British Journal of Clinical Psychology 28: 97-107.

Beutler LE, Clarkin J (1990) Differential Treatment Selection: Toward Targeted Therapeutic Interventions. New York: Brunner Mazel.

Beutler LE, Harwood TM (2000) Prescriptive psychotherapy: a practical guide to systematic treatment selection. New York: Oxford University Press.

Beutler LE, Consoli AJ, Williams RE (1995) Integrative and eclectic therapies in practice. In B Bongar, LE Beutler (eds), Comprehensive Textbook of Psychotherapy: Theory and Practice (274-95). New York: Oxford University Press.

Beutler LE, Engle D, Mohr D et al. (1991) Predictors of differential and self-directed psychotherapeutic procedures. Journal of Consulting and Clinical Psychology 59: 333-40.

Blanck PD (1993) Interpersonal Expectations: Theory, Research, and Applications. New York: Cambridge University Press.

Blatt SJ, Brenneis C, Schimek JG, Glick M (1976) Normal development and psychopathological impairment of the concept of the object on the Rorschach. Journal of Abnormal Psychology 35: 364-73.

Blatt SJ, Stayner DA, Auerbach JS, Beherends RS (1996) Change in object and self-representations in long-term, intensive, inpatient treatment of seriously disturbed adolescents and young adults. Psychiatry 59: 82-107.

Borkovec TD, Castonguay LG (1998) What is the scientific meaning of empirically supported therapy? Journal of Consulting and Clinical Psychology 66: 136-42.

Brockman B, Poynton A, Ryle A, Watson JP (1987) Effectiveness of time-limited psychotherapy carried out by trainees: comparison of two studies. British Journal of Psychiatry 152: 602-10.

Dobson KS, Bachs-Dermott BJ, Dozois DJA (2000) Cognitive and cognitive-behavioral therapies. In CR Snyder, RE Ingram (eds), Handbook of Psychological Change: Psychotherapy Processes and Practices for the 21st Century (409-28). New York: John Wiley & Sons, Inc.

Fairbairn WRD (1952) An Object-Relations Theory of the Personality. New York: Basic Books.

French TM (1933) Interrelations between psychoanalysis and the experimental work of Pavlov. American Journal of Psychiatry 89: 1165-1203.

Freud S (1953) On psychotherapy. In J Strachey (ed/transl), The Standard Edition of the Complete Psychological Works of Sigmund Freud (Vol. 7, 257-68). London: Hogarth Press. (Original work published 1905.)

Garfield SL (1990) Issues and methods in psychotherapy process research. Journal of Consulting and Clinical Psychology 58: 273-80.

Gelso CJ, Johnson DH (1983) Explorations in Time-Limited Counseling and Psychotherapy. New York: Teachers College Press.

Glass CR, Victor BJ, Arnkoff DB (1993) Empirical research on integrative and eclectic psychotherapies. In G Stricker, JR Gold (eds) Comprehensive Handbook of Psychotherapy Integration (9-26). New York: Plenum Press.

Gold JR (1993) The socio-historical context of psychotherapy integration. In G Stricker, JR Gold (eds), Comprehensive Handbook of Psychotherapy Integration (3-8). New York: Plenum Press.

Gold JR (1996) Key concepts in psychotherapy integration. New York: Plenum Press.

Gold JR, Stricker G (1993) Psychotherapy integration with character disorders. In G Stricker, JR Gold (eds) Comprehensive Handbook of Psychotherapy Integration (323–36). New York: Plenum Press.

Gold JR, Stricker G (2001) A relational psychodynamic perspective on assimilative integration. Journal of Psychotherapy Integration 11: 43–58.

Gold JR, Wachtel PL (1993) Cyclical psychodynamics. In G Stricker, JR Gold (eds) Comprehensive Handbook of Psychotherapy Integration (59–72). New York: Plenum Press.

Goldfried MR, Newman CF (1992) A history of psychotherapy integration. In JC Norcross, MR Goldfried (eds), The Handbook of Psychotherapy Integration (46–93). New York: Basic Books.

Goldfried MR, Wolfe BE (1996) Psychotherapy practice and research: repairing a strained alliance. American Psychologist 51: 1007–16.

Guntrip H (1969) Schizoid Phenomena, Object Relations and the Self. New York: Basic Books.

Haaga DAF, Stiles WB (2000) Randomized clinical trials in psychotherapy research: methodology, design, and evaluation. In CR Snyder, RE Ingram (eds), Handbook of Psychological Change: Psychotherapy Processes and Practices for the 21st Century (14–39). New York: John Wiley & Sons, Inc.

Henry WP, Strupp HH, Schacht TE, Gaston L (1994) Psychodynamic approaches. In AE Bergin, S Garfield (eds), Handbook of Psychotherapy and Behavior Change (4th edn, 467–508). New York: John Wiley & Sons, Inc.

Jussim L (1986) Self-fulfilling prophecies: a theoretical and integrative review. Psychological Review 93 : 429–45.

Jussim L, Eccles J (1995) Naturalistic studies of interpersonal expectancies. Review of Personality and Social Psychology 63: 947–61.

Kazdin AE (1995) Methods of psychotherapy research. In B Bongar, LE Beutler (eds), Comprehensive Textbook of Psychotherapy: Theory and Practice (405–33). New York: Oxford University Press.

Klein M (1975) Envy and gratitude and other works, 1946–1963. New York: Delacorte Press.

Klerman GL, Weissman MM (1993) Interpersonal psychotherapy for depression: background and concepts. In GL Klerman, MM Weisman (eds), New Applications of Interpersonal Psychotherapy. American Psychiatric Press: Washington, DC.

Klerman GL, Weissman MM, Rounsaville BJ, Chevron ES (1984) Interpersonal Psychotherapy of Depression. New York: Basic Books.

Lambert MJ (2001) Psychotherapy outcome and quality improvement: introduction to the special section on patient-focused research. Journal of Consulting and Clinical Psychology 69: 147–9.

Lambert MJ, Bergin AE (1994) The effectiveness of psychotherapy. In AE Bergin, S Garfield (eds), Handbook of Psychotherapy and Behaviour Change (4th edn, 143–89). New York: John Wiley & Sons, Inc.

Lampropoulos GK (2001) Bridging technical eclecticism and theoretical integration: assimilative integration. Journal of Psychotherapy Integration 11: 5–19.

Lazarus AA, Messer SB (1991) Does chaos prevail? An exchange on technical eclecticism and assimilative integration. Journal of Psychotherapy Integration 1: 143–58.

Luborsky L, Barber JP, Crits-Cristoph P (1990) Theory-based research for understanding the process of dynamic psychotherapy. Journal of Consulting and Clinical Psychology 58: 281–7.

Luborsky L, Crits-Cristoph P, Mintz J, Auerbach A (1988) Who Will Benefit from Psychotherapy? New York: Basic Books.

Mahler M (1968) On human symbiosis and the vicissitudes of individuation, Volume 1, Infantile Psychosis. New York: International Universities Press.

Margison F (2000) Editorial: Cognitive Analytic Therapy: a case study in treatment development. British Journal of Medical Psychology 73: 145–50.

Marmar CR (1990) Psychotherapy process research: progress, dilemmas, and future directions. Journal of Consulting and Clinical Psychology 58: 265–72.

Messer SB (1992) A critical examination of belief structures in integrative and eclectic psychotherapy. In JC Norcross, MR Goldfried (eds), Handbook of Psychotherapy Integration (130–65). New York: Basic Books.

Messer SB (2001a) Introduction to the special issue on assimilative integration. Journal of Psychotherapy Integration 11: 1–4.

Messer SB (2001b) Empirically supported treatments: what's a nonbehaviorist to do? In BD Slife, RN Williams, DH Barlow (eds), Critical Issues in Psychotherapy: Translating New Ideas into Practice (3–19). Thousand Oaks, CA: Sage.

Messer SB, Warren CS (1995) Models of Brief Psychodynamic Therapy: A Comparative Approach. New York: Guilford.

Norcross JC, Newman C (1992) Psychotherapy integration: setting the context. In JC Norcross, MR Goldfried (eds), Handbook of Psychotherapy Integration (3–46). New York: Basic.

Orlinsky DE, Howard KI (1986) Process and outcome in psychotherapy. In SL Garfield, AE Bergin (eds), Handbook of Psychotherapy and Behaviour Change (3rd edn, 311–81). New York: John Wiley & Sons, Inc.

Priel B, Besser A (2001) Bridging the gap between attachment and object relations theories: a study of the transition to motherhood. British Journal of Medical Psychology 74: 85–100.

Prochaska JO, DiClemente CC (1992) The transtheoretical approach. In J Norcross, MR Goldfried (eds), Handbook of Psychotherapy Integration (300–34). New York: Basic Books.

Rosenzweig S (1936) Some implicit common factors in diverse methods of psychotherapy. American Journal of Orthopsychiatry 6: 412–15.

Russell RL, Orlinsky DE (1996) Psychotherapy research in historical perspective: implications for mental health care policy. Archives of General Psychiatry 53: 708–15.

Ryle A (1979) The focus in brief interpretative psychotherapy: dilemma, traps, and snags as target problems. British Journal of Psychiatry 134: 46–64.

Ryle A (1990) Cognitive-Analytic Therapy: Active Participation in Change. Chichester: Wiley.

Ryle A (ed) (1995) Cognitive Analytic Therapy: Developments in Theory and Practice. New York: Wiley.

Ryle A, Golynkina K (2000) Effectiveness of time-limited Cognitive Analytic Therapy of borderline personality disorder: factors associated with outcome. British Journal of Medical Psychology 73: 197–210.

Ryle A, Low J (1993) Cognitive Analytic Therapy. In G Stricker, JR Gold (eds), Comprehensive Handbook of Psychotherapy Integration (87–100). New York: Plenum Press.

Sexton T, Whiston S (1994) The status of the counselling relationship: an empirical review, theoretical implications, and research directions. The Counselling Psychologist 22(1): 6–78.

Shapiro DA, Firth JA (1987) Prescriptive vs. exploratory psychotherapy: outcomes of the Sheffield Psychotherapy Project. British Journal of Psychiatry 151: 790-9.

Shapiro DA, Firth-Cozens JA (1990) Two-year follow-up of the Sheffield Psychotherapy Project. British Journal of Psychiatry 151: 389-91.

Sherman SJ, Judd CM, Park B (1989) Social cognition. In MR Rosenzweig, LW Porter (eds), Annual Review of Psychology (Vol. 40, 281-326). Palo Alto, CA: Annual Reviews.

Smith AE, Jussim L, Eccles J (1999) Do self-fulfilling prophecies accumulate, dissipate, or remain stable over time? Journal of Personality and Social Psychology 77: 548-65.

Snyder M (1984) When belief creates reality. In L Berkowitz (ed), Advances in Experimental Social Psychology (Vol. 18, 248-305). New York: Academic Press.

Snyder M (1991) Motivational foundations of behavioural confirmation. In MP Zanna (ed), Advances in Experimental Social Psychology (Vol. 25, 67-114). New York: Academic Press.

Stricker G (1994) Reflections on psychotherapy integration. Clinical Psychology: Science and Practice 1: 3-12.

Stricker G, Gold JR (1996) Psychotherapy integration: an assimilative, psychodynamic approach. Clinical Psychology: Science and Practice 3: 47-58.

Strupp HH (1993) The Vanderbilt psychotherapy studies: synopsis. Journal of Consulting and Clinical Psychology 61: 431-3.

Strupp HH, Binder JL (1984) Psychotherapy in a New Key: A Guide to Time-Limited Dynamic Psychotherapy. New York: Basic Books.

Task Force on Promotion and Dissemination of Psychological Procedures (1995) Training and dissemination of empirically validated psychological treatments. The Clinical Psychologist 48 (1): 3-23.

Vakoch DA, Strupp HH (2000) Psychodynamic approaches to psychotherapy: philosophical and theoretical foundations of effective practice. In CR Snyder, RE Ingram (eds), Handbook of Psychological Change: Psychotherapy Processes and Practices for the 21st Century (200-16). New York: John Wiley & Sons, Inc.

Wachtel PL (1977) Psychoanalysis and Behaviour Therapy: Towards an Integration. New York: Basic Books.

Wachtel PL (1997) Psychoanalysis, Behaviour Therapy, and the Relational World. Washington, DC: American Psychological Association.

Wampold BE (1997) Methodological problems in identifying efficacious psychotherapies. Psychotherapy Research 7: 21-43.

Wampold BE, Mondin GW, Moody M et al. (1997) A meta-analysis of outcome studies comparing bona fide psychotherapies empirically: 'All must have prizes'. Psychological Bulletin 122: 203-15.

Weinberger J (1995). Common factors aren't so common: the common factors dilemma. Clinical Psychology: Science and Practice 2: 45-69.

Weiss J, Sampson H (1986) The Psychoanalytic Process. New York: Guilford Press.

Westen D (2000) Integrative psychotherapy: integrating psychodynamic and cognitive-behavioural theory and technique. In CR Snyder, RE Ingram (eds), Handbook of Psychological Change: Psychotherapy Processes and Practices for the 21st Century (217-42). New York: John Wiley & Sons, Inc.

Wildgoose A, Clarke S, Waller G (2001) Treating personality fragmentation and dissociation in borderline personality disorder: a pilot study of the impact of Cognitive Analytic Therapy. British Journal of Medical Psychology 74: 47-55.

Winnicott DW (1965) The Maturational Process and the Facilitating Environment. New York: International Universities Press.

Wolitzky DL, Eagle MN (1997) Psychoanalytic Theories of Psychotherapy. In PL Wachtel, SB Messer (eds), Theories of Psychotherapy: Origins and Evolution (39-96). Washington, DC: American Psychological Association.

Chapter 4

An object relations based integrative psychotherapy: the use of conceptual analysis in understanding change

Hilde Rapp

Introduction

> [A theory of therapy should bring about] an understanding of the relationship between certain kinds of operations and interventions, and the occurrence or failure of occurrence of certain kinds of specific changes. It seems to me to be ironic that psychoanalytic writers attempt to employ clinical data for just about every purpose but the one for which they are most appropriate - an evaluation and understanding of therapeutic change. (Eagle, 1984, p. 163)

We live in a time where many societies are becoming increasingly multicultural, and where a multiplicity of perspectives is valued for the richness and diversity they bring to our understanding of the human condition.

Integrative object relations based approaches to psychotherapy combine an understanding of object relations developed within psychoanalysis with developments in integrative psychotherapy, philosophy, the human sciences, and the arts and humanities. One of the most significant advances within this group of approaches is the degree to which they have striven to formulate theoretical principles, which conceptualize change processes and clinical practices, which bring about therapeutic movement.

Because these approaches draw on a diversity of frames of reference it is important to make underlying assumptions transparent with respect to the contexts within which certain concepts are used and how they should be defined.

It is important to be mindful of how we use words to help us think about our client work (Bion, 1962; Rapp, 2001), if cumulative inaccuracies are not to seriously hinder open and intelligent discourse.

Similarly, unless we pay heed to how our choice of words shapes which values and beliefs we communicate in our therapeutic work with clients, unreflective use of theory laden concepts may amount to 'theoretical abuse', which can seriously harm clients (Basseches, 1997) by doing violence to their meaning systems.

A number of illustrations are provided to show how asking questions about context and detail may help to improve our communication about the essential features of our chosen approach with clients and colleagues alike.

I make the case for examining different approaches on a spectrum between bio-medical and social-constructivist positions. Reflective practice depends on being clear about the purpose of any theoretical or practical enquiry with respect to what kind of knowledge is being sought, and what kind of methods are used for obtaining it. This requires that we formulate clear and precise questions about the values, beliefs and practices enshrined in the customary 'theoretical' orientations represented by psychoanalytic, humanistic, cognitive behavioural or systemic approaches or 'schools'. It is vital that we look beyond these traditional 'labels' to explore and deconstruct what we are actually doing in practice.

Much confusion can be averted by distinguishing between theories of the human condition, theories of disturbances of human functioning, theories of change processes and theories of therapeutic action. Similarly we need to recognize that there is an increasing shift from the use of 'grand' theories embodying an all-inclusive vision of the human condition, towards the construction of theories which function as (postmodern) 'families' of partial models of key aspects of the field defined by contexts of use.

By analysing the concepts of internalization and projective identification, I will illustrate how distinguishing between contexts of use can improve both understanding and communication in the rapidly evolving field of psychotherapy.

I conclude by suggesting that integrative object relations focused psychotherapies can be viewed as innovative vehicles for promoting accelerated emotional learning.

A complex, multidimensional map for the reflective practitioner

We are used to distinguishing between approaches to psychotherapy in terms of psychodynamic, humanistic-existential, (cognitive-) behavioural and systemic orientations or 'schools'.

From such a perspective, psychodynamic approaches or 'schools' focus on motivational processes. Behavioural approaches emphasize learning processes. Humanistic-existential approaches bring into the foreground the importance of the self in relation to meaningful others, embarking on a search for meaning. Cognitive approaches focus on intentionality and intentional stance (Dennett, 1987). Systemic approaches pick out contextual dimensions. Thus each approach focuses differentially on such factors as motivation, learning, the co-construction of meaning and situational context.

As soon as we look at the implicit theories in use – as distinct from theories 'officially' espoused – we find that an increasing number of contemporary practitioners of psychotherapy appear to be integrating features from other 'schools' into their clinical practice (Najavits, 1997). Therefore the diversity within any one of these traditional 'schools' is as great as are the differences observed between 'schools'. In addition, across approaches, modifications in technique have become less theory driven and are increasingly informed by research findings from academic psychology, as well as by critical thinking both in the sciences and in the humanities.

We are faced with a complex multidimensional matrix. Traditional 'schoolist' labels serve to define only one axis. A number of perspectives ranging from extreme bio-medical to extreme social constructivist views of the human condition can be arranged along a second axis. Very particular lines of enquiry may be specified along a third axis. Such a matrix could allow us to locate certain questions in a common meta-theoretical framework. (A lucid illustration of the spectrum from bio-medical approaches to narrative co-construction of meaning in a multi-perspectival psychoanalytic universe is presented by Wallerstein, 1992.)

Typical examples of the sorts of questions practitioners might want to ask, using such a matrix, might be:

- Could similar aspects of the human condition, such as motivation, or motivational disorders, for example melancholia or depression, be explained with equivalent force and plausibility by different theories?
- Could 're-moralization', that is, motivating people to gather new hope, be one of a number of common factors, which promote 'healing' when offered by various professional groups from diverse 'schools', working in different contexts? Likewise, could common practices, such as 'motivational interviewing', be shown to be effective change agents, irrespective of their theoretical framing, their contexts of application, and client target problems?
- Can a humanistic-existential approach tell us something useful about empirically validated clinically effective interactions, interventions or techniques for facilitating change?
- What can we learn from systemic models about clinical strategies, which help people to manage, think about, and respond to particular kinds of distressing events and experiences?

- What kinds of rationale would be acceptable to psychoanalysts for actively intervening to help people formulate better coping strategies, and for providing tools to help them initiate changes in their behaviour?

The weight and importance which we attach to any one of these lines of questioning will interact with the kind of methodology we devise for collecting, recording, analysing, categorizing and theorizing both clinical and non-clinical observations.

Complex integrative object relations based bio-psychosocial approaches

Integrative object relations based psychotherapies tend, overall, to espouse complex, systemic, multi-factorial, bio-psychosocial positions. Complexity affords greater sufficiency and flexibility, while at the same time jeopardizing congruence, compatibility, coherence, transparency and the linkage between theoretical principles and clinical practices.

Integrative object relations based therapies need to demonstrate a good fit between their fundamental ethical and philosophical values, the principles of the espoused theory, and the body of observations the theory claims to organize. In addition both the actual clinical strategies and practical interventions which are claimed to have been derived from the theory, as well as the assumed principles and processes of change, should be both internally consistent and firmly grounded in available empirical evidence, demonstrating the clinical effectiveness and appropriateness of the approach. These basic requirements are consistent with current trends towards 'assimilative integration' in the field of psychotherapy integration in general (Messer, 2001).

A paradigmatic example of such a thoroughgoing integration of multiple perspectives is Paul Wachtel's landmark book *Psychoanalysis and Behaviour Therapy* (Wachtel, 1977), especially the entirely new second part (Wachtel, 1997; see also Chapter 3 in this volume). By integrating psychoanalytic understandings of object relations with modern learning theory and cognitive developments, Wachtel achieves an innovative integrative object relations based approach, finely balanced between the biomedical and the social-constructivist poles.

For clinicians the value of deconstructing traditional 'schoolist' approaches along the lines of assimilative integrationism proposed here, consists in its practical utility for helping to formulate more precise questions about micro aspects of the therapeutic process.

As practitioners we wish to understand more minutely, for example, what possible psychological mechanisms might be at play in a particular 'defensive' response? What exactly do we mean by 'barriers' and 'defences'? What will help a person to relinquish outdated and 'maladaptive' protective responses and motivate them to learn new ways of coping and behaving? Are all or only some people motivated by positive goals which open up the future by giving new hope, or should some be helped to let go of their self definition in terms of lifelong pain and victimhood?

As object relations based integrative therapists are becoming more and more responsible for giving a coherent account, providing evidence for their knowledge and skills base for providing safe, high quality services to the public, questions such as these will need to be addressed.

Cognitive Analytic Psychotherapy (CAT) is a typical example of an integrative object relations based psychotherapy accountable in just this way (Ryle, 1990, 1995). (See also Chapter 9 in this volume.)

Distinguishing between different kinds and uses of knowledge

How we use and generate knowledge has implications for how we apply theories, devise methods for testing their usefulness and explore the clinical effectiveness of certain practices, interventions and techniques.

The task of psychotherapy and counselling in general is, where possible, to help a person to restore, manage or put in place for the first time a culturally appropriate repertoire of human responsiveness associated with a sense of self mastery and well-being within a meaningful web of social relationships.

As I have argued above, the hallmark of a reflective practitioner is the commitment to scrutinize our practice, to generate and use scientific and experiential evidence, in order to ascertain what makes what we do therapeutically effective. This 'knowledge' is normally enshrined in a number of interrelated theories. We need to be very clear about the context within which a given theory is used and to what end.

Confusions often arise because there is a lack of clarity about the difference between what is a theory and what is a model, what is the scope of the theory (what sort of phenomena are being theorized), whether the theorist aims to generate or to test hypotheses, and whether the purpose of theory construction is to improve practice or to advance scientific explanations.

We need to be clear about what particular needs or interests are to be served, and therefore what sort of knowledge we are seeking to collectively co-construct within a given domain of knowledge.

The kind of knowing that will inform a general theory of the human condition is best thought of as declarative knowledge, that is, 'knowing that'.

Such a theory should cover human development, growth, fu
behaviour, and may include indigenous 'folk beliefs' about the
the human psyche.

This needs to be clearly distinguished from a particular and m
theory of disturbances in human psychic and social function. ₀, or in
Freudian terms, a theory of the neuroses, which also draws on declarative
knowledge, and which also may include 'folk beliefs' about possession states,
madness and so on.

The task of collecting a body of observations about how human beings
relate to one another inside and outside the therapy room, and what sort of
conditions help or hinder learning from experience, may best be served by
procedural knowledge: 'knowing how'.

Our biologically primed capacity to adapt to changing social, cultural and
economic circumstances may best be subsumed under a general (evolu-
tionary) theory of change processes.

Morris Eagle (Eagle, 1984) has argued that the legitimate field of enquiry
for practising therapists ought to be the understanding of change and of
change processes. A theory of change involves knowledge both about natural
change processes and about artificially accelerated experiential learning
mediated by the kind of meta knowledge transmitted and propagated via
psychotherapeutic work (Rapp, 1998).

In order to assess the special contribution made by psychotherapy to this
process, we need to have baseline observations of normal human growth and
development in naturalistic conditions. These observations are organized by
a general theory of the human condition.

Theories serve to organize and engender knowledge

What Freud called a 'theory of the neuroses', that is a theory of disturbances
in human psychic and social functioning, needs to describe and explain
'pathological' development. This occurs when people do not develop and
behave in 'normal' ways despite the absence of what are normally considered
to be extreme conditions.

I illustrate in the following section how the failure to make these crucial
distinctions between 'normal' and 'abnormal' development has engendered, especially concerning Kleinian object relations theory, the confusion of a specific theory of the neuroses with a general theory of human
behaviour.

Any theory has the purpose of organizing and making sense of a body of
observations. The theory needs to exhibit an internally consistent coherent
relationship between principles of organization and the categories used to

describe what is observed and in need of being organized into some symbolic representation of 'reality'. In order to be externally relevant, any novel integrative theory must be capable of generating new observations which support, enrich, weaken or disconfirm the espoused theory, and it must lead to novel understandings of the phenomena it seeks to explain. In line with the scope of a given theory, relevant observations should serve either to substantiate or to question its scientific validity and/or its clinical utility.

Theoretical models are biased – the map is not the territory

The observations which serve to constitute and to question the knowledge base which informs a given theory must therefore be very carefully selected if the theory is to provide us with a means for interrogating and understanding 'reality'.

Since 'reality' is complex (and, strictly speaking, unknowable) we tend to construct simplified models or maps of reality which include only those variables that we consider to be absolutely essential to account for the phenomena covered by the theory which organizes the knowledge which underpins the model. This is well expressed by Korzybski's (1933) famous dictum that 'the map is not the territory'.

It is crucial that we do not forget that in order to model a particular part of the whole for a particular purpose, we are deliberately representing key processes and relationships in a simplified form, leaving out aspects of 'reality'.

For example, we know as clinicians that much maladaptive behaviour occurs because we have forgotten why we once chose a particular behaviour, usually aimed at self protection.

In forgetting this initial choice, we are liable to apply a schema for organizing our understanding and behaviour to other situations to which this protective behaviour is irrelevant or inappropriate. The same process of unwitting or deliberate distortion operates in scientific knowledge. As long as we collectively value lifelong learning, and share a commitment to being aware of the unavoidable distorting influence of human interest on knowledge, we can create a culture in which we can openly and respectfully challenge one another's blind spots.

Observations are never theory neutral or value free. What we observe adds weight to or detracts from the very categories of observation we have constructed in order to sharpen our focus. Everything that I assert in this chapter is influenced by my own ways of seeing (the original meaning of theory) and hence open to challenge and debate.

Psychotherapy knowledge as the product of the continual interaction of theory, observation and practice

Our interpretation of what we have observed often changes how we look at phenomena. It actually alters the manner of our looking. It may also change the way we ask further questions.

Theory, observation and practice continually interact to make up the body of knowledge of psychotherapy. This method of cyclical or helical scientific enquiry, known under the term 'hermeneutic circle', was used by Freud in the footsteps of both Jewish and Protestant theology, where it provided the key to the interpretation of texts. 'Hermeneutics' was developed into a method by its leading modern exponent Hans-Georg Gadamer (1965), and gained wider currency through members of the 'Frankfurt school'.

A good example of the hermeneutic circle in action is how practice has changed in psychoanalysis in relation to the 'treatment' of 'victims' or 'survivors' of sexual abuse. Analysts can only do analytic work if clients 'produce clinical material'. In analysis this is done by means of free association, facilitated by lying on the couch. People traumatized by abuse cannot always 'produce clinical material' while lying on the couch. In those instances no observations can be made which can be analysed in order to advance analytic work and an impasse develops which used to be falsely attributed to the patient's resistance.

In part inspired by integrative, object relations focused therapists, a radical change in technique has become common in the way analysts work with sexual abuse, encouraging clients to sit face to face, engaging with them in 'active interventions'. By becoming more active participants in change, patients or clients have been able to tell their story more freely and have thus been enabled to produce 'clinically relevant material'. While this can probably not be sufficiently analysed, it still allows enough of the traumatic experience to be worked through, yielding valuable insights into the workings of the traumatized psyche as well as alleviating some suffering and psychic pain.

In this way a body of knowledge is constructed in psychotherapy, psychoanalysis and counselling which continually makes use of meta-knowledge. This is the knowledge about how we know, how we observe our observing, how we advance or block our learning from experience, and how we think about thinking. This body of knowledge is in turn illuminated by the theory, which it has enriched, and it is continually augmented by the fruits of an ever-diversifying practice.

Defining concepts within their context of use

In the following section I will illustrate how clarity about the use of words to denote clearly defined concepts, categories, theoretical scope and context of application might help us to communicate more clearly what sort of phenomena object relations focused psychotherapies intend to theorize.

A common error found in some psychoanalytic writings is to equate a theory of the neuroses with a general theory of the human condition.

According to S. Freud (1933) neurosis is a disturbance in the workings of the unconscious, which manifests in distortions in the normal workings of the resistance, transference, amnesia, and repression, which are influenced by biologically primed motivational forces (often translated as 'instinctual drives' from the German *Triebkraefte*).

As Freud originally intended it, a theory of the neuroses is meant to extend and deepen, but not to substitute for, the corpus of observations, models and theories of the human condition which constitute the discipline of psychology. Within psychoanalysis this was to be achieved by using a very particular method for obtaining data, namely free association.

Collapsing these crucial distinctions between a general theory of the human condition and a specific theory of the neuroses has led to a misperception of for example Kleinian psychoanalysis as claiming that all human beings are in the grip of atavistic forces (Klein, 1933). However, in the main, the clinical descriptions provided by Kleinian analysts make a significant contribution to the theory of the neuroses by extending the scope of their theory to also cover psychotic or 'borderline' phenomena.

First, Kleinian observations concern abnormal human responses to abnormal circumstances. A sample of patients have been victims of such severe early trauma that the normal course of psychic and social development has been perverted. This has led to so-called 'pathological organizations' associated with the subjective experiences of terror, psychotic ('mad') states, and anti-social behaviour.

Secondly, we are dealing with abnormal responses to normal circumstances, in that the client sample also contained patients who despite the absence of any discernible extreme conditions in their lives have developed a repertoire of responses, which lies outside the normal range and which also includes psychotic states.

Thirdly, we find normal human responses to abnormal circumstances. Observations relate to normal people who had to cope with extreme situations outside the normal range of human experience, such as war, torture and the holocaust, and whose responses to this trauma are normal in the sense of understandable and expectable. However, these responses are not (statistically) common and they are maladaptive when applied in normal situations.

Lastly the sample contains a small number of normal people with relatively normal developmental histories who tend to be practitioners in training.

As far as I can see the Kleinian theory does not distinguish adequately between these four very different person by situation conditions.

Distinction between intra- and interpersonal aspects of object relations

Not only are observations within the Kleinian theory drawn from four different kinds of client populations, but they also relate to two different realms of human experience.

The first concerns presumed intrapsychic structures and processes pertaining to the internal world of the person. The second relates to interpersonal and intersubjective phenomena, sometimes referred to as the 'real event'.

While intra- and interpersonal aspects of object relations are inextricably intertwined in life, they need to be described separately in the literature. It is useful, for the purpose of definition and description, to deal with these phenomena as if they belonged to two separate classes.

Sandler et al. (Sandler, 1988) have examined some of the complexities and confusions in the field of object relations within psychoanalysis. They have pointed out that it is important to distinguish between different contexts of use. With this in mind we need to be clear whether we seek to explain or to describe the phenomena in question. Next we need to decide whether we want to focus on intrapersonal factors or on interpersonal factors.

At a practical level, these decisions significantly influence the choice of ways of working. In working with clients who had already achieved most of the usual developmental milestones prior to some traumatic experiences, we need to create a facilitating environment in which emotional experiences relevant to interpersonal factors related to external events can be understood, and a sense of mastery over the environment can be re-established.

Conversely, the deep restructuring of intrapersonal experiences and 'phantasies' in a person who has got caught up in early vicious cycles of responding in catastrophic ways to normal (as distinct from blatantly abusive or neglectful) parenting requires a very different facilitating environment. Very special conditions will be needed to facilitate the achievement of certain developmental tasks for the first time, involving the capacity to think and to link concepts and experiences while tolerating the full range and intensity of human feeling states. Anna Freud in a conversation with Joe Sandler talked about this in terms of 'the house has not been built yet' (Sandler and Freud, 1985). This is quite different from the previous situation, where, so to speak, the house had been damaged.

Distinguishing between intra- and interpersonal phenomena becomes crucial when we want to communicate clearly what we mean by concepts such as internalization, externalization, identification, incorporation, introjection, projection and projective identification.

I will illustrate, using the concepts of internalization and projective identification, how the making of such distinctions can be useful. I will start with the concept of internalization because it in turn will help us to define what we mean by identification, which can be seen as a special case of internalization. Unless we can define what we mean by identification, we will be hard pressed to explain what we mean by projective identification, which must be the most hotly disputed term within the field of object relations theories, integrative or otherwise.

Without being able to define projective identification, we will be hampered in our understanding of what we mean by transference and countertransference (Heimann, 1950; Racker, 1953), role responsiveness (Sandler, 1976), reciprocal role relationships (Ryle, 1990), core conflictual relationships (Luborsky and Crits-Cristoph, 1990) and interpersonal schemata (Weiss and Sampson, 1986), to name a few descriptive labels.

At the outset of any discussion of concepts within any object relations focused approaches, some clarity needs to be achieved with respect to the following:

1. logical scope and definition (descriptive)
2. context of use (explanatory)
3. history of usage (originator, timeline)
4. function of the proposed affective mechanism (constitutive, differentiating, defensive/protective, aggressive/destructive)
5. assumed or proven clinical utility.

In the following sections I will use this outline of a conceptual analysis to examine the concepts of internalization and projective identification.

Conceptual analysis of internalization

In general 'internalization' covers all forms of 'taking in', and covers the family of concepts which has as its members introjection, identification and incorporation.

Historically, over the course of about 50 years, the concept of internalization has been used in roughly five different contexts and hence it has acquired five different meanings, each related to a particular function.

Over a period of 12 years between 1927 and 1939, Freud used the term to describe how a moral agency or superego is established by internalizing external prohibitions and regulations (Freud, 1933). At an explanatory level, internalization in this instance has a constitutive function – it adds to and gives shape to what at that time was hypothesized in terms of internal psychic structure.

The clinical utility of such a concept was thought to lie in providing an explanation and justification for how, first the child, and later the analysand acquire and exercise moral faculties. In a successful 'treatment or cure' the patient internalizes the analyst's realistic and compassionate superego which then gets substituted for the harsh and forbidding superego the patient had originally internalized from a critical or cruel parent.

A further use of the concept of internalization defines it as the retroflexion of aggressive impulses towards an external object on to the self (Perls, Hefferline and Goodman, 1951/1973, pp. 183-4). The function and purpose of this mechanism is defensive or protective with respect to the external object.

In 1939, Hartmann added a further use of the concept of internalization as a process for achieving individuation from the environment. Its psychic function is to improve the capacity to think as a way of mastering internal danger and to generate affective responses rather than 'instinctual' reactions to external stimuli. I mean by 'affective' the entire range of the biologically primed, socio-culturally constructed, intersubjective emotional repertoire, which underlies how we interrelate with others (Rapp, 2002). The clinical utility of this concept is to differentiate between what is adaptive and what is maladaptive.

In 1962, Loewald made a very important contribution, which paved the way for a much more interpersonal use for the concept of internalization. Projective identification is not usually an interpersonal process, because it does not represent a true social transaction which requires that the other do something which could be considered an explicit, negotiated social act. Rather what is involved is an unspoken psychological demand that the other should perform some inner psychological work and that this work is not to be acknowledged as of social value within the relationship (unless, as in an analysis it is eventually interpreted).

Loewald (1962) proposed that it is important to recognize that identity formation depends not only on the internalization of the personal qualities of role models via conscious or unconscious imitation, but that it is vital to internalize relationships themselves.

Mutuality and the capacity for concern require some process whereby the baby or analysand can experience, internalize and then use the capacity to love and care for others as well as to accept love and care from others.

Lastly, Rapaport (1967) and Schafer (1968) introduced the vital distinction between the internal world of psychic structure on the one hand and the inner world of mental representations on the other. Vygotsky's (1962) notion of 'inner speech', or Meichenbaum's (1977) 'self talk' are examples of the internalization of words, voices, and symbolic representations of action schemata, which help the child or analysand to respond appropriately to situations with the help of an 'inner guide' who, so to speak, tells them what to do or not to do.

In the case of psychosis, this benign function becomes persecutory, and the voices frighten and make mad rather than organize and guide. This would be an example of a mechanism which may be used aggressively and destructively, as when a person, in a desperate attempt to silence the voices, becomes violent towards either themselves, or another into whom such voices may have been projected as a last resort.

Space does not allow for the exposition of related terms, such as identification, incorporation and externalization, to the same length and detail. Externalization, like internalization, is also an umbrella term which covers all forms of putting out, externalizing a feeling, thought or behavioural intention, and covers such concepts as projection and projective identification.

Conceptual analysis of projective identification

I will now deconstruct some aspects of projective identification to make it possible for practitioners to distinguish between contexts of use, psychic function and clinical utility.

Broadly speaking, projective identification can serve several functions across the whole range from constitutive to aggressive. It can take an interpersonal form, as when it involves symbolic transaction between two people (A. Freud, 1937), or an intrapersonal form, when it is used to manage inner conflict.

To illustrate briefly why projective identification is such a thorny subject, let me take you through one particular context of use. Strikingly, in this context the concept involves both internalization and externalization within the same process. Sandler (1988) added a further use of the concept of internalization to cover the organizational activity involved in the developing perceptual and cognitive activities of the child. The psychic function here is constitutive, differentiating and defensive/protective. It adds psychological substance to the child's psyche. However, if the affect is very strong, the panicked baby/analysand may resort to an aggressive/destructive manoeuvre in order to displace the perceived unmanageable danger from the inside to the outside, resorting to externalization.

This manoeuvre is usually called 'projective identification', as this term has been developed by Bion (1962) and his followers. The baby or analysand externalizes intolerable feelings associated with a sense of danger by projecting them into the mother or analyst. The mother or analyst, without being aware of doing so, accepts these dangerous internal stimuli which are projected into them by the baby or the analysand. They then do some (inner) cognitive-affective work on this affective state, which still feels as if it were a state of their own. They identify with the baby or analysand in an empathic way without warding off the other's projection.

This inner work, so-called 'reverie', consists in the mother's or analyst's attempt at understanding what it is that they are themselves now feeling, what experience or event might have given rise to the feeling, and what should be done about it.

What felt to the baby or analysand like an internal object characterized by 'nameless dread' now becomes thinkable as the internal representation of an external object because of the transformative role, played by the mother or analyst. This work transforms the baby's or analysand's experience and thereby makes the raw, unnamed, unprocessed emotional material less intolerable because it can now be attributed correctly to an external cause of real or imagined danger.

The baby or 'patient' can now re-internalize their nameless dread as the nameable, understandable fear of an external object. This makes the dread tolerable, because, in its modified form as either a specific fear or a so-called signal anxiety, they can begin to gain mastery of it.

This is the function of naming in CAT, of interpretation in psychoanalysis, and affect restructuring in Short Term Anxiety Regulating Psychotherapy (STARP) (McCullough Vaillant, 1997).

Keeping pace with change through learning to learn

In the spirit of this chapter I will not offer a conclusion. Rather I will invite therapists to commit to lifelong learning, continually revising their thinking and their practice in order to stay abreast of the challenges of working in a fast changing multi-perspectival society requiring us to ask new questions.

Therapy offers persons suffering from problems with living the opportunity to learn how to use the principles of managing dynamic change processes to effect accelerated emotional learning.

In the same way the practice of conceptual analysis invites reflective integrative practitioners to apply their insights into evolving therapeutic practices to their own intellectual work of conceptualization, theory building and hypothesis testing.

Change and resistance to change is mediated by unconscious or unwitting resistances, transferences, repressions, fantasies and motivational forces which are the common properties of our psychic functioning.

Therapists learn from clients about their unwillingness or inability to learn from experience via the analysis of dreams, fantasies in the form of intrapersonal relations between the internal objects, and the transferential interpersonal relations between the client and their external objects of desire.

In the same way, as therapists we can learn from one another by means of dialogue and conceptual analysis, how as theoreticians and practitioners we also have attachments to important mentors, transferences on to cherished beliefs and an investment in safeguarding the fruits of years of effort perfecting certain practices, even if these are no longer deemed to meet current needs.

A practitioner of integrative object relations based approaches to psychotherapy knows how to convey (by being who he is) and to demonstrate (by doing what she does) how human beings learn to learn from experience. The real gift of psychotherapy is this second order learning, this meta-knowledge.

Clients can then use this meta-knowledge to accelerate their self-healing, and to maintain and manage their capacity to work, love and play (Bohart and Tallman, 1999).

Therapists can use this same knowledge to hone the leading edge of their own conceptual knowledge and practical skills in order to create a community of reflective practitioners. This paves the way towards loosing one's emotional defences against providing and accepting both intellectual challenge and emotional support.

References

Basseches M (1997) A developmental perspective on psychotherapy process, psychotherapists' expertise, and 'meaning-making conflict' within therapeutic relationships: a two-part series. Journal of Adult Development 4(1): 17–33; 4(2): 85–106.

Bion W (1962) Learning from Experience. London: Maresfield.

Bohart A, Tallman K (1999) How clients make therapy work. Washington DC: American Psychological Society.

Dennett DC (1987) The Intentional Stance. Cambridge, MA: Bradford/MIT.

Eagle M (1984) Recent Developments in Psychoanalysis: A Critical Evaluation. New York: McGraw-Hill.

Freud A (1937) The Ego and the Mechanisms of Defense. London: Hogarth.

Freud S (1933) New Introductory Lectures on Psycho-analysis. Standard edition, vol. XXII, 1–182.

Gadamer HG (1965) Wahrheit und Methode. Anwendungen einer Philosophischen Hermeneutik. Tuebingen: Mohr.

Hartmann H (1939) Ego Psychology and the Problem of Adaptation. New York: International Universities Press.

Heimann P (1950) On countertransference. International Journal of Psycho-Analysis 31: 81–4.

Klein M (1933) The early development of conscience in the child. The Writings of Melanie Klein, vol. 1, 248–57. London: Hogarth.

Korzybski A (1933) Science and Sanity. Chicago: International Non-Aristotelian Library.

Loewald HW (1962) Internalisation, separation, mourning and the superego. In HW Loewald (1980) Papers on Psychoanalysis. New Haven, CT: Yale University Press.

Luborsky L, Crits-Cristoph P (1990) Understanding Transference: The CCRT Method. New York: Basic Books.

McCullough Vaillant L (1997) Changing Character: Short-term Anxiety-Regulating Psychotherapy for Restructuring Defenses, Affects and Attachment. New York: Basic Books.

Meichenbaum D (1977) Cognitive-Behaviour Modification. New York. Plenum.

Messer SB (2001) (ed) Assimilative integration. Journal of Psychotherapy Integration 11(1). Special issue. March.

Najavits LM (1997) Psychotherapists' implicit theories of therapy. Journal of Psychotherapy Integration 7: 1–16.

Perls FS, Hefferline RF, Goodman P (1973) Gestalt Therapy: Excitement and Growth in the Human Personality. London: Penguin Books (originally published in 1951, New York: Julian Books).

Racker H (1953) A contribution to the problem of transference. International Journal of Psycho-Analysis 34: 313–24.

Rapaport D (1967) The Collected Works of David Rapaport. New York: Basic Books.

Rapp H (1998) Healthy Alliances to Promote Mental Health and Social Inclusion. London: British Initiative for Integrative Psychotherapeutic Practice.

Rapp H (2001) Learning from Wilfred Bion: learning from experience. Paper presented at the 17th International Congress of the Society for the Exploration of Psychotherapy Integration, 16 June 2001, Santiago, Chile.

Rapp H (2002) Fostering emotional intelligence. In C Feltham (ed), What's the Good of Counselling and Psychotherapy? The Benefits Explained. London: Sage.

Ryle A (1990) Cognitive-Analytic Therapy: Active Participation in Change. New Integration in Brief Psychotherapy. Chichester: Wiley.

Ryle A (1995) (ed) Cognitive-Analytic Therapy: Developments in Theory and Practice. Chichester: Wiley.

Sandler J (1976) Countertransference and role-responsiveness. International Review of Psychoanalysis 3: 43–7.

Sandler J (1988) (ed) Projection, Identification, Projective Identification. London: Karnac,

Sandler J, Freud A (1985) The Analysis of Defence. New York: International Universities Press.

Schafer R (1968) Aspects of Internalisation. New York: International University Press.

Vygotsky L (1962) Thought and Language. Introduction by JS Bruner, transl E Hanfman, G Vakar. Cambridge, MA: MIT Press.

Wachtel PL (1977, 1997) Psychoanalysis and Behaviour Therapy: Toward an Integration. New York: Basic Books.

Wallerstein R (ed) (1992) The Common Ground of Psychoanalysis. Northvale, NJ: Jason Aronson.

Weiss J, Sampson H, Mount Zion Psychotherapy Research Group (1986) The Psychoanalytic Process: Theory, Clinical Observation, and Empirical Research. New York: Guilford.

CHAPTER 5

Integration of theory: methodological issues

MIKAEL LEIMAN AND WILLIAM B. STILES

Integrating the conceptual models underlying different psychotherapeutic traditions, such as object relations theory and cognitive therapy, is a complex task that calls for explicit methodological principles. In this chapter, we suggest that the theory of tool-mediated activity, as articulated by Vygotsky and the Russian school of activity theory (Engeström, Miettinen and Punamäki, 1999; Wertsch, 1991) can serve as a meta-theory for comparing and integrating object relations theory with other approaches. Activity theory is sufficiently general to be applied in any practical mode of human activity, and we suggest that it can be fruitfully used to study psychotherapy.

Our thesis is that different psychotherapeutic approaches have evolved into distinct forms of activity, in which basic concepts have taken on distinct meanings. Empirical coding of recorded therapy sessions has shown that therapists using different approaches have sharply different profiles of verbal interventions, which correspond to theoretically-based prescriptions of what a therapist should do and should not do (e.g. Stiles, 1979; Stiles, Shapiro and Firth-Cozens, 1988). We suggest that the conceptual divergence is equally sharp. Each term or concept used within each approach has developed meanings that are dependent on other elements of the approach. Consequently, concepts cannot be extracted from one approach and transposed unchanged into another approach. Integration of theories, then, cannot be a matter of merely selecting compatible concepts from different approaches but must be an active, practical process in which all concepts develop new meanings and the product is a new form of activity.

The concept of tool-mediated activity

Activity theory proposes that the basic unit of psychological analysis should connect the person as an active agent (Wertsch, 1998) with his or her (social) context. Tool-mediated activity is such a unit. It represents an alternative to, for example, stimulus-response chains or schema templates as fundamental psychological units.

Structural elements of activity

An analysis of tool-mediated activity requires specifying the agent, the target, and the mediating tools.[1] An activity is defined by the relations among these three structural elements. A simplified illustration may clarify the triadic nature of the activity:

A man is splitting a log with an axe. In this context, the target of the activity is the log as a source of heat (a salient aspect of the target), and the splitting will make it suitable for burning. The qualities of the axe, for example, the shape of its blade and the way the shaft is united with the blade, embody the specific qualities of wood (relation of the tool to the target) and the muscular force required to split the wood (relation of the agent to the tool). The axe is thus a mediator, pointing simultaneously into three directions. Its shaft is an extension of the man's arms. Its blade is the meeting point of the splitting energy with the resistance of the wood. The third direction is the intended outcome of the act, the new shape of the wood at which the act is aimed.

Historicity of activity

Every activity has a developmental history – its origins and the transformations it has undergone (Wertsch, 1998). The development of an activity reflects continually evolving tensions among the three structural elements. Each use of a tool connects aspects of the target and the agent and reveals the limitations and potentials of the tool in this context. For example, a new log or a stronger arm may reveal limitations or new potentials of an axe, leading to changes in the tool or how it is used. Reshaping the tool may transform the activity, which may reveal still more new properties in the target, which may, in turn, call for a reorganization of the agent (e.g. new or refined skills).

Because tools mediate the contact between the target and the agent, they accumulate this developmental history and incorporate it into their structure. For example, the specific form and composition of a modern axe (shape, size, hardness, sharpness, weight etc.) incorporates thousands of years of history of human interactions with logs. This history can be approached and partially understood by studying the archaeological record, which contains innumerable axes of different forms and compositions. More generally, by studying the mediating tools, we can understand something of how an activity has developed. Development of any activity proceeds on both a societal and an individual plane. Cultural and technological development (e.g. the archaeological record of axes) illustrates the first aspect, while personal learning and growth of experience (e.g. growth of skill in splitting logs) illustrates the second.

Psychotherapeutic activity

We now use this general tripartite formulation to examine the activity of therapist and patient in psychotherapy.

The agent

In different understandings of psychotherapeutic activity, the agent may be considered as the therapist or the patient or, frequently, the dyad as a collective agent. The agent is dyadic when the patient and the therapist jointly focus their attention on a target that is an aspect of the patient's life or experiencing.

The target

Each model of psychotherapy construes the target of its work by concepts that focus on one or another aspect of human life and its problems. Freudian psychoanalysis targets the patient's unconscious, conceived as the realm of repressed conflicts and instinctual wishes. Traditional behavioural therapy targets the patient's directly observable actions, such as compulsive hand washing, and defines the aim of therapy in terms of reducing the frequency of the actions. Cognitive therapies target the thinking and feeling patterns of the patients, described as maladaptive schema structures. In each theory, the target is intimately tied with the concepts therapists use to distinguish it and to understand what they are doing.

The mediating tools

Psychotherapeutic tools include the verbal and non-verbal communication between patient and therapist and the concepts that the therapist uses to make sense of this communication. The latter are the models and theories about psychological problems and the psychotherapeutic process, which define the proper target of activity, spell out the relevant observations to be made, and organize the therapist's reflective thinking and interventions.

Verbal interaction is fundamental to all psychotherapies, but it is combined with other tools that shape therapeutic practice differently within each approach. Art therapy uses visual and tactile forms of expression, while verbalizations are used to reflect and make sense of the patient's productions. Behavioural therapies use verbalizations to instruct the patient or to induce appropriate mental states, with an aim to shape and restructure the patient's actions. The therapeutic setting itself can be regarded as an important tool domain, geared to facilitate activities regarded central to the thera-peutic task. For example, in Winnicott's set situation (Winnicott, 1982), the paediatric consulting room was laid out to permit an optimal observation of the early interaction between baby and mother.

Psychotherapy as activity: implications for integration

Considering concepts and theoretical statements as tools is central in activity theory, but it is different from the usual understanding of them as generaliza-tions of facts or as representations of reality. As mediators of activity, concepts point in three directions, like any tool. They reflect the nature of the agent and target, but only in the context of this activity, with its specific goals. In the context of a different activity, with other aims, their meaning is different. Each activity is distinct, with a different individual and social history, and the concepts change if they are transposed into the context of another activity.

According to activity theory, concepts develop in the practical encounter of the agent with the target. Schools of psychotherapy represent a collective experience of practice, in which participants have developed sets of concepts that have proved useful in treating psychological problems. The concepts each school uses for understanding psychological disorder and health, along with the verbal and non-verbal tools of treatment, thus embody the qualities and competencies of the persons who have participated in the treatment and the particular problems they have encountered.

This historical accumulation of meaning makes it difficult to compare conceptualizations of the target within different approaches. The Freudian unconscious is not quite the same as the Kleinian unconscious (Homer, 2000). Internal object relations are not equal to internalized working models, as Bowlby (1988) believed. Transference cannot be subsumed under the notion of alliance ruptures (Safran et al., 1990). These concepts developed within different contexts of activity and make sense in their own context, but they are likely to be misunderstood outside it.

Viewing psychotherapy as activity underlines the interdependence of agent and target across schools – the different understandings of who is doing what to whom. If the target is understood as the patient's dynamic unconscious, the patient's subjectivity must be divided into an observing part that is allied with the therapist (a dyadic agent) and to another less accepted and perhaps more hidden part (an alien target) that presents itself for joint observation. However, if the target is understood as the patient's dysfunc-tional action patterns in the world, the patient is invited as a whole person into a collaborative relationship with the therapist. Thus the structure of therapeutic alliance appears different depending on the understanding of the target.

The practical origin of object relations notions: Klein and Winnicott

Klein's child analysis

Melanie Klein's development of child analysis offers an interesting illustration of the interdependence of agent, target, and mediating tools. In the beginning, she conceived the target of her work with children largely in classical Freudian terms, as the repressed unconscious. However, because she began her treatment by talking to children and answering their questions concerning the sexual life of their parents (Hinhselwood, 1991), she was impressed by the important role of children's fantasies. This led her to emphasize the content of anxiety instead of regarding it as a sign of libidinal tension, which was the prevailing psychoanalytic understanding.

This shift in the target (from repressed libidinal impulses of adults to the unconscious fantasies of small children) opened up a radically new way of approaching conscious and unconscious mental processes. Klein had to invent tools that were able to uncover mental contents in ways that respected the child's particular ways of expression. The introduction of small toys permitted the children to embody their fantasies in play activity and helped to uncover the contents of early anxiety. Thus, the introduction of new tools exposed new phenomena that, in turn, called for further reformulations of the target.

The new tools also changed the relationship between the therapist and the child and hence the nature of the agent. In the classical psychoanalysis of adults, the agent of activity was realized in the working alliance. The analysand expressed his or her mind's movements in free association, following the fundamental rule of analysis. The analyst attended to the material and interpreted it. There was, thus, a joint or a dyadic agent of two persons with clearly differentiated tasks aiming at exploring the patient's unconscious processes. In play technique, this dyadic agent became differently structured. The child acted out and expressed his or her fantasies without conscious reflection. This put the task of observation and reflection on the therapist. In addition, the play required the participation of the therapist, who had to combine observation with enactment. Thus, the roles of the participants in the dyadic agent of Klein's child therapy (i.e. the therapeutic pair) differed considerably from those in adult psychoanalysis.

Kleinian child analysis also transformed the meaning of the classical psychoanalytic conceptual tools by which the mental life of patients and the process of therapy had been described. For example, the concept of object changed from being the object of libidinal satisfaction into an internal being that was active and responsive in the unconscious fantasy life. In addition to their defensive functions, introjection and projection acquired the role of fundamental mechanisms in all mental development. To make things more complicated, Klein claimed that the children's fantasies enacted in play therapy were equal to the patients' dreams in adult analysis. She also held that she interpreted the child's unconscious processes, when verbalizing the child's expressions and acts in play. She developed her ideas about internal object relations around the same time as Freud worked with the concept of the superego (Hinhselwood, 1991), and she equated them in her writing (Klein, 1929), leading her to claim a very early origin of the superego and the Oedipus complex.

Clearly the activity of child analysis had become very different from classical psychoanalysis, and Klein's choice to retain the classical psychoanalytic terms even though the meanings had changed caused much criticism and opposition among the classical Freudian analysts. When the discussion took place on a purely conceptual level, there were intense doctrinal disputes involving confusion and debates over the proper meaning of the terms that reached a peak in the great controversy between the Kleinians and the Freudians in the 1940's (Hinhselwood, 1991). By using the terms differently, the Kleinians interfered with the mutual understanding that had grown up among the classical analysts. If they allowed her to prevail, they couldn't talk with each other any more. It could legitimately be asked whether Kleinian analytic practice still could be regarded as psychoanalysis or whether it represented a distinct approach to treating mental problems.

Winnicott's semiotic reformulation of object relations theory

In his major revision of psychotherapy in the object relations tradition, Winnicott reconceptualized the target of work by introducing such ideas as early dependency and environmental provision, the potential space, transitional objects, and the change from object relating to object use (Winnicott, 1974). His practice also involved controversial modifications, for instance, allowing physical contact with the patient (Jacobs, 1995). These changes offer another important illustration of the interplay among the tools, the target and the nature of the joint therapeutic agent, leading to the development of a distinct type of therapeutic activity.

Winnicott entered the psychoanalytic tradition as a paediatrician, with experience in making detailed clinical observations and an appreciation of the importance of how parents responded to their infants' bodily needs. Modifying the usual contextual tools, he arranged his consulting room so that he could observe semiotic qualities (communication of meanings) as well as nurturing qualities of the parent–baby interaction. The desk was at the far end of a large room, which created an opportunity to observe how the mother and the baby approached. On the desk, a shining tongue depressor eventually attracted the baby's attention. The game that ensued richly illustrated how the baby handled objects and made the spatula a medium for communication and how the parent responded.

With older children, Winnicott frequently used another semiotic tool, the squiggle game (Jacobs, 1995; Winnicott, 1971). He placed a white paper between him and the child. He then drew a free flowing line (a squiggle) and asked the child to turn it into something else. Then the child was asked to draw a squiggle, and Winnicott developed the line in a responsive way, transforming it into something with a new meaning potential. His case histories (Winnicott, 1971) illustrate his use of the squiggle to create non-verbal comments, responses, and interpretations that developed throughout the game.

Introducing these semiotically sensitive technical tools, as well as the practice of seeing young patients with their parents (a new configuration of the agent), changed the target of the psychotherapeutic work. In order to account for this, Winnicott had to develop new conceptual tools. He did not create systematic theory of human development and interaction; however, there seems to be an underlying unity in descriptions of the developmental trajectory from early joint action and extreme dependency toward independence and object use. In place of the Kleinian emphasis on the internal world, he postulated a third area of living within which development and the acquisition of cultural experience happen, using such concepts as transitional phenomena and the potential space (Leiman, 1992).

Winnicott changed the concept of the internal object by tracing its developmental trajectory from the 'subjective object' to the object as 'objectively perceived'. Even at the outset, his definition of the internal object was structurally different from the Kleinian object. The baby creates the object as a subjective act, but this act is impossible without the environmental object (the parent) (Winnicott, 1974). Winnicott transferred the internal object from the realm of instinctual representations into the early interaction between baby and mother. Thus, in Winnicott's conception, 'in between' and 'within' interpenetrate each other. The baby's caretakers already provide the objects that are there 'to be created'. They invest these objects with meanings that stem from their own experiences and fantasies. These parental experiences are transferred to the baby by semiotic mediation, that is, by the exchange of (mainly non-verbal) signs. Subsequently, children may display or enact the unresolved or repressed problems of their parents.

Winnicott's work is a vivid example of the evolving interplay between agents, targets and tools. His practice of seeing babies together with their caretakers pushed him to an intersubjective direction, which found its way to his psychoanalytic work with adult patients and led to radical reformulations of the nature of the target as a joint area of playing, which provides for the patient's creative development. Through Winnicott's conceptualizations, rather than Klein's, we may approach the currently important issues of early interaction and developmental promotion and parental collaboration in child and adolescent psychotherapy.

Integrating object relations and cognitive views: evolution of the target in CAT

Attempts to combine theories must confront the problem that the meanings of terms depend on other aspects of each theory and hence on the history of that theory. The process can be illustrated by the evolution of the target across Ryle's (1978, 1982, 1985, 1991, 1995) and Leiman's (1992, 1997) attempts to integrate object relations theory with cognitive psychology in Cognitive Analytic Therapy (CAT; see also Chapter 9 in this volume).

Ryle (1978, 1982) began with a view that object relations concepts could be translated into cognitive terms. He saw value in such concepts as early object relations, splitting, and projective identification, and he sought to use these to improve upon cognitive therapy's reliance on belief systems in explaining dysfunctional action patterns and feelings. In his 1982 book, the target of psychotherapy was defined as the patient's maladaptive procedural sequences – repeated sequences of aim-directed actions. The new conception differed from Kleinian object relations views. Instead of unconscious fantasies, sequential action patterns became the focus of joint observation in therapy.

The emphasis on cognitive-behavioural sequences overshadowed the dialogic aspects of patients' activity, which had been so important in the object relations tradition. Object relations theory, in its Kleinian and Winnicottian expression, viewed the target as dialogically structured – the internal object relations of the patient's unconscious fantasy world (Klein) or the intersubjective space with real and fantasized others (Winnicott). The contemporary cognitive-behavioural models had no room for the role of another person – real or fantasized – in shaping the sequences.

In an attempt to deal with this problem, Ryle introduced the concept of reciprocal role patterns – sequences that incorporated other people – and the model came to be called the procedural sequence object relations model (PSORM; Ryle, 1985, 1995). The concept of reciprocal roles recognized transference-countertransference phenomena and suggested that people's mental processes are dialogically constructed. However, the sequential and dialogical aspects were often simply juxtaposed in the describing patients' problems, so the theoretical integration of the target remained incomplete, and the target of CAT's therapeutic activity was ambiguous.

As an illustration consider the PSORM formulation depicted in Figure 5.1. This type of pictorial case representation is called a 'Sequential Diagrammatic Reformulation' (SDR) (Ryle, 1995, p. 90). (a) The centre of the diagram is called the core of reciprocal roles. It represents an internalized reciprocal relationship pattern and is explicitly dialogic. (b) The loops represent action in the world, and describe non-dialogic sequences of action – typically the enactment of one of the positions. The circular shape of the loops reflects the underlying theoretical understanding of self-reinforcing action sequences, as formulated in the earlier procedural sequence model.

That is, the PSORM took as the target *both* the patient's dialogically-constructed internal world, in the form of internalized reciprocal roles, *and* the sequential action patterns in the world. These incompatible views of the target informed the therapist differently. When examining the reciprocal roles, the therapist was alerted to the importance of the other. When examining the procedures, the therapist was directed to the sequential and repetitive aspects in the patient's accounts.

Eventually, activity theory was used to help reconcile these conflicting concepts of CAT's target by placing them in a more general meta-theoretical

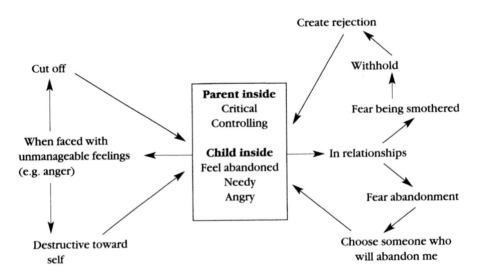

Source: Ryle, 1995, p. 90

Figure 5.1. An example of patient SDR.

frame – a dialogical account based on Bakhtin's and Vygotsky's theories of semiotically mediated activity (Leiman, 1992, 1997; Ryle, 1991). As part of the reconciliation, Leiman (1997) proposed a modification of the procedural sequences that was based on the idea of dialogically mediated activity. Instead of grouping relationship patterns and action sequences into the core and the loops (see Figure 5.1), the analysis should begin by examining the dialogical patterns of the patient's personally important activities, including dialogic aspects *within* the sequential action patterns. In the case depicted in Figure 5.1, for example, it is possible to recognize that 'Destructive toward self' holds a dialogic relation, which might be spelled out as a reciprocal role pattern, 'Enraged – Victim', or as a variant of the 'Critical – Abandoned' pattern in the core. Because external and internal activities have a common structure, dialogical qualities can be recognized both in patients' interpersonal relationships and in ways they relate to themselves.

Concluding remarks

Applied to psychotherapy, activity theory's tripartite analysis (agent, target and mediating tools) represents an alternative to the traditional distinction between theory and practice. In this view, a theory of therapy emerges within a specific mode of practical therapeutic activity and remains an integral part of practice in two senses. First, by identifying and describing the target, the theory addresses the question of what there is to be acted upon. This is the traditional function of theory, which emphasizes its validity and scientific verifiability. Secondly, however, by focusing the therapist's attention and action on what is most relevant, the theory functions as a practical tool, organizing the material as it emerges in the discourse. Such conceptual tools shape the therapist's understanding of and responses to the patient's utterances. An object relations theory, for example, invokes a very different practical approach to the patient's problems than does a cognitive theory of action sequences. Thus, in activity theory, the *what* and the *how* are intimately connected, as illustrated in the example of Klein's play therapy.

Insofar as theories are the tools of psychotherapists, their mediating function in organizing practice needs careful attention in any attempt to integrate different theories. A practitioner attempting to integrate without thoroughly examining or reflecting on the fundamental aspects of each theory can resemble a tailor attempting to sew with needle and scissors welded together. Integrative practice must choose its target; it must attend selectively to the aspects of the patient's experiences and actions deemed important while, necessarily, leaving something aside. Attending unselectively to aspects deemed important by different theories is likely to be intellectually bewildering and practically confusing.

Acknowledgements

We thank Meredith J. Glick, Michael A. Gray, Raimo Puustinen, and Anthony Ryle for comments on earlier versions of this chapter.

Note

[1] In some English translations of activity theory, what we here call the *target* is called the *object*. We substitute the word target in this chapter to avoid confusion with the internal object of object relations theory. The term 'agent' is now commonly used to denote the subject of activity (e.g. Wertsch, 1998). The concept of agent tends to emphasize the power of getting things to happen, which may eclipse some important aspects in the concept of a subject, for instance, the possibility to 'act differently'. There are elements of choice, even a choice not to act, that characterize the subject position with regard to the object of activity.

References

Bowlby J (1988) A Secure Base: Clinical Applications of Attachment Theory. London: Routledge.

Engeström Y, Miettinen R, Punamäki R (eds) (1999) Perspectives on Activity Theory. Cambridge: Cambridge University Press.

Hermans HJM (1996) Voicing the self: from information processing to dialogical interchange. Psychological Bulletin 119: 31–50.

Hinhselwood RD (1991) A Dictionary of Kleinian Thought. London: Free Association Books.

Homer S (2000) The Kleinian unconscious. Paper presented at a seminar on psychoanalytic studies. University of Joensuu, Department of Psychology, September.

Jacobs M (1995) D.W. Winnicott. London: Sage.

Klein M (1929) Personification in the play of children. The Writings of Melanie Klein. Vol. 1. 199–209. London: The Hogarth Press, 1975.

Leiman M (1992) The concept of sign in the work of Vygotsky, Winnicott and Bakhtin: further integration of object relations theory and activity theory. British Journal of Medical Psychology 65: 209–21.

Leiman M (1997) Procedures as dialogical sequences: a revised version of the fundamental concept in Cognitive Analytic Therapy. British Journal of Medical Psychology 70: 193–207.

Ryle A (1978) A common language for the psychotherapies. British Journal of Psychiatry 132: 585–94.

Ryle A (1982) Psychotherapy: A Cognitive Integration of Theory and Practice. London: Academic Press.

Ryle A (1985) Cognitive theory, object relations and the self. British Journal of Medical Psychology 58: 1–7.

Ryle A (1991) Object relations theory and activity theory: a proposed link by way of the procedural sequence model. British Journal of Medical Psychology 64: 307–16.

Ryle A (1995) Cognitive Analytic Therapy: history and recent developments. In A Ryle (ed), Cognitive Analytic Therapy: Developments in Theory and Practice (1–21). Chichester: John Wiley.

Safran JD, Crocker P, McMain S, Murray P (1990) Therapeutic alliances rupture as a therapy event for empirical investigation. Psychotherapy 27: 154-65.

Stiles WB (1979) Verbal response modes and psychotherapeutic technique. Psychiatry 42: 49-62.

Stiles WB, Shapiro DA, Firth-Cozens JA (1988) Verbal response mode use in contrasting psychotherapies: a within-subjects comparison. Journal of Consulting and Clinical Psychology 56: 727-33.

Wertsch JV (1991) Voices of the Mind. Cambridge, MA: Harvard University Press.

Wertsch JV (1998) Mind as Action. New York: Oxford University Press.

Winnicott DW (1971) Therapeutic Consultations in Child Psychiatry. New York: Basic Books.

Winnicott DW (1974) Playing and Reality. Harmondsworth: Penguin Books.

Winnicott DW (1982) The observation of infants in a set situation. In DW Winnicott, Through Paediatrics to Psycho-analysis. London: The Hogarth Press.

CHAPTER 6

Developmental theories in the process of change

MARGARETA BRODÉN

The aim of this chapter is to present findings and theories which attempt to integrate clinical knowledge of early development with modern research from developmental psychology. The need for a theory of early relationship development which integrates both the progressive unfolding of behaviour and capacities of the infant as well as the subjective experience of self and self in relation to other is long overdue. Such a theory was presented in 1985 by Daniel Stern and will be summarized in this chapter. Attachment theory, starting with Bowlby, has come to play an important role in the area of infant mental health, in the nineties. Theories of inner working models of relationships and intergenerational transmission of relationships grew out of attachment theory. These lead to some test methods, which enable us to differentiate patterns of clinical relevance, and have proved to be relatively stable over time. They will be described here as they have advanced research in this field.

During the last 25 years there has been an explosion of studies into infants' capacities and interactional skills and of parents' inborn sensitivity and capacity to regulate those. Apart from the development of self, patterns, quality and mutuality of these processes of early relationship building have been documented. In light of this new research, the early view of the preverbal period of development in psychoanalytic theory has been revised (Stern, 1985). A revision of the way in which we view early development is required together with an integration of this new knowledge into psychoanalytic theory. In this chapter there will be a short review of the view on infant development at different periods in the history of psychoanalytic theory.

As a psychotherapist and clinical child psychologist and researcher, I have worked for 30 years in the field of early intervention and parent–infant psychotherapy. In the early days of working closely with mother–infant dyads it became obvious to me that the clinical theories that I had at my disposal were not sufficient to understand what I saw and thus had limited value in explaining this dynamic. In building a treatment model and starting a clinic for therapeutic intervention in infancy (Berg Brodén 1989, 1992) my belief in the need to integrate different theoretical and methodological perspectives led me to explore this new and exciting field of knowledge.

All schools of individual psychotherapy are based on a developmental theory. In order to assist in the healing process and in the reconstruction of the client's past there is a need to understand present problems within a developmental context. It is essential for psychotherapists to review their theories of early development and to integrate new knowledge of the preverbal period in both theory and practice. Studies from the field of infant development have also generated new ways to view change in psychotherapy. This perspective also offers possibilities to integrate new methods in psychotherapy and also new ways of viewing the patient–therapist relationship.

The view of early relationship development in the history of psychoanalysis

Pine has presented an interesting description of the view of infancy in the history of psychoanalysis in the form of a metaphor of 'four waves of development' (Pine in Havnesköld, 1992).

The first wave

Freud's drive theory represents the first wave. For Freud, infancy did not seem like an interesting source of study in developing psychoanalytic theory, since at that time the infant was viewed as autistic and thus asocial and closed off from his environment. Concepts like 'stimulus barrier' were introduced, signifying an inborn filter which was thought to protect the infant from incoming stimuli. Basic needs of warmth, food and protection were the essential and only needs of the baby. The infant was described as being totally dominated by its biological instincts and a totally dependent, primitive organism. The baby was seen as having little or no ability to interact with the mother or to behave intentionally in the here and now.

The second wave

Anna Freud and the development of ego-psychology heralded the second wave. She was the first psychoanalyst to focus interest on children through her treatment of them. Systematic psychoanalytically oriented observations of children were initiated during that period. The view of early development was still rather static in that the child was seen as going through defined phases of development, regardless of relationships and influences from his environment. Concepts of interaction and processes of relationship building were still lacking. It was the interest in psychoanalytic treatment of patients with severe psychological disturbances that opened up an interest in early development. Still the focus of interest was on the study of pathology rather than on normal development.

The third wave

The third wave is represented by object relations theory, which brought the mother and the early mother–child relationship into focus. The importance of close ties to the mother for healthy development was emphasized. Winnicott's assertion that: 'There is no such thing as a baby' is a good example of the perspective of the object relations theorists. Thus the development was now viewed within the context of the mother–baby unit. This development brought about a shift, from concepts of drives and ego-development to an emphasis on relationships and representations of both inner and outer objects. Melanie Klein's work was important here in that she highlighted the impact of early object relations for both normal and pathological development. Fairbairn's pioneering work described the infant as object seeking rather than pleasure seeking. The works of Spitz and Bowlby had an important impact on the theory of early development. Their studies on maternal deprivation in children in orphanages in Europe after the war showed the devastating effects on children who had been separated from their mothers early in life.

Mahler (even if she represents ego-psychology) provided important contributions to the field of developmental theory with her observational studies of small children. She formulated a theory of early psychological development with observations of normal children as the main source of information. Systematic observations became an important source of knowledge in developing psychoanalytic theory. This is in contrast to how information on early development had been gathered previously, namely by recording patients' narratives of their childhood.

Observations of infants of 0–6 months were not a part of Mahler's systematic empirical study. That period is therefore the weakest part of her theory and the one that has required most extensive revision in the light of new research.

The fourth wave

The 'fourth wave' came out of object relations theory, but was also inspired by self-psychology, systems theory, and cognitive theory. Infant psychiatry, or infant mental health, became a new multidisciplinary research field. Research from a diversity of disciplines like psychology, developmental psychology, psychoanalysis, biology, neurobiology, physics, genetics, obstetrics, neo-natology, paediatrics, psychiatry, sociology, anthropology and linguistics are represented in this development. Knowledge about child development was rapidly growing thanks to new technology, which made it possible to study infant behaviour more closely. The finely tuned regulation between mother and child, competencies of infants and their capacity for relating have been possible to describe in more detail.

The object relations school was now criticized for defining 'the other' in a relationship as 'an object'. There was a move from concepts like 'subject–object' and 'mother–child symbiosis' to concepts of 'subject–subject', in short from object to subject.

The focus for study is now child development in the process of mutual interaction and relationship development. Development of self and self-with-others are central concepts in the building of new theories. The self is now being viewed as an organizing principle, which takes the infant's inferred subjective experience as a starting point in development of a sense of 'self-and-other'. The infant is viewed as a person in his own right, with a sense of self and a sense of 'the other' from the beginning of life.

Daniel Stern's theory of early development

Daniel Stern, psychoanalyst and researcher in developmental psychology, has presented a coherent theory of development during the pre-verbal period, in his book *The Interpersonal World of the Infant* (Stern, 1985). The book represents an important shift of paradigm in the theory of early development and focuses on development of self and self-with-others as parallel processes from the beginning of life. Stern has merged a perspective from develop-mental psychology ('the observed infant') with a theoretical perspective from psychoanalytic thinking ('the clinical child') into a theory of early relationship development.

As the infant's capacities unfold they are organized in subjective perspec-tives of sense of self and self-with-other. Stern describes five domains of development, one following the other, each having a sensitive period of formation. Each domain represents a new sense of self and a new sense of relatedness in which the self and the world around are experienced differ-ently, as a new form of social experience. Each of these modes of social experience stays with the child for the rest of his life, even after more mature and complex modes of experiencing develop. Subjective social experience can be defined as the sum of experience in all domains. In earlier develop-mental theories, like Freud's, Ericson's and Mahler's, specific phases of devel-opment, one following after the other, were thought to be defined by clinical issues, like autonomy, trust or orality. There have been no prospective studies to support the notion that psychological insults at a specific age should result in specific types of clinical problems later on. There are no grounds to consider basic clinical issues as definers of phases of development. On the contrary, Stern argues that clinical issues should be viewed as life issues that humans deal with at many different stages of life.

Domains of development of self and other

The first domain described by Stern is the sense of emergent self. During the first two months the social experiences are organized around the parents helping the infant to regulate sleep, wake and hunger cycles in order to establish some basic rhythm and structure. Parents do this by being sensitive and being able to read and respond to the infant's signals. When this is achieved, a more relaxed state in the relationship follows the domain of a core sense of self, in which experiences of the infant's own action, feelings and a sense of coherence manifest the self. Face-to-face affective interaction is the dominant social experience. This is the time for learning how to regulate feelings and for establishing the first dialogue.

The next domain is the sense of intersubjective self where mental states can be shared and intersubjectivity develops. Around seven months the infant becomes aware that other people have an inner psychic world and it is now possible to share subjective experiences as well as sharing meaning and experiences beyond the dyad. The domain of the sense of verbal self begins around 18 months and ways of being with others increases immensely. A new organizing subjective perspective develops and leads to a new area of relating. Symbolic play becomes possible as well as communication about and with people who are not present. Reflection becomes possible. When language is rich enough, the infant can share his experience and construct a simple narrative about himself. He has reached the domain of narrative self. He can explain his actions and thoughts and with that can also change his representation of self. The pre-verbal period is over.

Attachment theory

John Bowlby's important pioneering attachment theory has made an enormous contribution to the understanding of early parent–child relationships. He began exploring biologically based behaviours in the infant in the 1960s (Bowlby, 1969). His understanding of infant development was based on awareness of the existence of several genetic motivational systems, which meet different vital needs. Bowlby chose to focus on the systems that had to do with the development of relationship. He reasoned that a long period of vulnerability in the human infant demanded the existence of an innate system for securing parental protection. This protective system is biologically based in evolution and provides the infant from birth with a behaviour-system, which functions to secure physical proximity to the primary caretaker. The infant is biologically designed to attach and cannot choose not to attach.

The infant's attachment behaviour activates the 'care-giving system' in the parent and security is a mutual developmental task during the first year of life (Solomon 1996). The two interconnected systems of the attachment system in the infant and the care-giving system in the parent, operate from the start (George and Solomon, 1996).

Development of attachment

In the beginning, before the child can move, the care-giving system dominates. The protection depends on the parents' ability to observe and to react to the signals from the infant. When the infant starts to move about, fear of separation and fear of strangers activate the infant's attachment system, which includes a need to keep close to the parent and to seek protection.

Parallel to the attachment system the innate motivational system of curiosity and exploration develops. The infant explores his environment from birth, but the preoccupation with seeking security dominates during the first half year. Following this period the exploratory motive takes over except at times of danger. The child who feels safe will feel free to explore and the child who feels insecure will be preoccupied with seeking protection and therefore explore less, which will have an effect on his development. These processes are mutually organized and negotiated between parent and child.

Internal working models

With cognitive maturation and experience, the child can start to internalize representations of self and others during the second year. The attachment system will be internalized in the form of an 'internal working model of attachment' (Bretherton, 1987). This internal model will secure the attachment even when the parent is not present. It will also help the child to organize himself, to interpret events, to predict the near future and to find coping strategies. The existence of an internal working model facilitates autonomy and also guides the child's interaction with other people.

The concept of internal working model is not static, unlike the similar concept of internal object. It is rather one in a process of change and one that will be updated as new information is added (Lyons-Ruth, 1998; Main, Kaplan and Cassidy, 1985).

The quality of the attachment pattern varies according to the sensitivity and availability of the caregiver. The secure child will have a model of positive expectations of himself and meet others in that frame of mind. The insecure child will form a working model of himself as not worthy and of the parent as cold and untrustworthy.

Methods to assess attachment

Attachment research has received intense interest in recent years partly because of the development of test methods, which have been shown to have a prognostic value. Interest in finding individual differences in attachment patterns made Mary Ainsworth construct 'The Strange Situation Test'. This assessment tool differentiates between secure and insecure patterns. The insecure patterns are then categorized in terms of insecure ambivalent, insecure resistant and disorganized patterns (Ainsworth et al., 1978). These patterns have been shown to have stability over time and to have predictive value, especially the secure pattern and the disorganized pattern (Main and Cassidy, 1988). Since around 40 per cent of a normal population show insecure attachment patterns, one could not assert that they are predictive of later pathology or determinants of later behaviour problems in children. They are rather precursors, which many follow-up studies of early attachment have indicated. Grossman did a follow-up study and found that 75 per cent of the children securely attached at one year had a good adaptation to everyday situations and peer relations at the age of ten, as compared with only 25 per cent of the insecurely attached (Grossman, 1992). It has also been shown that the child's attachment pattern is specific to each parent which means that the child can have an insecure attachment to mother and a secure one to father.

To explore if there was convergence between children's and parents' attachment patterns, Mary Main developed a structured interview, the 'Adult Attachment Interview' (Main and Goldwyn, 1985). This was designed to study parents' mental representations of their childhood. The basis for categorizations was how parents described and reflected on their childhood. Four distinct patterns in the way of thinking about their childhood were identified and categorized: autonomous, dismissing, preoccupied and disorganized patterns. These adult attachment patterns have been shown to correlate well with the patterns found in their children (IJzendoorn, 1995).

Intergenerational transmission of attachment pattern

These results have generated many studies on the intergenerational transmission of attachment patterns which show that attachment patterns are to a large extent transferred from one generation to the next (Bretherton, 1990). One way to change the cycle of intergenerational transmission is the ability to reflect on one's past experiences. Adults who demonstrate an autonomous attachment pattern in spite of growing up with disturbed parents have had the capacity to reflect on both their situation and on their parents'. With the help of reflective functioning they have freed themselves from repeating the destructive patterns of their parents. The capacity for reflection is thus the key to a possible change of attachment patterns.

Capacities in the newborn child

We have come a long way from the description of the infant as a passive recipient of care with no control over his or her environment. It has been shown that the infant can use all his or her senses competently at birth. S/he sees, smells, tastes, hears, feels and has an awareness of internal bodily changes and some of these senses are well developed long before birth. The auditory capacity is, for example, formed already in the fourth month of pregnancy. The infant can hear sounds inside and outside the womb and can also remember. It has been shown that babies can recognize stories and music that they have heard before birth.

Infants can recognize their mother's voice and differentiate that from other women's voices already at birth (De Casper and Spence, 1982). The baby can also recognize his mother by the taste and smell of her milk (MacFarlane, 1975), her touch and after a few weeks also visually, by her face (Field, 1984). This early ability to recognize the mother serves the bonding process. This imprinting-like quality in relation to the mother at birth shows that there is an awareness of human qualities. This serves to establish a unique intentional relationship to the mother, a relationship that will support his future development.

Feelings are transferred with special precision via qualities from all the senses of the parent. These qualities have a high value in the infant's perception. For example qualities of the voice such as pitch, intonation, intensity, and volume are important in the affect regulation of infants. This is also true for how parents use their mimics, with slower pace, exaggerated forms, closer to the child's face and intensity of eye contact. This ability to convey affective information to an infant goes outside awareness and is inborn in parents and called 'intuitive parenting'.

Amodal perception – the world is seen as whole

The newborn infant is not only able to separately register and use information from his senses. He also has a capacity to combine his sensory modalities from the start (amodal perception). Infants appear to experience their world as one of perceptual unity. The infant forms and acts upon abstract representations of qualities of perception from birth (Bower, 1974). These are more global qualities of experience, not only sight, or sounds or touch per se but rather the basic elements of early subjective experience such as shapes, intensities, temporal patterns, vitality affect and category affects. Through the capacity for amodal perception the infant perceives the world around him as unified and global (Stern, 1985).

An example of this ability is when the infant hears a sound and turns his eyes to look for the source of the sound. Auditory information is then transferred to visual information. Having had a pacifier in his mouth without having seen it, the baby can visually identify that pacifier among others, by recognizing the form. Information from tactile senses is transferred to visual senses (Meltzoff and Borton, 1979). This inborn capacity to transfer information from one channel to another in order to orient himself makes the infant less vulnerable to incoming stimuli and more able to organize himself in the complex world around him. This new knowledge about the inborn integrating capacity challenges the old notion about the infant 'having a relationship to the breast' as separate from that to 'the mother as a person' and having experiences of 'a good and a bad breast'. The infant can not experience as separate 'the seen breast' and the 'sucked breast'. With the knowledge of amodal perception the breast would emerge for the infant as an already integrated experience of a part of the mother, as a result of the transference between tactile and visual sensory information. Infants do not need repeated experience to learn this. They are pre-designed to integrate at this level and do experience the world as whole, not in fragments and split off experience as was previously believed

Vitality affects

In every interaction active feelings of vitality are elicited and shared by both mother and child. Vitality affects are described as emotions that arise directly from encounters with people and differ from discrete affects like those of surprise and joy (Stern, 1985). They are the sensations or feelings, which accompany all actions. These qualities of feeling are better described in dynamic kinetic terms, like 'fading away', 'explosive' and 'fleeting'. Dance and music are good examples of expressions of vitality affects.

These qualities of 'forms of feelings' are of great momentary importance to infants and are always present, while regular affects come and go. Vitality affect can be experienced by the manner in which the mother picks up the baby, the way she feeds him or by the way she puts the baby to bed.

Social competencies in the infant

Infants are innately programmed to seek other humans for security and protection as attachment theory has taught us. Recent infant research has shown that the infant is able to engage in interpersonal communication from birth, and the parent and child mutually attend and attune bodily to each other's affective expression. This is demonstrated by the newborn's capacity for imitation and 'proto-conversation' in the first month (Bateson, 1975). Trevarthen (1979) has identified an innate primary intersubjective ground for socio-emotional communication. He proposes an inborn capacity for inter-subjectivity in the human infant. At birth infants appear ready to enter into a feeling engagement with another – 'felt immediacy'. Breastfeeding is a typical situation when mother and child can engage in this 'felt immediacy'. It involves the immediate mental presence and engagement of both partners. Bodily touch in itself does not necessarily involve 'felt immediacy'. It is the mental presence that provides the necessary condition. The frequency and quality of moments of 'felt immediacy' with another person will affect maturation and come to colour feelings and distinctions of self and others in the infant (Bråten, 1992).

Self-other differentiation

Self-other differentiation begins at birth. Stern makes a point of not viewing separation of 'self-from-other' as phase-specific, nor does he view it the most important developmental task. He turns the argument around and proposes that formation of affective ties with others in increasing depth and quality, is the most important task in early development (Stern, 2000).

Infants demonstrate a different strategy when encountering a person as compared with an object. Recent research has described two parallel systems of perception, operating from birth: cognition memory and affectivity. This is an argument for a differentiation of self from other at the beginning of life. One system is designed to 'do with object', to explore, manipulate and make sense of things in the physical world. The other system operates in order to make sense of the human world and to follow and respond to communica-tion with others. The two systems are in dynamic interaction (Trevarthen, 1980). To describe this specificity of accumulating knowledge is a new notion and a major step forward in the way of thinking about development. It has gained evidence and been a valuable starting point in studies of patholog-ical development, especially on autism (Stern, 2000).

The transfer of affect between infants and parents

The preverbal period is dominated by affective interchanges between infant and parent and the parent's role is to regulate the infant's inborn capacities. Parent–infant interaction is a goal oriented reciprocal system with a shared motive to reach a positive emotional state. The infant plays an important and active role, being able to modify his communication in response to feedback from the parent. Tronick et al. (1986) termed this early transfer of affect the 'mutual regulation model' (MRM).

Mutual regulation model

This model states that the infant attempts to control his relationships through active use of his inborn emotional signals. Expansion of the infant's state of consciousness is enhanced by the process of mutual regulation of affective states, which create a dyadic state of consciousness. Dyadic consciousness is something more than adding the input from each of the individuals. The dyadic system is more complex, more coherent and carries more information than the parent's or the infant's own system. In this dyadic union both partners experience an expansion of their own consciousness. To expand and 'to be larger than oneself' is a fulfilling, powerful, and a sought after experience.

When the infant succeeds in communicating, positive feelings arise. This generates a sense of mastery. When the infant fails, he experiences both negative feelings and a sense of helplessness. Not being able to signal one's needs to the parent over time creates communication failures at a basic level and also results in the infant distrusting of his own capacity to communicate. Success depends on the sensitivity of the parent, in noticing, understanding and responding to his signals. The system works both ways and when the interaction goes well the parent experiences a feeling of success in parenting and a sense of failure in parenting when it fails.

Capacity to repair

Since there are countless spontaneous everyday interactions between the parent and infant, it is comforting to know that an important aspect of mutual regulation contains the potential for repairing. Miscommunications are normal events and they occur when one of the partners doesn't understand the other's emotional signals and therefore reacts inappropriately. An interactive repairing takes place when the partners move from a mis-coordinated state to a coordinated state. That process of reparation is also a mutually regulated process and success depends on parental sensitivity and competence of the infant. A study demonstrated that sensitive mothers had children whom at six months made strong and persistent efforts to overcome interactive stress and failures. The opposite was true for children of controlling mothers, who prevented the infants from having an effect on the interaction. That style of interacting produced a sense of being non-effective in the infants. To learn how to repair and redirect the interactional process is one of the main hidden agendas of parent–infant interaction (Tronick and Cohn, 1989).

The effect of parents' internal representations on interaction

Each encounter reflects the quality of the present relationship. Of course parents and children are not in interaction on equal terms and one difference is that parents bring their history of relating into this new relationship. Parents' past relational experiences will have an influence on their interaction with the child. If negative experiences dominate the parents' past, then their sensitivity towards the child may be blocked and their behaviour disrupted. The parents' past emotional experiences thus have an effect on how they behave towards the infant in the present. We know that parents' internal representations play an important part in creating disturbances in parent–child relationships and in child behaviour. Selma Fraiberg (1980) called this phenomenon 'ghosts in the nursery'. How parents' internal representations are organized and transferred in interaction is a topic of great importance to the field of infant psychiatry. The literature on the subject is vast, but it will not be elaborated further here.

The effects of interruptions within an early interaction

To show the sensitivity of the early interactive system and to demonstrate what happens when the expected reciprocity in the dyadic-interactive system is violated, an experimental procedure called still-face experiments was designed. Mothers of three-month-old babies were asked to sit face to face to their infants, to keep a still face and not to respond to their baby in any way (Tronick et al., 1978). The infants' reaction to this disruption of expected reciprocal interaction was intense. The general pattern of reaction was first to invite a response from mother by signalling more and more intensely. When all attempts failed to bring the mother out of her immobilization, the infant withdrew, turned his face and body away, and withdrew with an expression of hopelessness. This 'micro-depression' happens within minutes in an experimental situation with normal children, which shows how sensitive the parent–infant system is. These experiments support the MRM model and demonstrate how the quality of the interaction does affect the infant's emotional state and the extent to which the infant feels successful or helpless in his effort to communicate. This is how helplessness is learned. Seligman (1975) has proposed that this process of learned helplessness may also account for depression in adults.

Effects of maternal depression

These experimental studies initiated interest to study what happens to children who have depressed mothers or mothers who for other reasons are not emotionally available to their infants. The hypothesis was that the infant who over time does not succeed in getting his mother to respond, and who does not have someone else to turn to, will give up trying, turn inwards and imitate the mother's depressed affect.

Lynn Murray (1991) took the MRM hypothesis a step further and studied the effect of maternal depression on infants, since depression has a powerful effect on interrupting and breaking states of relatedness. The results have been important in understanding normal as well as pathological development. She found that the quality of mother–infant interaction was dramatically affected by the mother's depression. As shown in the still-face experiments, infants reacted strongly to the mother's lack of mental presence, which is a violation of the mutually regulated system of interaction. At 18 months these infants' attachment patterns were insecure and their social and cognitive development was delayed. They vocalized less, their ability to concentrate was reduced and they showed little positive affect. Furthermore they were tense, sensitive to stress and seemed unsatisfied or avoiding. Depressed mothers in interaction with their infants were self-centred, silent, and unresponsive and showed little expression of affect and physical contact. The child was left to organize himself as best he could. This is important information since post-natal depression is very common in western societies. It has been shown that 10–15 per cent of a normal western population will suffer from this condition (Field, 1984). Untreated post-natal depression lasts longer than other types of depressions. For half of the depressed mothers the depression lasts longer than six months, with serious effects on the emotional regulation of the infant (Murray and Cooper, 1997). Thus the rationale for early intervention into the mother–infant interaction, not only treating the mother, is obvious. It is important to mention that if the father or another close person enters into a close and continuous relationship with the baby, the negative effect on the infant's development can be drastically reduced.

From infancy studies to psychotherapeutic processes

There is no verbal understanding of the early mother–infant interaction as most of what is going on happens out of awareness. This emotional and intuitive communication operates on a bodily level and rarely becomes symbolically coded or expressed in words. 'Knowing how to do things with others' is a form of procedural knowledge that has been termed 'implicit relational knowing' and is represented in the child long before the beginning of language. It operates in an implicit way outside focused attention and conscious experience throughout life. It guides the child's intimate interactions and is not language based. It is in this domain of implicit relational knowing that emotional change occurs in the child, as well as in therapeutic relationships (Stern, 1998). Through these insights infant research has brought a perspective that has been of value in understanding change in the psychotherapeutic relationship.

What is change in psychotherapy?

Most clinicians would agree that therapeutic change ⸺ 'something more' than effective interpretations whi⸺ scious conscious and gives insight.

More recent explanations in relation to this question emphasize shifts ⸺ the organization of consciousness. These shifts are brought about through moments of shared awareness. A study-group in Boston consisting of psychoanalysts involved in the field of infant mental health has been exploring the process of change in psychotherapy (Tronick, 1998). Their starting point has been to describe how mutual regulation of affect creates states of dyadic consciousness in the mother–infant interaction. Tronick proposes that the process of mutual regulation of affect, which we observe in mother–infant interaction, might be the 'something more' that we are searching for to explain change in the psychotherapeutic process. A dyadic expansion of consciousness can be achieved between patient and therapist in creating a system for mutual regulation of affect. It is a purely emotional and implicit process. It operates as a force and vehicle for change in the mental organization of the patient. Furthermore it does not require interpretation. When this dyad is formed, the state of consciousness of the patient expands and change is facilitated. In this state of expanded consciousness, implicit knowledge of 'how to relate' can possibly be reorganized.

The client's wealth of implicit knowledge will be transformed by this new and real experience with the therapist. This type of interaction demands a relationship between patient and therapist that is characterized by authentic personal engagement and a reasonably competent ability to tune into the other person's present psychological and emotional state. Lyons-Ruth has named this 'a real relationship' as opposed to a therapy in which the emphasis is on semantic representations and giving verbal interpretations (Lyons-Ruth, 1998). 'Real relationships' form in the field where both client's and therapist's implicit relational knowing meet. That is affected by, but also goes beyond, the transference–countertransference relationship.

Another important concept developed by this group to help in understanding the process of change in psychotherapy is 'moments of meeting'. Moments of meeting are those moments in therapy when participants interact in a way that creates a new implicit intersubjective understanding of their relationship. This affords a new way of being with another (Morgan, 1998). The moment of meeting is the event that rearranges the patient's relational knowing through changing the intersubjective field between patient and therapist, for example, their dyadic state of consciousness. This allows for the possibility to elaborate on more complex and coherent states of consciousness. Moments of meeting may or may not be subject to interpretation. These moments are the key elements in bringing about change in plicit relational knowledge, just as interpretations bring about change in explicit knowledge (Stern, 1998).

Non-verbal methods in psychotherapy

As infancy research is being integrated into new theories of development there is a growing interest among psychotherapists to develop therapeutic methods which can take into account and reach the preverbal domains. New therapeutic techniques are needed to explore and bring about change in the domain of implicit relational knowing.

As experiences during the preverbal period never entered the semantic domain they can only be alluded to and cannot be fully described. Painters, musicians and poets can evoke the feeling, tone and affective memory of these early experiences. In order to reach the patient's preverbal experiences we need to develop therapeutic methods, which would convey and structure affect in a more complete way. In this respect body psychotherapy, movement therapy, dance therapy, art therapy and music therapy can offer valuable ports of entry. Tools from these methods could be integrated in the psychotherapist's repertoire to facilitate access to the preverbal domains of experience.

References

Ainsworth M, Blehar MC, Waters E, Wall S (1978) Patterns of Attachment. Hillsdale, NJ: Erlbaum.

Bateson MC (1975) Mother infant exchanges. In D Aronsson, D Rieber (eds), Developmental Psycholinguistics and Communication Disorders. Annals of the New York Academy of Sciences 263.

Berg Brodén M (1986) Therapeutic treatment of early disturbances in mother–child interaction. Paper presented at the Third World Conference of Infant Psychiatry (WAIPAD), Stockholm.

Berg Brodén M (1989) Mother and Child in No-Man's Land. Dublin: The Irish Institute for Integrated Psychotherapy.

Berg Brodén M (1989, 1992) Psykoterapeutiska interventioner under spädbarnsperioden. Dissertation (in Swedish), University of Lund.

Bower TGR (1974) Development in Infancy. San Francisco: Freeman.

Bowlby J (1969) Attachment and Loss: Vol. 1 Attachment. New York: Basic Books.

Bråten S (1992) The Virtual Other in Infants' Minds and Social Feeling, in the Dialogical Alternative. Oslo: Scandinavian University Press.

Bråten S. (1999) From intersubjective communication in infancy: virtuous and vicious circles of intergeneration re-enactment. Paper presented at the First International Conference on Existential Psychotherapy, Aarhus.

Bretherton I (1987) New perspectives on attachment relations: security, communication and internal working models. In J Osofsky (ed), Handbook of Infant Development. New York: John Wiley & Sons, Inc.

Bretherton I (1990) Communication patterns, internal working models, and the intergenerational transmission of attachment relationships. Infant Mental Health Journal 11(3): 237-52.

De Casper AJ, Spence MJ (1986) Prenatal maternal speech influences newborns' perception of speech sounds. Infant and Behavior and Development 9: 133-50.

Fairbairn WRD (1954) An Object Relation Theory of the Personality. New York: Basic Books.

Field TM (1984) Early interaction between infants and their post partum depressed mothers. Infant Behaviour and Development 7: 527-32.

Field TM, Cohen D, Garcia R, Greenberg R (1984) Mother-stranger face discrimination by the new-born. Infant Behaviour and Development 7: 19-26.

Fraiberg HS (1980) Clinical Studies in Infant Mental Health: The First Year of Life. New York: Basic Books.

George C, Solomon J (1996) Representational models of relationships; Links between caregiving and attachment. Infant Mental Health Journal 17(3): 198-216.

Grossman K (1992) Emotional sequel on early attachment pattern. Paper presented at WAIPAD World Conference in Chicago.

Havnesköld L (1992) Daniel Sterns Teorier. Stockholm: Almquist & Wiksell Förlag.

IJzendoorn HM Van (1995) Adult attachment representations, parental responsiveness and infant attachment: a meta-analysis of the predictive value of the adult attachment interview. Psychological Bulletin 117: 387-403.

Lyons-Ruth K (1998) Implicit relational knowing: its role in development and psychoanalytic treatment. Infant Mental Health Journal 19(3): 282-89.

MacFarlane J (1975) Olfaction in the development of social preferences in the human neonate. In IM Hofer (ed), Parent-Infant Interaction. Amsterdam: Elsevier.

Mahler M, Pine F, Bergman, A (1975) The Psychological Birth of the Human Infant. New York: Basic Books.

Main M, Cassidy J (1988) Categories of response to reunion with the parent at age 6: predictable from infant attachment classification and stable over a one-month period. Developmental Psychology 24(3): 415-26.

Main M, Goldwyn R (1985) Adult attachment classification system. Unpublished manuscript, University of California, Berkley, Dept of Psychology.

Main M, Kaplan N, Cassidy J (1985) Security in infancy, childhood and adulthood: a move to the level of representations. In I Bretherton, E Walters (eds), Monographs of the Society of Research in Child Development 50 (1-2, serial no. 209): 66-140. Chicago: University of Chicago Press.

Meltzoff AN, Borton W (1979) Intermodal matching by human neonates. Nature 282: 403-4.

Morgan A (1998) Moving along to things left undone. Journal of Infant Mental Health 19(3): 324-32.

Murray L (1991) Intersubjectivity, object relations theory and empirical evidence from the mother-infant interaction. Infant Mental Health Journal 12: 219-32.

Murray L, Cooper P (eds) (1997) Post Partum Depression and Infant Development. New York: Guildford.

Seligman MEP (1975) Helplessness: On Depression, Development and Death. San Francisco: Freeman.

Solomon J, George C (1996) Defining the caregiving system: towards a theory of caregiving. Infant Mental Health Journal 17(3): 183-97.

Stern D (1985) The Interpersonal World of the Infant. New York: Basic Books.

Stern D (1998) The process of therapeutic change involving implicit knowledge: some implications of developmental observations for adult psychotherapy. Infant Mental Health Journal 19(3): 300-8.

Stern D (2000) Introduction. The Interpersonal World of the Infant. Pbk edn, transl into Danish. Copenhagen: Reitzel Forlag.

Trevarthen C (1979) Communication and co-operation in early infancy. In M Bullowa (ed), Before Speech. Cambridge: Cambridge University Press.

Trevarthen C (1980) The foundations of intersubjectivity. In D Olson (ed), The Social Foundation of Language and Thought. New York: Norton.

Tronick EZ (1998) Dyadically expanded states of consciousness and the process of therapeutic change. Infant Mental Health Journal 19(3): 290-9.

Tronick EZ, Cohn J (1989) Infant–mother face-to-face-interaction: age and gender differences in coordinations and the occupancy of miscoordination. Child Development 60: 85-92.

Tronick EZ, Als H, Adamson L et al. (1978) The infant's response to entrapment between contradictory messages in face to face interaction. American Academy of Child Psychiatry 17(1): 1-13.

Tronick EZ, Cohn J, Shea E (1986) The transfer of affect between mothers and infants. In TB Brazelton, MW Yogman (eds), Affective Development in Infancy. Norwood: Ablex.

Winnicott DW (1956) Collected Papers. London: Tavistock.

CHAPTER 7

Integrating object relations narratives in analytic work with children and adolescents

PAUL SEPPING

> The initiation of object-relating is complex. It cannot take place except by the environmental provision of object-presenting, done in such a way that the baby creates the object ... the baby develops a vague expectation that has origin in unformulated need. The adaptive mother presents an object or a manipulation that meets the baby's needs, and so the baby begins to need just that which the mother presents. (Winnicott, 1965, p. 62)

The integrating of different versions of object relations

There is no single version of 'the object relations story'. Like so much else in the subject of the psyche, object relations stories are plural (Samuels, 1989). Thus the account of the child's object relations given by Klein in 1932 was superseded by her own 'modifications' of the object relations story of 1948 (Klein, 1948, p. xiii). Klein acknowledges that Anna Freud gives a different account or version of the child's object relations, one where the child cannot develop a full transference to the therapist because 'the old edition (of its love relationships) ... is not yet exhausted ... its original objects, the parents, are still real and present as love objects' (Freud, 1927, p. 34). Then, unable to agree on the timing of the Oedipus complex (among other things), the two versions remain side-by-side within the Institute of Psychoanalysis on a sort of gentle-women's agreement. Winnicott has summarized their different contributions in several papers (1958 and 1965) and has added numerous modifications and additions, so richly that it could be said that there is a Winnicottian version. Another early and notable contribution came from Fairbairn (1952) who hypothesized an 'original inherent unitary ego' which introjected its objects before splitting, thus disagreeing with Abraham's modifications of Freud's initial (and then finalized) version of libidinal development (published posthumously in 1940). Then came the further versions of object relations summarized by Guntrip (1971), Green (1975, 1987), Sandler and Sandler (1978), Kohut (1984), Kernberg (1988, 1993), Steiner (1989) and Sandler (1992). The complications of articulating a common theory or version of the object relations story are well summarized by Schafer (1990) who divides the problems into linguistic, methodological and ideological considerations. He thus highlights the differences of meaning that analytical therapists might reveal in their wording of even their most central concepts (such as 'analysis of transference'). He considers that we should not necessarily be aiming for a 'single master text for psychoanalysis'. Rather, 'we should work with a sense that our differences show us all the things that psychoanalysis can be even though it cannot be all things at one time or for any one person. The alternative is the blindness of conformism' (Schafer, 1990, p. 52).

Psychoanalytic contributions to object relations theory have a prominent place, but not a monopoly, and it is possible that ethologists and geneticists will make modifications and, perhaps, new versions of the object relations story (Bateman and Holmes, 1995, p. 48). For example, Bowlby's attention to attachment theory has stimulated experiments by Mary Main and others, which have resulted in the refining and standardizing of research instruments, such as the Strange Situation and the Adult Attachment Interview or AAI (Main in Goldberg et al., 1995). The use of these instruments has yielded results that support the doctrine of the constancy of internal objects, i.e. that there is relative stability in the type of attachment status to the most significant figures in the child's life (ibid., p. 438). It has also been shown that prospective parents 'pass on' attachment behaviour to their offspring, i.e. that prospective parents' attachment status on their AAI is a reliable predictor of their future infant's attachment status on their Strange Situation test (ibid., p. 446).

A simple example of the narrative use of object relations

The following youngster's treatment illustrates how discussion in a narrative style, using little interpretation, can more naturally inform an object relations perspective. Stephen was a rosy-cheeked boy of 10 with sparkling dark eyes. His bad moods got him into trouble at home and school. He didn't know why he got bad moods. His parents brought him to the Child Guidance Clinic with his younger twin brother and sister. His mother didn't tell me at first that I had seen her as a girl of 17 when her mother had died of a brain tumour. She had felt I hadn't heard her story at that time, as I asked the family as a whole to come, and after the initial interview, I had invited the father only to return.

He hadn't done so, and the case had been closed. The 17 year old had been bright, and had thrown herself into her schoolwork to stave off her depression. She had grown up to study law and got her degree during Stephen's early tears as a toddler (what an interesting parapraxis!). Then she had the younger children and felt forced to become a full-time mother. This resulted in her suffering several major depressions and making several determined suicide bids. Stephen had seen police and ambulance men carrying his mother out of the house and off to mental hospital. He told me he wanted to be a policeman like his father, or a presenter of children's programmes on the BBC.

The first individual session included a story about 'Queenie'. Stephen, using the building blocks, enacted a drama where Queenie's home got blown up by a man with dynamite, who then got blown up himself by Queenie with dynamite, in revenge. Stephen invented many more stories around the theme of the blowing up of the home of the king and queen. He also used my supply of paper clips to construct a chain that was used for rescuing the royal couple from being blown up. A Jungian version of object relations would likely include the royal couple as a type of combined object, although it could also stand for the Self (Jung, 1964).

At about the 12th session, Stephen's dollhouse stories changed to a family where the mother was very strict. The father eventually attempts to run away with them, but the mother discovers the plan and punishes all the family, both children and father. Then came changes in the ending where the mother gets her punishment by being put in gaol for a year, on a diet of bread and water. Then the nightmares were brought, involving mad dogs, goblins and burglars. These sessions were punctuated by mum's further admissions to mental hospital. Eventually, mother's depression became controllable and Stephen's moods and nightmares subsided. He started reading *The Lord of the Rings*, and his sessions could tail off, with subsequent discharge from the clinic and the offer of further contact, if it was needed.

Much of Stephen's therapy was conventional, though very little interpretation was needed. His dollhouse stories indicated his unconscious anger at his mother and this sharing of it with another who seemed to understand him had the effect of a less troubling introject and a consequent improvement in his mood. Winnicott (1971) shows how the child can be helped to get back over a phase of loss of the object, back to an earlier phase of satisfactory relation to the object, by the ability of the therapist to act as a transitional object. It is not just the therapist's ability to interpret which enables the child to use this object to bridge the gap. Rather, it is the therapist's ability to survive and to continue relating to the child in an understanding and interested way. Bion refers to this activity of the mother (and subsequently the therapist) as her 'reverie'. Reverie requires the mother's (or therapist's) *alpha* function, the function of making *beta* elements (or 'pre-thoughts') available for thoughtfulness. The mother or therapist receives impressions from the child and converts these into material for the couple to think about, enabling the child to read the other's response as attempts to realize the quality of the child's distress (see Bion, 1962, p. 17 for a detailed account).

In the case of Stephen above, a narrative slant required no great modifications to a contemporary 'middle group' or 'British Independent' version of an object relations approach.

Children whose objects have frozen

It is more difficult with children who find it impossible to communicate, who are frozen and watchful and expressionless, not because of overt abuse, and not only because it is their first experience of psychotherapy, but because they have developed a habit of emotional inhibition. One such teenager (Roderick) whom I treated in Child Guidance was a 14-year-old encopretic (i.e. soiling) boy, who was academically bright but emotionally repressed. His soiling had begun when he was six, his father having left the family one year before. His stepfather had moved in one year after his soiling commenced. He had an older sister and two younger (half) brothers. In object relations terms, he had developed a compliant false self (Winnicott, 1965) in his relationships within the family and also in his schoolboy relationships at an academic, selective school. One could say he had developed an academic persona using the ego defence mechanism of intellectualization. The aggressive aspect of his personality seemed entirely missing, though the faecal problem certainly 'punished' his family.

After I saw him with his mother (his stepfather didn't attend), we began individual psychotherapy. *Or at least I did!* Roderick remained expressionless and quite still and silent ... absolutely tongue-tied in response to the invitation to use the time as he wished. I tried to maintain a benign neutrality, 'without memory or desire' (Bion, 1967, 1988). After several sessions, during which I played the squiggle game[1] with him, I invited him to draw whatever he wished (and/or use the toys within the room: building blocks, set of small human figures, model house etc.). He would take up the coloured pencils but pause over the blank paper ... and then ... freeze. He would say he didn't know what to draw. After several attempts at this, I suggested he lie on the couch. I gave him the choice to lie either end, so he could see me or have me out of sight, and I slightly averted my chair. The room filled with silence ... and then ... it stayed tensely silent for the remainder of the session. I suggested he consider joining my weekly group-analytic older teenager's group, although on entry he was the only male (apart from myself as conductor). It was at the time full of rather chatty girls and they gently encouraged him to communicate by their easy interpersonal ways. He had found the right setting and had begun his psychotherapeutic journey. Was this a case of frozen internal objects, or was it the delay required for the patient to re-access the little-used and frozen pathways between the real self and the external world?

When the object lacks a real external dimension

While Roderick had difficulty getting into a verbalized narrative of any kind, there are some children who can only survive in someone else's narrative, much like Sophie in *Sophie's World* (Gaarder, 1994), whom I have discussed previously (Sepping in Mace, 1999). Gordon, aged 12, is an example of such a child who is stuck inside stories. I had seen him for an assessment of his encopresis. (Perhaps children stuck outside of stories, like Roderick, or inside stories, like Gordon, have a tendency to the anal inhibition of consti-pation and overflow soiling.) Gordon, from age 5–11 years of age, had been seeing nurse therapists who worked with him and his single-parent mother in (unsuccessfully) treating him for his soiling and for being bullied. Gordon had two half-brothers aged seven and three. Only the last boy's father had stayed with the family for any time and had recently married Gordon's mother.

But now, aged 12, at reassessment, Gordon was not only soiling, he was practically friendless, had been given the diagnosis of Asperger's Syndrome[2] by a senior paediatrician, had also developed the habit of pulling out his eyebrows and eyelashes, had started rocking in a foetal position in the school playground, and writing notes saying he felt unsafe and that he'd rather live away from home, to join up with his paternal aunt and cousin in Wales. He was bullied by other boys because of his rather bizarre appearance. Though his mother was a good-hearted person, this family was going through difficul-ties at the time, and his name was put on the Child Protection Register.

At the reassessment interview, Gordon's eyes never met mine. Not untyp-ical of Asperger's syndrome, I thought. His mother brought him (his stepfa-ther did not attend). If I asked him a direct question, mother attempted to speak for him. I pointed this out and I asked Gordon another direct question. Although he didn't look at me, he answered clearly and without hesitation in a factually coherent and correct way. What was more interesting was that his prosody and his intonation were quite normal and emotionally fully present. This was very promising from a prognostic point of view. It also made me wonder if the diagnosis of Asperger's was correct, though it was easy to see how the diagnosis had been made, considering Gordon's solitariness, his total avoidance of eye contact and his public display of foetal rocking in the school playground.

Again, in object relations terms, Gordon seemed to have given up on most human relationships. A compliant self had taken over the usual requirements of factual communication in the home and school. He had settled into a lifestyle of taking senna to avoid constipation, pulling out his eyelashes and eyebrows, and continuing to feed his true self with wonderful stories. Instead of the intellectual defence of the previous patient (Roderick), Gordon developed the 'narrative defence'. He lived in stories rather than living his own life story. He wasn't at all sure, he said, if he would take up my offer for individual psychotherapy, which I made at the end of the reassessment.

However, within a week or two, his mother phoned to say he would do so. Why had I left it so much up to him? I think I had initially felt that he was used to his mother making decisions for him and his compliant false-self responding to whatever arrangements she protectively made for him. By my emphasizing to her (in his presence) that it had to be his decision to enter therapy, I felt I had a better chance of an enhanced treatment alliance with my possible future patient. Another way of saying this is that I wanted to create the optimal situation for eventually qualifying as a (transitional) object worth him introjecting. Although Kernberg (1999) sees little possibility that once weekly therapy can be analytically effective, all the children that I discuss here are in that sort of therapy and I find it can be therapeutic enough for many of our Child Guidance referrals, though not for all. The real issue is whether the child is able to use the therapist as an introjectible object.

Gordon had decided to compose a family with four children and two adults. He was to stick with this basic family structure over several months. He structured his fantasy family, which he called the Hughes family, as follows: the only wooden faceless armless figure in the toy collection (I have only one collection that all my patients share) was chosen as the oldest boy, then came twins (a boy and a girl), then the baby. The boy twin was good at schoolwork, Gordon said, and had to do extra homework. He crept downstairs at night to eat some crisps in the kitchen. Here Gordon paused, as if expecting me to contribute to the story. I responded. 'His mum doesn't let him steal too many,' I said, and Gordon seemed to approve of this, an admittedly intuitive guess on my part. Why did I participate in the story construction when I felt bidden by the patient? According to Sandler (1992), the therapist can experience a sense of 'role responsiveness' as a way of getting in touch with the patient's projections, but the therapist should re-establish his neutrality as soon as the information about the nature of the projection is evident to him (and to the patient, hopefully)! It may be that very severely disturbed children should be responded to more circumspectly.

Perhaps I had used my intuition that Gordon's family situation involved a withdrawal of maternal oral gratification as he was nearing his teens. Gordon seemed to appreciate this interactive and co-constructive approach

(Papadopoulos and Byng-Hall, 1997) by showing me more meaningful eye contact, and perhaps it was no coincidence that time was up for this session. When he was leaving, he told me he wanted to be a paediatrician! Was he indicating a positive transference and if so to what extent is this necessarily defensive? Why didn't I interpret this? After all, Spence (1993) shows how transference interpretation can increase objective measures of free association. And free association is regarded by Bollas (1999) as being the goal of all psychoanalytic technique.

In any case, the next session again had mother in the room, with her son, and this time with the school tutor. I noticed Gordon absorbing himself in *Harry Potter and the Prisoner of Azkaban* and C.S. Lewis's *The Voyage of the Dawn Treader*, while the two women described their concerns about Gordon. These shared sessions pay dividends for the viability of long-term treatment, as they help allay the possible maternal envy and jealousy when the child starts to grow away or individuate from a previously fused relationship with his mother (or father). Once alone with me, Gordon seemed preoccupied with Prince Caspian's escape from his uncle (who had taken his father's throne, much as Hamlet's uncle had). Gordon told me that Caspian had taken refuge in the forest with the wild animals warning him and hiding him from the Trolls who roamed the area. What was he trying to communicate to me about his internal objects? Was he a prey to persecutory phantasies of troll-like monsters who forced him to hide his true self, while his false compliant self tried to copy his 'uncle' (stepfather), who had usurped his father's 'crown and throne' (as his mother's partner)?

Whatever the answers to these object relations questions, the next session saw Gordon bringing in two books, ignoring the play things I routinely lay out, and reading quietly for the whole session! Would he like to share the reading of alternating paragraphs with me? No! Would he like to share where he had got to in the story? No! But he knew, without looking up, exactly when the session had five minutes to go and told me that the band of Caspian's men were entering a village on one of the Lone Islands and didn't know what they would find. Gordon started to make furtive eye contact with me. I told him I was retiring in two years but we could see one another in sessions until then, if he wanted. He smiled and seemed pleased.

You will have observed that I avoided direct interpretation both of his decision to read for the session and of his story about Caspian's entering an unknown village on a Lone Island. Why? I did it to promote the treatment alliance. I could have interpreted that he was retaliating to my ignoring him while attending to his mother and school tutor in the previous session. But one unfortunate aspect of models which concentrate on analysing the transference (meant for daily therapy) was that it was applied to weekly therapy, where it was inclined to sound to the patient as if he were being blamed.

Interpretations of the patient's part-objects (often depicted as body parts or body excretions) can sometimes leave the patient bamboozled, outraged, embarrassed or simply wanting to disagree. All these possible reactions can put the treatment alliance at risk, and, in any case, there are now other ways of proceeding (Alvarez and Reid, 1999; Hurry, 1998) which can often avoid unnecessary confrontations.

It is often hard for the therapist if a patient chooses to engage in an alternative to a talking behaviour for most of the hour. During my attempts to stay in 'reverie', I occasionally passed a remark, almost in soliloquy (Gans, 1994). My remarks were about having known Gordon for seven years, having seen that he had had to put up with a succession of father figures, and wondering aloud if he had nightmares. He had furtively glanced at me between the pages of *The Voyage of the Dawn Treader*, said he slept fine, with no dreams. But the following session, Gordon seemed much less depressed and talked a lot about Harry Potter. I tried to link Harry Potter's experience of parenting with that of Gordon, only to be corrected curtly that Harry Potter's parents were dead while his own were very much alive, though often absent or unavailable. (His mother by this time was giving more attention to her new husband and younger sons.)

Next, Gordon turned up looking sad, and after a silence I asked whether he was missing his father and he nodded. He said he'd tried the last phone number he had but the line was discontinued. His aunt in Wales might have the new number or address of his Dad. He then asked me where *The Hobbit* fitted into *The Lord of the Rings* and took down my copy of it to check. He then drew an accurate map of the West Country and Wales railway network.

The Hughes family dollhouse story went into further episodes, where the parents were twinned with the names Daniel and Danielle and checked their twin daughter's homework, and where the older (but still under-age) brother takes his sister for a trip in the family car without the parents' knowledge. What is Gordon trying to tell me? He then mentions that he's finished *The Voyage of the Dawn Treader*, and that he specially likes Harry Potter's friend Hermione. By now my head is reeling from the possible and myriad meanings of this narrative camouflage and self-protectiveness. Is Gordon trying to indicate anything, or am I dealing with an organic syndrome characterized by the neural defect in sequencing and social signalling of Asperger's Syndrome? My eyelids begin to grow heavy (Brown, 1977), and I struggle against an overwhelming desire to sleep ... Gordon looks at me in a concerned way and says, 'I hope it isn't Dumbledore that dies.' I become more alert at this remark, made with direct and intense eye contact. He then looks relieved and, after a pause, adds, 'I don't think he'll die, because it says somewhere that wizards live to a great old age.' This felt like a clearly transferential remark, perhaps expressing his fears that he might lose my attention and possibly the whole therapeutic relationship.

Meanwhile the paediatricians were responding to mother's anguish that she regularly heard him crying in his bedroom by increasing his antidepressants.

Gordon came to his next session carrying the railway timetable for Wales and the West. He tells me he intends to run away to Monmouth and not tell his mother. This is clearly a conspiratorial bid in the transference. How much would my silence be an implied assent to a phantasized collusive relationship? I interpret that he is expressing his desperation at missing his father. He nods. For the first time, I notice that, at the end of the session, he is extremely reluctant to finish.

Mother phones before the next session to say, in an agitated voice, that Gordon has exposed himself at school and has 'snogged' another boy. She is very upset.

At the start of the next session, a smiling Gordon, clearly in denial, announces that he has finished volume four of Harry Potter, and that an important character does die. Using what Casement (1990) calls 'my internal supervisor' and my 'trial identification with the patient', I suspect he's telling me that the child in him is dying and that he's having trouble giving birth to the man. I ask him how old he is, and he says, 'Thirteen.' I pause, then, almost in a soliloquy, add, '... Yes ... that's around the age that boys get big willies, isn't it?' My patient hides his face for most of the remainder of the session. After ten minutes, I again get very sleepy, and in fact close my eyes for a few seconds, and I think I go into REM visualization.[3] *I briefly see a man who is putting a folded blanket on a shelf...* I 'start' as I come to, and wonder aloud if Gordon might feel as if his dad has shelved the important task of talking to him about sexuality at this particular age. He nods. I ask him if he feels embarrassed that I am not his father talking to him like this. He nods, and I notice that he no longer has to hide his face. In object relations terms, Gordon is showing a weakness in the relation he has with his internal paternal object, and he indicates that he is able to use me as a transitional object in this regard (see Meltzer, 1972, 1976, for a detailed discussion of the problems of distinguishing between inspired interpretations and the risks of megalomania).

In one of his last books, *The Piggle*, Winnicott (1977) illustrated a similar use of the patient's projective identification in his account of the analysis of a little girl. In the use of this technique, it is important that the projection goes into (emotively felt), as well as on to (consciously known), the interpreting therapist, otherwise the interpretation may lose impact. The complex object relations movements underlying this way of working with difficult patients have been recently described by Newirth (2000).

The following meeting, Gordon announces it's his 13th birthday. He says he's 'gutted' that Harry Potter hasn't moved in with Sirius Black (his godfather) yet. I avoid the obvious transference interpretation. He again adds, 'Somebody dies.' He draws a fun park. Suddenly I realize that he's been drawing fun parks for the last few sessions as he's been chatting to me, and I wonder aloud if he'd really like to spend 52 weeks a year living in fun parks. (This is my way of trying to get it across to him that he's tending to shelter in stories rather than use them as a way of relating to real life. I'm not sure that it succeeds!) He again speaks of running away but, significantly, does not put a date on it this time. He is smiling more and, for the first time, he gets down on the floor to draw (he has gone to considerable trouble previously to avoid this symbolic regression, and has remained cooped up and protected in his chair). He draws a watchful eye and a caption, cleverly using letter abbreviations: 'I.C.U. ... Baby I'm watching U'. Clearly, regression in the transference was making Gordon vulnerable, and therefore anxiously watchful.

Next session, Gordon asks about my family. I answer him truthfully, and not with silence, or with a reflected question about why he's asking me. I am aware that this departs from almost all analytical definitions of neutrality. But before I answer Gordon's questions about myself, I have consulted the countertransference, or that part of it that is conscious, and it feels intuitively correct to proceed with the simple truth about myself, without hedging or other complicated ways of avoiding directness and factual accuracy. Gordon then reports happily that his mother is taking him on a local scenic railway trip. Is this displacement of the search for the father, or could it be a rapprochement with his mother as now less of a persecutory internal object, now that his masculinity has been validated and affirmed (i.e. been introjected into the true self)?

The long summer break occurs.

I return from holiday to find that Gordon has threatened to kill himself and his baby brother with a knife. His stepfather had needed admission to an alcohol detoxification unit and his mother had become preoccupied with him and Gordon had felt a loss of the combined object (i.e. the internal image of both parents together). Mother says she feels excluded from the sessions I have with her oldest son and the locum consultant on holiday duty encourages her to contact me about it on my return.

Next session, Gordon is quiet. We discuss what happened. He says he is angry with his younger brothers, who call him names. I remember that he has been bullied in the past about his effeminate gait, and I wonder whether he has been called 'gay' or 'poof', and has retaliated with the knife threats. I notice that he holds a fun park brochure in his hand for the entire session. Is this his transitional object? Is he halfway out of his compulsive need to take constant refuge in fantasy and story?

Different ways of using an object

In each of the three examples given above, the therapist was made into a different type of object. Stephen needed the analyst to understand what his dollhouse stories were about. He needed to portray a graphic account of his unspeakable anger at the experience of losing a mother who was otherwise engaged with her own delayed mourning process, which was about her own mother's death. He needed a 'container' for his own psychotic anxiety at the threatened loss of the maternal object (Bion, 1970). Roderick, on the other hand, could not use the therapist in individual therapy as the required object, but could begin to use the analytic group as the required or introjectible object (see Winnicott, 1971, for a more detailed account of the use of an object).

The third patient, Gordon, comes to therapy with the inability to use any external person(s) as introjectible, but instead uses the fantasies of another person's mind (that is, the author's fictional stories) for his (internal) objects. Only later in his therapy does he begin to projectively identify the therapist with some of his internal objects (e.g. Dumbledore and Sirius Black), and thus start on the road to developing his transference neurosis.

Object relations as a basis for integrating different dynamic psychotherapies

From the family therapy point of view, the first patient, Stephen, could have used his parents as the containers of his rage, but they were already in individual therapy themselves, and may not have had the ego strength to 'hear' his communication at that time, though most families can and do act as the 'holding function' (Winnicott, 1965) for their children's anxieties. In other words, for Stephen to experience an alteration in his internal objects, his family would have had to provide a 'minimum sufficient network' (Skynner, 1989, 1991) for the family therapist to work with.

With regard to Gordon's psychotherapy arrangements, it could be that the mother needed to take a step back from her previous and traditional level of involvement ... one could say, over-involvement ... with her first-born son. An early term that attempted to link systems theory to the analytic terminology, to describe this sort of family problem was 'undifferentiated ego mass'. That is, the problem in this case was the intrusive nature of the patient's experience of the mother, in conjunction with the desperately felt need of her attention, not an uncommon ambivalence for children with only one effective parental introject or object.

Freud had been the first to note that the most common cause of failure to progress to a satisfactory conclusion of analysis was resistance from quarters outside the analytic couple, i.e. the family surrounding the patient. This extension of the object relations paradigm to dynamic considerations outside the therapy couple, however, is the weakest area of application of the object relations metaphor. For example, Samuels (1993) has pointed out that the metaphor of object relations is biased toward seeing individuals as the fundamental unit, whereas he has suggested the model of psyche as a network. In this model, a collection of individuals would resemble the different stalks of a rhizome (i.e. a single organism with subterranean connections between its scattered members). Samuels's model replaces the lost horizontal dimension, which the developmental model marginalizes in favour of the vertical relations of parenting and 'childing'. In this way, Samuels's suggestion provides for the relational possibilities of the peer-group interactions of bargaining and exchange (Brown and Zinkin, 1994).

Foulkes was also aware of the West's traditional philosophical bias of marginalizing the group in favour of centralizing the individual. He proposed that individuals be considered as 'nodes' within a network or plexus (1964), and he referred to the totality of the object relations between all members of the analytic group as the group's *matrix*. This line of basic philosophical criticism was taken further by Brown and Zinkin (1994) who commented,

> the contributions of systems theory to understanding individual development ... is to provide a framework for what actually happens in families: for connecting the internal world of the individual to the interactions of the social context, for relating the internal object to the external object. (pp. 42–3)

The object relations story is currently a contested one, and this is a sign of healthy plurality. But the disagreements within this field are comparatively small compared with the wide-ranging differences between the various approaches of the dynamic psychotherapies. In order to compare the relative merits of these assorted traditions of psychotherapy, a common language is needed. At present, the language of object relations (with an expanded vocabulary of group and family therapy terms) appears to be the strongest candidate to help us to integrate our knowledge and evaluation of these differing approaches. The choice of object relations for this integrative task is supported by recent research findings, which show that it is possible to distinguish reliably between object relations categories (Hobson et al., 1998). It is also supported by the findings on the stability of our attachment behaviours (Holmes in Mace, 1999), which are the external correlates of our internalized relations to our objects.

Perhaps we should also be thinking of the possibility that a person's objects can become his subjects as well, and be recognized as such, thus opening him to the enjoyment and enrichment of intersubjective relations (Benjamin, 1995).

Notes

[1] Winnicott's squiggle game is a turn-taking, pencil-and-paper game where the therapist make a rapid and spontaneous squiggle and invites the child to complete the squiggle into something that the child thinks it could become. Then it is the child's turn to do a squiggle, and so on. And often a conversation goes on while the game proceeds.

[2] Thought to be a neurological disorder, characterized by difficulty recognizing social cues and gestures.

[3] REM stands for 'rapid eye movement' and denotes a stage normally occurring in sleep when one dreams in images. The visual experience can occur in the waking state, though it is rare.

References

Alvarez A, Reid S (eds) (1999) Autism and Personality. London: Routledge.

Bateman A, Holmes J (1995) Introduction to Psychoanalysis. London: Routledge.

Benjamin J (1995) Like Subjects, Love Objects: Essays on Recognition and Sexual Difference. New Haven: Yale University Press.

Bion W (1962) Learning from Experience. London: Maresfield Library, Karnac.

Bion W (1967) Notes on memory and desire. The Psychoanalytic Forum 2: 272-3; 279-80; also in E Bott Spillius (ed) (1988) Melanie Klein Today, Vol. 2: Mainly Practice (17-21). London: Routledge.

Bion W (1970) Attention and Interpretation. London: Maresfield Library, Karnac.

Bollas C (1999) The Mystery of Things. London: Routledge.

Brown D (1977) Drowsiness in the countertransference. International Review of Psycho-Analysis 4: 481-92.

Brown D, Zinkin L (1994) The Psyche and The Social World. London: Routledge.

Casement P (1990) Further Learning from the Patient. London: Routledge.

Fairbairn WRD (1952) Psychoanalytic Studies of the Personality. London: Tavistock.

Foulkes S (1964) Therapeutic Group Analysis. London: George Allen & Unwin.

Freud A (1927, 1946) The Psychoanalytical Treatment of Children. London: Imago.

Freud S (1940) An Outline of Psychoanalysis. Standard Edition 23. London: Hogarth.

Gaarder J (1994) Sophie's World. A Novel about the History of Philosophy. London: Phoenix.

Gans JS (1994) Indirect communication as a therapeutic technique. American Journal of Psychotherapy 48(1): 120-40.

Goldberg S, Muir R, Kerr J (eds) (1995) Attachment Theory: Social, Developmental, and Clinical Perspectives. London: The Analytic Press.

Green A (1975) The analyst, symbolisation and absence in the analytic setting (on changes in analytic practice and experience). International Journal of Psycho-Analysis 56: 1-22.

Green A (1987) Changes in psychoanalytic ideas: transference interpretation. Journal of the American Psychoanalytic Association 35: 77-98.

Guntrip H (1971, 1977) Psychoanalytic Theory, Therapy and the Self. London: Karnac.

Hobson RP, Patrick MPH, Valentine JD (1998) Objectivity in psychoanalytic judgements. British Journal of Psychiatry 173: 172-7.

Holmes J (1999) Narrative, attachment and the therapeutic process. In C Mace (ed), Heart and Soul: The Therapeutic Face of Philosophy. London: Routledge.

Hurry A (ed) (1998) Psychoanalysis and Developmental Therapy. London: Karnac.

Jung CG (1964, 1990) Man and his Symbols. London: Arkana Penguin.

Kernberg O (1988) Object relations theory in clinical practice. Psychoanalytic Quarterly 57: 481–504.

Kernberg O (1993) Convergences and divergences in contemporary psychoanalytic technique. International Journal of Psycho-Analysis 74: 659–73.

Kernberg O (1999) Psychoanalysis, psychoanalytic psychotherapy and supportive psychotherapy: contemporary controversies. International Journal of Psycho-Analysis 80: 1075–91.

Klein M (1932, 1948, 1975) The Psycho-Analysis of Children. London: The Hogarth Press.

Kohut H (1984) How does Analysis Cure? Chicago: University of Chicago Press.

Mace C (ed) (1999) Heart and Soul: The Therapeutic Face of Philosophy. London and New York: Routledge.

Main M (1995) Recent studies in attachment. In S Goldberg, R Muir, J Kerr (eds), Attachment Theory: Social, Developmental, and Clinical Perspectives. London: The Analytic Press.

Meltzer D (1972) Temperature and distance as technical dimensions of interpretation. Psychoanalysis in Europe 9: 39–45.

Meltzer D (1976) Routine and inspired interpretations – their relation to the weaning process in analysis. Contemporary Psychoanalysis 14(2): 210–25.

Newirth J (2000) Impasses in the psychoanalytic relationship. Journal of Clinical Psychology 56(2): 225–31.

Papadopoulos RK, Byng-Hall J (1997) Multiple Voices. London: Duckworth.

Samuels A (1989) The Plural Psyche. London and New York: Routledge.

Samuels A (1993) The Political Psyche. London: Routledge.

Sandler J (1992) Reflections on the developments in the theory of psychoanalytic technique. International Journal of Psycho-Analysis 73: 189–8.

Sandler J, Sandler A (1978) On the development of object relationships and affects. International Journal of Psycho-Analysis 59: 285–96.

Schafer R (1990) The search for common ground. International Journal of Psycho-Analysis 71: 49–2.

Sepping P (1999) Narrative and interpretation. In C Mace (ed) Heart and Soul: The Therapeutic Face of Philosophy. London: Routledge.

Skynner R (1989, 1991) Institutes and How to Survive Them. London: Routledge.

Spence DP (1993) Impact of interpretation on associative freedom. Journal of Consultation and Clinical Psychology 61(3): 359–402.

Steiner J (1989) The aim of psychoanalysis. Psychoanalytic Psychotherapy 4(2): 109–20.

Winnicott DW (1958) Collected Papers: Through Paediatrics to Psycho-Analysis. London: Tavistock.

Winnicott DW (1965, 1990) The Maturational Processes and the Facilitating Environment. London: Karnac.

Winnicott DW (1971) Playing and Reality. London: Tavistock.

Winnicott DW (1977, 1991) The Piggle: An Account of the Psychoanalytic Treatment of a Little Girl. New York: International Universities Press.

CHAPTER 8

The weave of object relations and family systems thinking: working therapeutically with families and couples in a community alcohol service

ARLENE VETERE AND MAVIS HENLEY

Working therapeutically with couples where one of them has a problem with drinking is complex and demanding. In this chapter we introduce our integration of the theories and practices of group analytic psychotherapy, object relations and systemic psychotherapy as our response to this complexity. We hope to show how we draw on ideas and practices that have stood the test of therapeutic time and which lend themselves to flexible and innovative use within our collaborative therapeutic partnership. We shall address some of the therapeutic issues that we encounter, and trace the development of our thinking about the impact on couple relationships and family groups of problem drinking. To do this, we shall describe our experience of therapeutic engagement in the context of the Prochaska and DiClemente (1992) model of the stages of change in giving up addictive behaviour. The Prochaska and DiClemente model has been adopted by the community alcohol service within which our couples and family therapy service is located.

Do we need a couples and family therapy service in a community alcohol service?

The complexity of the impact of problem drinking over time on family life and relationships led us to integrate ideas and practices from different social science disciplines and schools of psychotherapy. Understanding the nature of the attachments between couples where drink is the problem has become crucial in our work (Bowlby, 1979). Where these attachments are characterized by violence, coercion and emotional abuse, and underpinned by problematic gender assumptions and the overt and covert abuse of power, we needed a framework that would allow us to draw on different theoretical sources to help us with formulation and planning change in drinking habits. Systemic psychotherapy provided us with the framework within which we could explore the theory and practice connections with group analytic psychotherapy (Behr, 1994), personal relations theory (Berg and Clark, 1986), and feminist informed socio-political critiques of power and gender (Burck and Speed, 1995). Systemic psychotherapy with its emphasis on connection and meaning helps us to think about patterning and process in relationships in the past and present (Vetere, 1998); group analytic psychotherapy offers us a means to think about the development of the inner world and how that inner world is expressed in family groups and influenced in relationship with others, over time. The different perspectives on connection and meaning offered by these two major psychotherapeutic approaches enhance and complement each other (Behr, 1994). We are familiar with, and welcome, the literature on the rapprochement between family systems and analytic thinking (Larner, 2000). For us, integrative practice is an approach that recognizes no one explanatory model is sufficient when working with complex phenomena like addictions and their iterative effects within family relationships. Our integrative approach is guided by our respect for each other, what each new couple teaches us, our clinical experience, and most importantly, our commitment to familiarity with more than one theoretical perspective. Clinical examples of our integrative approach appear later in the chapter.

Orford and Harwin (1982) and Velleman (1992) have graphically documented the psychological effects of problem drinking on family members and their relationships. Impacts include disruption to family members' roles, routines, communications and family celebrations, with effects also on social life and family finances. Steinglass et al. (1987) made a helpful differentiation between family groups where problem drinking has become a central organizing feature of family life, and families where this systemic reorganization seems not to have occurred. In addition, they draw our attention to the effects on family relationships and on family life of alternating patterns of drinking and sobriety. Based on our clinical observations in our couples and family therapy service we wish to contribute further to ideas about the effects of problem drinking on couples' object relations using our synthesis of systemic psychotherapy and group analytic therapy theories as a framework.

Edwards and Steinglass's (1995) review of the treatment efficacy for couples and family therapy with problem drinking points out that most of the treatment outcome studies have involved men as the partner with the drinking problem and may well have excluded more complex cases. Kent (1990) has observed that a man's heavy drinking is likely to be tolerated for a longer period of time by his family and friends than is a woman's. In addition, she observed that a man is more likely to end his relationship with a woman who has a problem with drink, whereas women tend to stay in partnership with heavy drinking men for longer. In many ways, a woman partner is in a less powerful position, both financially and interpersonally, than the husband of a woman with a drink problem.

Brief description of our couples and family therapy service

Both permanent team members are women; one is a group analytic psychotherapist, the other is a systemic psychotherapist. We accept referrals from our community alcohol service colleagues only, thus ensuring that good convening practices and regular liaison underpin our service, thus minimizing the potential for splitting within staff and client relationships.

Our team uses in-room consultation and reflecting process conversations, derived both from systemic and group analytic practices. This is our preferred way of working for a number of reasons: (a) many of the families we see have been subject to professional scrutiny over long periods of time and the use of a one-way screen may elicit negative transference and interfere with therapeutic engagement; (b) the family can act as a harsh distorting mirror to its members and reflecting conversations can offer a gentler, kinder reflection, as part of the process of recovery and reparation; (c) reflecting conversations can be used as an opportunity to introduce new ideas, under-line and support what is going well, introduce challenging ideas in a non-confrontational way and offer suggestions; and (d) inviting family members to comment on the team's reflecting conversations privileges their observations and comments in a way that helps develop collaborative working practices. In group analytic thinking the family and reflecting team form a group which encompasses the norms and practices of the larger society in which we live. In Bion's terms (1962), the lead therapist and reflecting team provide a container within which overwhelming feelings can be actively processed. In systemic terms, we have created a context for reframing.

We synthesize our integrated therapeutic approach to working with couples and families with the stages of change model. Such a synthesis then allows us to match our thinking with the CAS alcohol treatment keyworkers and their individual clients, facilitating joint decisions on the timing of referrals to our couples and family therapy service, and in evaluating our treatment success.

The stages of change model

Prochaska and DiClemente (1992) posit that those who are attempting to change habitual behaviour go through five stages. The stages are described as:

1. Precontemplation – there is no intention to change in the foreseeable future.
2. Contemplation – people are aware that a problem exists and are thinking about making a change but have not yet made a commitment to do so.
3. Preparation – people intend to take action in the next month and have already made some small behavioural changes.
4. Action – people modify the problematic behaviour.
5. Maintenance – people work to prevent relapse and to consolidate what they have achieved in the action stage.

Most people who attempt to change their addictive behaviour make several attempts. Relapse is often the rule rather than the exception. Prochaska and DiClemente conceptualized change as a spiral pattern of movement through the stages. People progress through contemplation, preparation and action to maintenance, but most will relapse and return to earlier stages in the model. Some will return to precontemplation and effectively give up any idea of changing for varying lengths of time. Most people will return to contemplation or preparation and start to plan for their next action attempt, using their recent attempt as a learning experience. The spiral model suggests that people who relapse do not revolve endlessly in circles and neither do they go back to where they started. Rather, each time they move through the stages they have an opportunity to learn from their efforts and their mistakes and to try something different the next time. Prochaska, DiClemente and Norcross (1992) emphasize the need to assess the stage of a client's readiness for change and to tailor the interventions accordingly. The Prochaska et al. model is atheoretical, descriptive and focuses on the here-and-now. Our integrative approach weaves explanatory ideas of the causes and maintenance of problem drinking and its relational consequences for family life, which provides a richer formulation, and more options for intervention.

Engagement issues

Initially we offer one or more consultations before engaging in therapy. We use this as an opportunity to track the implications of working with us. We map the differences in motivation for change in the family members' relationships and their attitudes and responses to issues of responsibility and blame around problem drinking. The consultation meeting provides us with some opportunities to externalize the problem with drink, to track the effects on relationships of the drinking, while assessing the personal and relationship resources that can be harnessed in combating the effects of problem drinking on relationships, and to discuss the different treatment approaches available.

Experience teaches us that often the partner with the drinking problem has developed a primary attachment to alcohol (Vetere and Henley, 2001). The drinker becomes preoccupied with the need to obtain alcohol and everything becomes secondary to this need. Relationships and relationship-making skills deteriorate because of the ways in which the drinker behaves in order to maintain a supply of alcohol. Forming a relationship with the CAS worker whom they see on an individual basis may be the first new attachment the drinker has made since the need for alcohol took a hold and it tests their relationship skills. At the same time changing their drinking behaviour tests their relationships with the family. Coming into therapy with us may threaten the problem drinker and the family members because we focus on the less than optimum relationships in the family; secondly it involves the need to form a new attachment to the couples and family therapy team. Arroyave (1984) found it important to have several preparatory sessions with the person with a drinking problem to encourage the development of a strong attachment before they joined an analytic group. The resulting tension between continued drinking on the one hand and the wish to change on the other has to be managed by all participants carefully. It might take a couple up to a year of sporadic consultation meetings to decide to engage in a therapeutic process with us, where the commitment to change has been prioritized.

The therapeutic triangle

In dynamic terms, we form a triangle between our clients, ourselves and the CAS keyworker, with the latter acting as the stable 'third' in our relationship with our clients. The relationship developed with the keyworker may well be the first significant relationship that the partner with drinking problems has engaged in for some time, that is, a safe, new relationship external to the family. For some, relationship skills may have been held in abeyance for a long time. Thus the second step is to develop a relationship with us, while including their partner/family in this process. The leap involved in moving from a primary relationship with alcohol to a couples/family therapy attachment is so enormous that the person who is drinking needs to be in the action or maintenance phases of the stages of change model to sustain the transition. In our view, this leap is less likely to be successful if there is not a positive attachment with the alcohol keyworker already established.

Our acceptance of the long and complex engagement process, exemplified by missed appointments with and without notice, meetings with a partner absent, attending while under the influence of alcohol, and so on, means that we do not actively pursue couples to engage them in treatment – rather we are available for consultation, and often, couples use multiple opportunities to discuss the implications of working with us, before they actually do.

According to social attraction theory, the development of a therapeutic relationship would be facilitated by proximity, that is, the more we see of a person, the more our attitude toward them will be enhanced (Zajonc, 1968). Thus seeing people several times for consultation provides an opportunity to enhance the client's view of ourselves, so they might take the risk of entering therapy. The beginning of a therapeutic alliance is created. If the clients do not find something attractive about the family therapy team for them they will not engage with us. In object relations thinking, we provide people with an opportunity to bond.

The stages of change model guides us, the keyworkers, and the family members, in our day-to-day practice decisions about when to consult, when to engage in therapy, when to review and when to end our meetings. Analytic ideas about resistance and the defences against anxiety and emotional pain, help us to judge when the time is right to move from consultation to therapy (Brown and Pedder, 1991). For example, the countertransference experience for the in-room consultant of feeling bored, disappeared at the point when the partner with the drinking problem decided to make a commitment to therapy.

We ask people to attend our therapeutic sessions alcohol-free. We explain that intoxication might lead someone to volunteer information or express themselves in a way they might not when sober, thus increasing their vulnerability. This ground rule for attendance is intended to help the development of containment and a safe therapeutic space in which to work.

Theoretical issues: pattern and process in behaviour

A multimodal approach helps us integrate theory and practice when working with couples where there are longstanding patterns of drinking and abuse in the family. We are interested in the intersect between patterns of drinking and patterns in communication, relationships, and patterns over time, both the intergenerational transmission of family culture, particularly attitudes to alcohol consumption, and family life-cycle transitions (Carter and McGoldrick, 1989).

(a) Pattern in communication

We have observed differences in sober versus drinking patterns of communication with the couples we work with. Often the non-drinking partner will accuse the drinking partner of telling lies about drinking alongside the drinking partner's sober acknowledgement of the problem in the therapy session. The dilemma is often how to develop honest and straight talking about the problem drinking, the maintaining conditions and even perhaps the causes of drinking, as they are constructed and deconstructed by the couple over time.

Social penetration theory views the personal and private area in a person's personality as gradually penetrated as a relationship develops (Taylor and Altman, 1987). At the periphery of social interaction can be found information about the self that is visible, socially acceptable and common to most people. Less visible therefore, would be more intimate information which social penetration theory suggests is more central to personality development, and may be construed by some people as information which makes them vulnerable or less socially desirable. The process of penetration is believed to be ordered and rule governed, and includes the stages of orientation: exploratory affective exchange, affective exchange and stable exchange. Social penetration theory might suggest that the stage of stable exchange in the couple's communication has disappeared. It seems to us, that one of the longer term effects of problematic drinking on a couple's communication style is to restrict what can be safely discussed by the couple. Thus in social penetration theory terms, the couple restrict their communication to exploratory affective exchange, often describing the experience as like walking on eggshells. The problem drinking can result in the withholding of intimate information, especially if shame is involved.

We have found it important to acknowledge the role of shaming and blaming in couples' relationships when tracking the effects of problem drinking. We discuss shame as both an internal experience, and as an interpersonal and social experience which conveys information about a person's status and standing in the family and community. The history of the emotion of shame and feelings of humiliation for the couple, can often prevent the development of openness and honesty in conversation and rebuilding trust in the relationship. The partner of the drinker knows when they are not drinking, but finds it hard to trust that the drinking will not begin again. This is where systemic reflecting processes can be so helpful in raising and addressing these issues in a non-blaming way.

(b) Pattern in relationships

We have noticed that we rarely see couples whose relationships can be described as reciprocal, rather they fall into patterns of (i) complementarity, where one partner dominates and holds most power; often this is the non-drinking partner; and (ii) symmetry, where the couple are constantly in competition for power, expressed as the one who gets the last word, or who knows best, or whose description of reality prevails. The lack of reciprocal rewards in the couple and family relationships can be psychologically discomfiting and differently acknowledged. For example, the drinking partner may well maintain their drinking to ease or avoid such psychological discomfort. The non-drinking partner may then use this as evidence that change is unlikely and to sustain the view that the problem lies with the drinking partner.

We find that the effects of living in relationships dominated primarily by patterns of complementarity or symmetry vary according to whether it is the man or the woman who is drinking. A woman who is the drinker in a complementary relationship with a male partner, can find herself the recipient of negative projections, where her drinking behaviour is used as evidence for her uselessness, inability to cope and/or her contemptibility, further reinforcing her sense of powerlessness to effect change in her self, her relationships, and so on. At these times, her attempts to be assertive of her point of view can often be interpreted as aggression by other family members, and further used against her, reinforcing patterns of blame. Paradoxically the male partner, apparently powerful, will in this situation often report feeling extremely powerless about being able to change his wife's behaviour, with consequent feelings of frustration and distress, all risk indicators for further abuse.

In these circumstances, we have to deal with the negative transference, using the sensitivity of psychodynamic understanding. For example, at short notice the lead therapist had to leave and the couple session was led by the in-room consultant. At the next session, with the lead therapist present, the wife was very critical of her, and said she preferred the in-room consultant as the therapist. This alerted us to the need to address and work through her feelings of abandonment in the session. We explored through the countertransference why we were unaware of the nature of her attachment to the lead therapist, identifying it as avoidant in style.

Alcohol can represent an escape from intolerable emotion; drinking can become entrenched as an over-learned pattern of coping, with different meanings ascribed to the drinking behaviour by different family members. When the primary relationship with alcohol shifts, into action and maintenance of change stages, there are systemic consequences for all family members, and consequences in the world of work and with friendships. People may be unprepared for the impact that stopping the drinking has on the family system relationships. For example, other methods of coping with stress and unhappiness are not always easily developed by the person who had been reliant on alcohol, and for the partner it can be difficult to learn to trust they will not drink again. Couples may then need to reassess the basis of their relationship. When the view of the future is filled with risk and anticipated loss, we often ask questions about the future that allow family members to explore one in which drinking continues and one in which drinking does not continue. Imagining a future without drinking, in a solution focused way (Miller and Berg, 1995), encourages people to step back and reflect on their view of drinking as organizing family life. In our experience, it is often when the woman partner with the drinking problem becomes more independent that their male partner agrees to work towards a more reciprocal relationship, shedding the entrenched patterns of complementarity.

Claire and Mike provide an example of a couple facing and exploring the possibility of separation as part of her recovery from a long-standing problem with drinking. Mike is a finance director and Claire is a homemaker. Their children are in the process of leaving home. Claire complained that she had always felt in a childlike role with Mike, experiencing him as more powerful in decision-making and controlling of her in both overt and subtle ways. In contrast, Mike complained that Claire would not put forward her views and left him to make major household decisions. In our couples work, as Claire maintained both her abstinence and her emerging assertiveness, Mike recognized that he needed to challenge certain assumptions he made about himself, about Claire, about their relationship and about their future together. It was our understanding that his enduring sense of insecurity in their relationship had led him to behave in controlling ways towards Claire, such as trying to control her activities, her friendships, and how she spent money. When he addressed this insecurity, its origins and maintaining factors, he became more confident, more assertive and more able to negotiate directly with Claire.

(c) Pattern over time and life cycle issues

Curiosity about 'why now?' in response to the request for consultation with us, can promote discussion about the changed demands on family members and their changed expectations of each other. For example, a wife drinking through her husband's career might be more challenged by him during the early stages of their retirement. Ideas about travel, shared activities, visits to grandchildren and so on may have to be shelved because she is unable to participate. He can no longer deny the extent of her problem, as his reliance on the outside world may shrink somewhat with retirement or, at least, he has fewer opportunities to locate his energies elsewhere and if he has just retired, he has to see what is under his nose.

Exploration of the intersect between life-cycle demands, life events and the crisis around drinking, for all family members, provides an opportunity to track with the family how they have organized themselves around the drinker and the drinking. In many respects they can be described as a problem determined system (Anderson, Goolishian and Winderman, 1986), with family members coping and organizing aspects of family life to deny or minimize the effects of drinking, to protect others from the effects of drinking, or to ostracize the drinker. Patterns of behaviour can be reinforced over time and take on an over-learned or habitual quality. The crisis that often precipitates the move into family and couples work is an opportunity to understand and unpack these problem determined patterns, in a non-blaming way, offering opportunities to reframe aspects of family members' motivations as helpful or protective, and at least as people capable of change. Recruiting supportive ideas and feelings from family culture and from positive past and present relationships sometimes helps when exploring fraught and shameful memories.

We find an example in our work with Bob and Janet, a couple in their sixties, married for ten years. Bob's previous marriage had ended in divorce, with no children. Janet was a widow with grown up children and grandchildren. When they were referred to us, Bob had been abstinent from alcohol for six months, following a lengthy period of problem drinking. As a couple they had many common interests and enjoyed each other's company, but there was one major area of conflict between them. Janet thought that Bob was too possessive, wanting her for himself, and that he resented strongly the time and attention she gave to her family. Bob, on the other hand, thought that Janet's family exploited her, and that she needed to slow down and enjoy a well-earned retirement. In particular he blamed Janet's daughters and the stress caused by their difficulties for some of his previous relapses into drinking. Janet believed that Bob should be grateful that she had continued to care for him when he was drinking, and that he should show his gratitude by letting her care for her family now that he was not drinking.

Over several sessions, Bob became more understanding of the roles that Janet filled and how she tried to balance being a wife, mother and grand-mother. This allowed Janet the space to reflect on how and why her children had come to rely on her so much. We asked Bob and Janet to tell us about their own grandparents and how their experiences of them might have influenced how they carried out the role of grandparent and stepgrandparent. Janet had two grandmothers who lived near her as a child. One was a warm affectionate grandmother with whom she spent a lot of time whenever she wished. The other grandmother was more distant but showed her caring in an altogether different way. She had a maid called Agnes who was sent to help out whenever there was a problem in the family. Janet realized that her internalized model of a grandmother was a composite of both grandmothers and Agnes, and that she was trying to be all three. We worked with Bob and Janet for a few months, maintaining contact over 18 months with several follow-up meetings. During this time Bob did not relapse.

Working with violence and abuse

Often we are challenged to find ways of working therapeutically within, and holding the tension between, legal processes, moral discourses around responsibility, psychological explanations for behaviour, and therapeutic practices. This tension is particularly evident in our work with couples who experience violence and abuse in their relationships. We find that both the drinker and the partner can be both victim and perpetrator and that the dynamics and consequences vary according to gender. We are informed by socio-political critiques of power in intimate relationships, and the privileged position of men in a patriarchal society, while we pay attention to individual experience within the couple and family relationships. Such violence includes: (a) physical assault (for example, a husband spitting food at his wife who drinks; a wife who hits her husband when he is drinking); (b) sexual abuse (for example, forced intercourse, or a husband masturbating over the face of his wife while she sleeps in a separate bedroom because of her drinking); and (c) psychological abuse (such as verbal abuse, denigration, humiliation, coercion and intimidating and controlling behaviours). Many controlling behaviours seem to develop out of an attempt to prevent further drinking and are reinforced intermittently in a manner that promotes and escalates their use. Often, this escalation leads to behaviours and attitudes designed to humiliate the drinking partner into stopping the drinking, usually to no avail, other than to deepen the gulf between the couple.

In our therapeutic work with couples, we hold people responsible for their abusive behaviours towards others (Vetere and Cooper, 2001). We are clear at the outset of the work that responsibility is not diluted by psychological explanations about the violent behaviours. We try to help people develop a sense of personal agency in their problem-solving and help prepare them for action, in the way they accept responsibility for their abusive behaviour and in how they develop a sense of responsibility for their own safety, and the safety of children. To facilitate this, we talk to couples in their individual roles as (a) partners, for example, we might ask of men and women 'What are your hopes for the future of your relationship?' 'How will your hopes be affected if the drinking stops/continues?'; or as (b) mothers and fathers: 'What do you want to teach your son or daughter about developing responsibility for their behaviour?' 'What do you want to teach your children about the use of alcohol?' 'What do/can they learn from you about being a man/woman?' The couples and family work provides an important context to explore the role of adults in teaching children about alcohol and violence, which emphasizes the responsibilities of adults towards children, paralleling our emphasis on individual responsibility for problem drinking and abusive behaviour. This emphasis on personal agency and responsibility directly challenges some lay beliefs which describe alcohol use and associated violence as being out of control and uncontrollable. We pay attention in the therapy to the language people use when describing their actions, for example, 'I lost it!', and their sense of personal agency and problem solving, helping them develop descriptions that accept responsibility for their abusive actions and for their own and others' safety.

We find that patterns of behaviour in which one partner feels morally superior about both the other's drinking and the effects of such drinking, are difficult and complex to disentangle. The psychodynamic concepts of projection and projective identification are helpful in understanding such processes in the relationship. The partner who does not have an identified drink problem may externalize their own shortcomings on to the partner with the alcohol problem (projection), who by virtue of their drinking is an easy target. The non-drinking partner then might feel superior, in control of their own impulses, and with a sense of entitlement to shame their drinking partner. Alternately, the non-drinking partner may project these split off feelings into the partner with the drinking problem (projective identification) in such a way that the drinking partner is moved to feel or act in ways that originate with the non-drinking partner. Thus it could be hypothesized that the non-drinking partner might need their partner to behave in a way that can be described as bad in order to defend their own inner world. The partner with the drinking problem, in this pattern, might move through the stages of contemplation, preparation for change and action, but never quite manages to move to the stage of maintenance of change.

We find an example of this process with Ann and James, a well-off, retired, middle-class couple, whose children have grown up and left home. Ann has a longstanding problem with drink, which worsened around the time of their joint retirement. James described himself to us as a reasonable and convivial chap, who only attended our meetings to support and help his wife overcome her drinking problem. He described Ann as a person without friends, who found it difficult to make relationships. This was not borne out by our countertransference, as we were able to warm to Ann, yet our experience of James was that he was difficult to relate to. Ann repudiated James's description of herself, telling us she was well able to make friendships, citing satisfying relationships while at work. Ann described James as controlling and patronizing of her, in her choices and actions and in his descriptions of her. Ann was clear that she wanted James to make changes in his attitudes and actions towards her in the direction of equity in their relationship. Ann told us she had discovered feminist ideas during her fifties and that these ideas helped her understand her relationship with James and her feelings towards him.

We were not able to engage this couple in therapeutic work, never moving beyond a consultative relationship with them. James told us that a professional worker – he would not say whom – had told him some years ago that his wife had a personality disorder and that it was incurable. This explained for him his view of his wife's interpersonal problems, and in our view reinforced his view of her and his more dominant position in the marriage. James could see no need for him to change in response to his wife's requests for change. It could be said that Ann's continued drinking was an exercise of power from a more subordinate position, in that he could not actually stop her drinking. With a mix of frustration and resignation, Ann told us there was no point in attending further meetings with us. She wrote us a full and thoughtful letter in which she said the meetings raised her expectations of change, only to be dashed by disappointment. In addition, Ann ended the individual sessions with her CAS keyworker.

We listen for couples' descriptions of behaviour, attitudes, decision-making and styles of conflict resolution, which help us understand how they share power within their relationship. Systemically, we think of power both as being in a position to define reality and have other people accept that definition, as well as relative influence and control in relationships (Burck and Speed, 1995). Thus we pay attention both to the use of language in the descriptions of drinking episodes and the partner's responses and the power base resources available to both partners, such as contained in James's words about his wife, Ann. 'It is such stupid silliness on her part to pretend she hasn't been drinking when I know she has!' We would deconstruct such a statement with a couple to understand the different positions contained within it, how people feel both powerless and powerful, and the strategies of contempt used in order to gain control. Power bases have been described as information, knowledge, economic power, physical strength, relational and affectional power, ascribed power and use of language (Williams and Watson, 1988). We explore with couples to what extent access to power is gendered and whether power balances in their relationship have changed over time, at different life-cycle stages, with adaptation to life events and at different times during the stages of change in stopping drinking. Once the partner with the drinking problem is in a period of maintenance of change, the role of alcohol in coping with change has diminished while the repertoire of alternative coping methods has broadened, often for all family members. Our emphasis is on helping people develop maturity, a sense of personal agency and responsibility, both for drinking behaviour and the responses to drinking behaviour. In dynamic terms, there has been some move from the paranoid schizoid position to the depressive position (Klein, 1946). Thus we believe problem-solving needs to be informed by a complex, integrated theoretical approach.

Conclusion

Working with couples in our service is both complex and demanding, largely because of the power imbalances in their relationships. We observe a lack of intimate communication in their relationships, whereby drinking has come between them. So instead of seeing stable exchange in their communication we see more tentative communication, with couples often fearful that any communication will make an already tense situation worse. In our experience therapeutic progress depends on both (a) the drinking partner re-establishing a relationship with their partner and other family members that is more important to them than the drinking itself, and (b) on the non-drinking partner moving from a position of believing that happiness will be attained when the drinking partner stops drinking, to a position where they recognize that they too need to change. We have learned to be aware that in some relationships the non-drinking partner has more invested in the characterization of their drinking partner as the bad one, rather than having an investment in the commitment to change. We find the integration of ideas from the schools of systemic psychotherapy and group analytic psychotherapy to be helpful when working with such complex attachment issues in therapy.

References

Anderson H, Goolishian H, Winderman L (1986) Problem determined systems: towards transformation in family therapy. Journal of Strategic and Systemic Therapies 5: 1–14.

Arroyave F (1984) Group-analytic treatment of drinking problems. In TE Lear (ed), Spheres of Group Analysis. London: Group Analytic Society Publications.

Behr HL (1994) Families and group analysis. In DG Brown, LM Zinkin (eds), The Psyche and the Social World. London: Routledge.

Berg JH, Clark MS (1986) Differences in social exchange between intimate and other relationships: gradually evolving or quickly apparent? In VJ Delega, BA Winstead (eds) Friendship and Social Interaction. New York: Springer-Verlag.

Bion W (1962) Learning from Experience. London: Heinemann.

Bowlby J (1979) The Making and Breaking of Affectional Bonds. London: Tavistock.

Brown D, Pedder J (1991) Introduction to Psychotherapy. London: Routledge.

Burck C, Speed B (eds) (1995) Gender, Power and Relationships. London: Routledge.

Carter E, McGoldrick M (1989) The Family Life Cycle: A Framework for Family Therapy (2nd edn). New York: Gardiner Press.

Edwards M, Steinglass P (1995) Family therapy treatment outcomes for alcoholism. Journal of Marital and Family Therapy 21: 475–509.

Kent R (1990) Focusing on women. In S Collins (ed), Alcohol, Social Work, and Helping. London: Routledge.

Klein M (1946) Notes on some schizoid mechanisms. In M Klein, P Heiman, S Isaacs, J Riviere (eds), Developments in Psychoanalysis. London: Hogarth (reprinted London: Karnac, 1989).

Larner G (2000) Towards a common ground in psychoanalysis and family therapy: on knowing not to know. Journal of Family Therapy 22: 61–82.

Miller S, Berg IS (1995) The Miracle Method: A Radically New Approach to Problem Drinking. New York: Norton.

Orford J, Harwin J (eds) (1982) Alcohol and the Family. London: Croom Helm.

Prochaska JO, DiClemente CC (1992) Stages of change in the modification of problem behaviours. In M Herson, RM Eisler, PM Miller (eds), Progress in Behaviour. Sycamore, IL: Sycamore Press.

Prochaska JO, DiClemente CC, Norcross JC (1992) In search of how people change: applications to addictive behaviours. American Psychologist 47: 1102-14.

Steinglass P, Bennett L, Wolin S, Reiss D (1987) The Alcoholic Family. New York: Basic Books.

Taylor DA, Altman I (1987) Communication in interpersonal relationships: social penetration processes. In ME Roloff, GR Miller (eds), Interpersonal Processes: New Directions in Communication Research. Newbury Park, CA: Sage.

Velleman R (1992) 'Oh, my drinking doesn't affect them': families of problem drinkers. Clinical Psychology Forum 48: 6-10.

Vetere A (1998) Family systems perspective. In R Velleman, A Copello, J Maslin (eds) Living with Drink: Women who Live with Problem Drinkers. London: Longman.

Vetere A, Cooper J (2001) Working systemically with family violence: risk, responsibility and collaboration. Journal of Family Therapy 23: 378-98.

Vetere A, Henley M (2001) Integrating couples and family therapy into a community alcohol service: a pantheoretical approach. Journal of Family Therapy 23: 85-101.

Williams J, Watson G (1988) Sexual inequality, family life and family therapy. In E Street, W Dryden (eds), Family Therapy in Britain. Milton Keynes: Open University Press.

Zajonc RB (1968) Attitudinal effects of mere exposure. Journal of Personality and Social Psychology 9: 1-27.

CHAPTER 9

Cognitive Analytic Therapy: a Vygotskian development of object relations theory

ANTHONY RYLE AND FIERMAN BENNINK-BOLT

Cognitive Analytic Therapy (CAT) is an active time-limited therapeutic model which has been applied across the whole spectrum of psychotherapy patients, from those treated in primary care to personality-disordered patients in the psychiatric and forensic services. One major source of CAT was object relations theory and the formation of the self and shaping of relationships during early development remains central to the model. However, these processes are described using concepts, which differ considerably from current psychoanalytic theories and many of the therapeutic techniques will be unfamiliar to most psychodynamic therapists. To help understand these differences this chapter will begin with an account of the evolution of the approach.

The early development of the model: integration of cognitive and psychoanalytic ideas

The origins

Cognitive Analytic Therapy originated in the 1970s and '80s in the course of A. Ryle's practising psychodynamic therapy and being involved in research into its effectiveness. This research involved the use of the repertory grid (Kelly, 1955), a method of psychological inquiry in which the subject systematically rates a number of individuals (elements) on a number of descriptions (constructs). Computer analysis of the resultant grid of figures yields correlations showing how far any two constructs (for example, 'strong' and 'I depend on') are seen as similar and how far any two of the people rated (for example, My Mother and My Wife) are seen to resemble each other. Such associations can indicate the individual's assumptions about people and these can be linked to his or her problematic behaviours and relationships. In the dyad grid the elements are relationships of self-to-others and others-to-self, rather than individuals. Either way, the dispersal of all the elements in terms of all the constructs is summarized in a 'map' which provides an overview of how this person sees the self and significant people in his or her world.

Although the language of grids can feel alien to dynamic therapists, it offers a parallel way of understanding familiar issues. Patients' grids can reveal things which, while not dynamically repressed, are not consciously known. Thus a male patient conceptualized psychoanalytically as displaying an unresolved Oedipus complex might describe people on his grid in two clusters, either as 'successful and nasty' (like his father) or as 'sensitive and submissive' (like his mother), locating himself in between. The aim of therapy would be to revise this false dichotomy. Or the coldness and inaccessibility of a patient described as schizoid might reveal, on a dyad grid, how relationships are seen as offering only a choice between 'dangerously angry', 'submissive dependency' or 'emotional isolation'. Here, therapy must enable the patient to risk exposure, making it safe to explore and revise the meaning of closeness.

Comparing clinical and grid-derived formulations of a large number of psychotherapy patients (Ryle, 1975) initiated a process of re-stating psycho-analytic ideas in a cognitive language (Ryle, 1982) and demonstrated the value of describing the unrecognized but not dynamically repressed processes determining self-processes and relationships. It became apparent that patients could both recognize these patterns and use the recognition to initiate change.

A second influence on the development of CAT was the practice of creating, with the patient, at the start of therapy, a description (reformulation) of the recurrent problems and of the patterns which maintained them. This practice was initially intended as a basis for devising research measures of dynamic change but it had such a marked positive impact on the process of therapy that it became a defining feature of the approach.

Reformulation

The reformulation resembles a dynamic formulation but in CAT it is made in full consultation with the patient, using accessible language and concepts. It focuses on identifying the features of persistent maladaptive patterns of action, in particular those which explain why revision does not take place. A study of the notes of a series of completed therapies showed that the following three general patterns explained non-revision in most cases.

1. Traps

Negative assumptions about the self and the world lead to forms of behaviour and relating which provoke consequences which seem to confirm the truth of the assumptions. For example, the reformulation of a depressed young woman might identify her problems as follows: 'It seems you feel you are a bad, unlovable person so you give in to others and try to please them. As a result you are often taken advantage of, and in the end you show your resentment of this in withdrawal or tantrums. This puts people off so they reject you, apparently confirming your belief that you are unlovable.'

2. Dilemmas

The apparent choices for action or relationships or self-management are polarized between extreme opposites. Two common dilemmas would be described as follows:

> 'You act as if, if you are not absolutely perfect, you are absolute rubbish' or
> 'In your relationships it seems you act as if you must either be a powerful caretaker or a dependent wimp'.

3. Snags

Appropriate goals are abandoned or undone, as if forbidden by others or the self. For example: 'It seems that when things go well for you, you somehow arrange for them to go wrong, as if you were guilty.' Sources for this might be added, such as 'Maybe the experience of being brought up with your Downs Syndrome sister made you feel you were not entitled to a life' or 'You have perhaps felt irrationally that your adolescent anger with your father were responsible for his death.' Current as well as past relationships may seem to disallow success or happiness and may block successful therapy.

It was surprising to see how patients, who in most instances were at best only partially aware of these patterns, were quickly able to recognize how such descriptions explained their difficulties and were able to use this understanding to control or replace damaging processes. To help in the reformulation process the Psychotherapy File was constructed, explaining the nature of traps, dilemmas and snags, with common examples. The File is reproduced in Ryle (1995, 1997a) and examples of particular items are given in the case example below. The File is given out at the first session and items which the patient recognizes as applying are discussed at the next session.

The development of formal models

Traps, dilemmas and snags are shorthand examples of 'procedural' descriptions. The theoretical basis of such descriptions was summarized in the Procedural Sequence Model (PSM). This suggests how the processes underlying problematic patterns need to be described in terms of the following sequence: the context or external event, perception, appraisal, aim formation, action planning, the prediction of outcome, enactment, the evaluation of the consequences and the revision or confirmation of the procedure. By linking external reality, mental processes and action in this way, and by combining thought, feeling and action, the persistence of maladaptive behaviour can be explained in a more adequate way than is offered by a focus confined to faulty cognitions or unconscious conflict. A full account of this model will be found in Ryle (1982).

In practice, procedural descriptions are derived from the details of the patient's story, discussion of the Psychotherapy File and the evolving therapy relationship. They are made in general terms and in practice are largely concerned with issues of care, dependency, control, submission and abuse. Such descriptions point out the consequences of following the maladaptive patterns and provide a basis for recognizing them.

Object relations ideas

The PSM is adequate as a way of analysing many problematic behaviours but it gives no account of personality development or structure. To overcome this restriction and because the main acts of concern to psychotherapists are to do with relationships to others and with the self, the model was extended by the explicit inclusion of object relations ideas. The Procedural Sequence Object Relations Model (PSORM) emphasizes how, in the enactment of a role procedure, the aim is the elicitation of the responses of the other. Based on this, the Reciprocal Role Procedure (RRP) became a key concept of CAT theory (Ryle, 1985, 1990).

Reciprocal role patterns are established and internalized in early development and shape both relationships with others and self-management; indeed the mature self is constituted from these early interactions. They are stable because they are stored in procedural memory, which is pre-verbal and unreflected upon, and because, in seeking relationships, we usually choose others from whom we can elicit the reciprocations we expect – even though, in many cases, these are damaging.

The use of procedural descriptions

While much of the time is spent in open-ended exploration in ways familiar to all dynamic therapists, in CAT the description and recognition of the individual repertoire of problematic role procedures is a priority in the first sessions. These descriptions enhance the patient's capacity for self-reflection, and, on their basis, the therapist is more able to avoid or correct collusive, reinforcing responses to damaging role procedures.

Consider, for example, a depressed woman patient in whom a childhood-derived core reciprocal role procedure has been identified as 'striving to please' in relation to 'inconsistent, partial care'. In therapy her initial attempts to be a good patient might switch to passively resistant behaviour, perhaps provoked by some shortcoming in the therapist's care. Or the patient might switch to the inconsistent role and from being appreciative of the therapist's need, might start missing sessions or might induce in the therapist feelings that he or she should work harder for the patient. Individuals can play either pole of a RRP but their options are limited by their particular repertoire and identifying this is the first step in achieving recognition and control for the patient and non-collusion for the therapist.

The basic practice of CAT

The early practice of CAT reflected this evolution of ideas and was also influenced by the wish to develop a mode of therapy which could be used in the public service or other poorly resourced settings. This pointed to the need for brevity but this was also justified on other grounds for, as Mann (1973) observed, working psychodynamically within pre-determined time limits has a powerful positive impact, even in severely ill patients and it avoids debilitating dependency. No therapy can provide all that the patient wants and in time-limited work this disappointment is explicit; termination is on the agenda from the start and is nearly always manageable.

In outpatient practice CAT is usually delivered in 16 weekly sessions (fewer for less disturbed patients, 24 or sometimes more for patients with Borderline Personality Disorder). The first four sessions are devoted to the reformulation process. This is an open-ended enquiry in which the therapist seeks to gain a sense of what it is like to be this patient and in which key experiences and informing myths and assumptions are identified. Patients will be involved in 'homework' such as diary keeping and self-monitoring of symptoms and discussion of these and of the patients' use of the Psychotherapy File will take up some of the time. At the fourth session (usually) the therapist presents, in draft:

1. a letter with a narrative reconstruction, describing how the history and current problems are linked;
2. a list of target problems and target problem procedures (traps, dilemmas and snags);
3. for all but the simplest cases problem procedures are also described in a Sequential Diagrammatic Reformulation (SDR); in these diagrams the reciprocal role procedures are listed in a box and the procedures reflecting their enactments are drawn as loops indicating the consequences (see below for an example). These diagrams provide the patient with a tool for self-reflection and the therapist with a clear indication of

likely transference-countertransference patterns. The letter and diagram are modified in full consultation with the patient and each keeps copies.

The reformulation process generates an emotionally powerful working alliance and the reformulation tools help patient and therapist to recognize and not repeat the damaging 'Reciprocal Role Procedures' in their relationship. The safety generated by these new understandings allows patients increased access to memories and feelings. These are often disturbing but their emergence in the therapy relationship has usually been anticipated in the reformulation letter, which makes it easier for therapists to recognize and contain the patients' distress or anger and their own countertransference reactions.

Throughout therapy, the active use of the reformulation tools in the sessions and in homework assignments involving self-monitoring and diary keeping is encouraged. This may sound mechanical to those used to conventional psychodynamic technique, but in practice, as the reformulation tools become part of a shared language, the exchange of feelings becomes freer. There need be no conflict between 'cognitive' and 'analytic' elements; good understandings allow affects and memories to be safely accessed and understood.

Termination is always difficult, for no therapy of whatever length can make up for the past, but the clear pre-determined time limit of CAT makes it more tolerable. In brief therapy there is little time for new understandings to be worked through; the work of therapy must be continued. To assist this, at the last session therapist and patient exchange 'goodbye letters' which aim to evaluate realistically the changes achieved. The therapist's letter will note both the positive achievements and the inevitable disappointments and will suggest what needs further consideration. This procedure ensures that mixed feelings are acknowledged and provides one more concrete tool, which assists the patient's internalization of a realistic image of the therapist linked with key understandings.

Case example

This basic pattern of practice is illustrated in the following summary of the case of 'Anne'.

Anne was referred by her general practitioner on account of longstanding depression. She was a 28-year-old teacher living with her father and stepmother. Before her first session her father telephoned to express his concern about her state; he accompanied her to the first meeting and seemed to want to come in with her. Anne spoke clearly for the first few minutes and then began to cry to the extent that it was hard to understand her, a pattern repeated in the next three sessions.

Background

The main event in her life was the death of her mother when she was aged 9. She had been a rather strict, perfectionist person but was a good and loved mother. Before she died she had repeatedly asked Anne to promise to look after her father and younger brothers. Anne had indeed done this, making a good team with her father, looking after the household, getting her younger brothers ready for school and doing her utmost to be a good daughter. She described her father as over-concerned, loving but somewhat self-centred. Father had remarried when Anne was aged 12, assuring her that 'life must go on'. Anne had experienced but had not expressed powerful mixed emotions at this change but she made a good relationship with her stepmother. She was still living in the family home and expressed the feeling, which her father reinforced, that she ought to be grateful and happy. She was offered a 16-session course of CAT.

The Psychotherapy File

Anne was given the Psychotherapy File at the first session and brought it to discuss at the second. She identified the following descriptions as applying to her:

1. Feeling fearful of hurting others we keep our feelings inside or put our needs aside. This tends to allow other people to ignore or abuse us, which leads to us feeling, or being, childishly angry. When we see ourselves behaving like this, it confirms our belief that we shouldn't be aggressive and reinforces our avoidance of standing up for our rights.
2. Feeling depressed, we are sure we will manage a task or social situation badly. Being depressed, we are probably not as effective as we can be, and the depression leads us to exaggerate how badly we handled things. This makes us feel more depressed about ourselves.
3. Feeling uncertain about ourselves and anxious not to upset others, we try to please people by doing what they seem to want. As a result we end up being taken advantage of by others, which makes us angry, depressed or guilty, from which our uncertainty about ourselves is confirmed, or we may feel out of control and start hiding away, putting things off, letting people down which makes them angry with us and increases our uncertainty.
4. Feeling worthless, we feel we cannot get what we want because we will be punished, or others will reject us, or it is bound to turn sour, or we must punish ourselves. From this we feel everything is hopeless so we give up trying which increases our sense of worthlessness.

In addition to these four traps Anne also identified the dilemma 'If I try to be perfect, I feel depressed and angry; if I don't try to be perfect I feel guilty, angry and dissatisfied.' These revealed her strongly critical view of herself.

She also identified from the File a tendency to cope with confusing feelings by blanking off and feeling emotionally distant from others.

The course of therapy

During the early sessions, in which her sense that she ought to be happy but was not was further explored, Anne avoided eye contact, cried most of the time and frequently apologized for being 'ridiculous'. By combining what she had conveyed about her family, her replies to the File and her demeanour in the room (where she seemed to feel she must please the therapist as she had to please her father), three problematic reciprocal role procedures were identified:

1. 'Striving' in relation to 'critical demand'. This could be seen to originate in her mother's character and demands and in her later responsible role in the family, and was most evident in her demands on herself.
2. 'Abandoned' in relation to 'abandoning'. Her mother's death seemed to have been incompletely mourned due to her having to take on her family role and to her father's keeping his feelings to himself. The loss of her special relationship with father had been experienced as abandonment.
3. 'Caring perfectly' in relation to 'insufficiently cared for'.

The reformulation

At the fourth session the following reformulation letter was read:

Dear Anne,

I am writing this on the basis of our first meetings to set out how I understand your problems and to suggest how it is that they have been hard to change. You have told me about the death of your loving but strict mother and of how she asked you to promise to care for your father and brothers when she was gone. It is clear that you did that very well, managing the house and shopping and getting your brothers ready for school and feeling, as you still do, grateful and devoted to your father, even though he can be over-concerned and a bit self-centred. I was moved when you described how, at your mother's funeral, you chose to stay alone in the car, and I wonder did you ever have the chance to fully grieve for her. Three years later your father remarried, saying that 'life must go on' and suddenly you were a child again, deprived of your special role. With this loss you were very much aware of feeling angry and abandoned but also felt very guilty for having such feelings; for a time in adolescence you dealt with these feelings by drinking heavily and bingeing. However, in the years since you have done well in the world, graduating from the University and holding a good teaching post, but in other ways your life has not progressed and you are very unhappy.

In therapy we will try to understand why this is so. Your main problems are your unhappiness and your inability to ask others for what you need; I think these are the understandable consequences of your childhood. It seems to me you still feel you need to care for others and do everything perfectly and you cannot know or express your own needs. Deep down you feel resentment that you do not get what you need from life and then you seem to feel guilty for having these feelings. With me you have several times apologised for being a bad patient, as if you must look after me like you felt you must look after your father. In therapy we will work together at recognizing how these old patterns are still operating in your life and in your work with me and will explore how you might become kinder to yourself.

Anne's procedures all led to depression or resentment, anger and guilt, and finally to self-destructive behaviour: bingeing, drinking, starving or cutting-off zombie (see Figure 9.1).

Anne accepted the letter without revision but remained emotionally cut off through sessions 5 and 6. She came to session 7 saying 'it had all clicked', by which she meant that she now knew that her tears were for her mother. From that time she changed markedly in how she was in the room and she proceeded to be assertive in the world. She arranged a discussion with her father and stepmother at which she spoke of her unmet needs for emotional support; father was angry at her ingratitude and she realized how much her

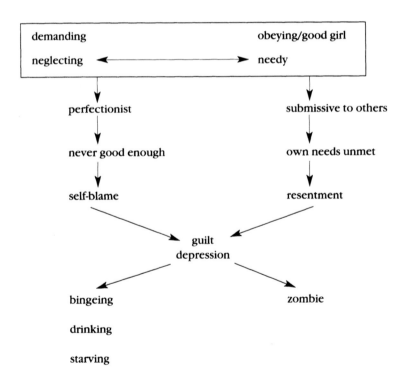

Figure 9.1. Sequential diagrammatic reformulation

own 'getting on with life' had represented her going along with his needs rather than her own. Following this she moved out into her own apartment. She was assailed by guilt and briefly returned to drinking heavily. She also had a brief affair which she terminated when she realized she was once more adopting a self-effacing role.

Termination and follow-up

The therapist wrote a brief goodbye letter, noting how she had been able to find her feelings for her mother and how she had been able to assert her needs to her father and encouraging her to go on working at change and to keep the therapy in mind and if need be to refer to her reformulation. Follow-up meetings at three and nine months were arranged. At these, she reported that she had no regrets at the decisions she had taken and that, despite being aware of the temptations to act in the old ways, she was holding on to the gains, was more able to seek support from friends and felt that 'maybe one day I will be able to find my own voice'.

The later development of the model: differentiation and introducing Vygotskian ideas

While drawing initially upon cognitive and psychoanalytic ideas the theory and practice of CAT became increasingly differentiated from both sources. Cognitive and behavioural therapy methods were seen to be of some practical use but their theory of human experience is impoverished. Psychoanalytic practice is impracticably long and lacks research evidence for its effectiveness; moreover, the accumulating evidence from observational studies of early development point to the need to revise radically much of the psychoanalytic account of early development. Thus Stern in his review of observational studies and their implications for psychoanalytic theory concluded that there was no evidence for the traditional developmental model of libidinal stages. Stern argued that patterns of thought and behaviour determining patients' problems, rather than being the products of innate unconscious conflict and fantasy, were manifestations of procedural learning derived from the developing child's 'actual experience' (Stern, 1985, p. 225).

In the evolving practice of CAT, collaborative descriptive reformulation describing the inter- and intrapersonal procedures derived from the individual's 'actual experience' became the main focus. Phenomena described in psychoanalysis as due to dynamic repression are deduced from manifest acts, omissions or intrusions or from non-verbal communications. These can be described and discussed without the need for speculative interpretation – a practice which often draws upon theories of pre-verbal development for which there is little evidence, and which imposes a passive role on the patient. It has been argued from a CAT perspective (Ryle, 1992, 1993, 1995) that this can have harmful effects. The introduction of Vygotskian and Bakhtinian ideas into CAT, in particular through the work of Leiman (1992, 1994, 1997), offers a different understanding of early development, of which the following is a summary.

Vygotsky and the social formation of mind and self

The biological evolution of man and our ancestors occurred during millions of years of social evolution. Natural selection favoured features aiding social cohesion in the face of changing circumstances, with the result that the human infant is uniquely adapted biologically to be socially formed (Donald, 1991). The genotypic self of the infant, with its evolved, innate predispositions and inherited temperamental characteristics, is geared from birth to be intersubjectively involved. Developed (phenotypic) self-structures and complex higher functions, notably the capacity for conscious self-reflection, are formed in the intensely active relationship between infants (each with an inborn temperament) and mothers and other caretakers (each with their temperament and their repertoire of reciprocal role procedures). In this interaction the mother and other caretakers convey both their personal meanings and values and those of the wider culture.

This social, dialogic view of the formation of the self is in contrast to the prevalent (Cartesian) idea that the individual self emerges in some sense from within. Temperament is inherited but the individual's self-processes are not pre-existing at birth, they are formed – and also potentially deformed – from this joint experience; psychotherapy is primarily concerned to correct the deformations. Both conscious and unconscious thought processes are deeply influenced by the values and assumptions transmitted through this dialogue and conversations with others and with the internalized others who form part of the self persist throughout life.

Vygotsky's understanding of the social formation of the individual offers psychotherapists four important insights:

1. In a famous quotation he stated that 'what the child does with an adult today she will do on her own tomorrow'. The individual learns first through external activity and only subsequently internalizes what is learned.
2. The role of parent, teacher and by extension, therapist is to provide a 'scaffolding' of support, tools and concepts which can be handed over as competence develops.
3. Learning takes place in the 'Zone of Proximal Development' (ZPD), defined as the gap between current performance and the level which could be achieved with the help of a more competent other. Proposed initially in

relation to intellectual development, the concept can be extended to self-knowledge (reflective capacity) where the ZPD is usually extensive.

4. Internalization involves sign mediation. In the pre-verbal 'conversation' of mother and infant and increasingly through speech the child's exploration of the world is accompanied and shaped by the provision and creation of signs. We do not store representations of reality so much as we know the world and ourselves through words, artefacts, rituals and so on which convey meanings and values. These signs become the instruments of the inner speech which is conscious thought and which allows self-reflection.

Clinical applications of the CAT model of personality

Joint description rather than interpretation is the key element in CAT. It provides an understanding of the processes which therapy aims to alter and initiates collaborative work. All therapy depends upon the establishment of a safe and productive relationship (the 'secure base' of attachment theory). In CAT, with its recognition of the way in which we cannot avoid being a powerful presence in the patient's life, security can only be established and maintained through the sustained, accurate, empathic understanding which is summarized in the reformulation. This involves both basic human attributes and honed skills. Thus:

1. Patients need to be understood historically, both so we may acknowledge their experience and so we may understand how that experience has shaped and distorted their current experience and activity. The retelling of the patient's life story and linking it to current problems is recorded in the reformulation letter. It is, to begin with, a daunting requirement on trainee therapists to write such letters but there is a safety in that patients will be encouraged to correct them; in fact in most cases they find them accurate and moving.

2. Patients need to be understood sequentially, in order to clarify and emphasize the consequences of present modes of proceeding and to demonstrate what has prevented revision of harmful modes. This process is initiated and encapsulated in the written and diagrammatic descriptions of procedural patterns, which are completed during the first four to six sessions; if later events can not be located, the initial diagram will be modified. Moods, symptoms, unwanted behaviours and defensive avoidance must be located on the sequential diagram so that the self-management and relationship procedures, which they accompany or replace, can be identified and addressed.

3. Patients need to be understood and described reciprocally in order to focus on the RRPs between self and others in the external world

(including in the therapy relationship) and on the related RRPs between parts of the self and internalized others, for these are the 'building blocks' of their personality. We internalize patterns of relating, not objects, and we are formed, exist and change essentially in terms of these inner and outer RRPs and of the dialogue which accompanies them, and we are capable of enacting either pole.

4. To this we must add one more element, the need to think structurally. The model described so far is implicitly hierarchical, that is to say, high level 'strategies' are reflected in a range of lower order 'tactics'. Reformulation aims as far as possible to describe these general, high-level patterns. In practice, of course, these high level patterns are deduced from the detailed accounts given by patients of particular events and relationships and from observing the 'in the room' interaction. But once identified, they provide a template whereby subsequent particular events can be located in what can be described as a 'top down' approach, through which learning can be generalized.

There is a second important structural aspect. In addition to hierarchy the degree of integration between different reciprocal role procedures (RRPs) needs to be described. In most people transitions between the different RRPs in their repertoire are relatively smooth and appropriate but, in patients with borderline personality organization, instability and sudden confusing switches between states are characteristic. In reformulating and treating these patients with CAT it became evident that diagrams had to be drawn in which RRP patterns were located in separate boxes, indicating partial dissociation between them.

Borderline personality organization

The CAT Multiple Self States Model (MSSM) of borderline pathology (Ryle, 1997a, 1997b) was developed from this work. It describes three associated forms of damage, based on extreme childhood adversity in those genetically predisposed, as follows:

1. The presence of one extreme, harsh RRP based on childhood neglect and abuse, for example 'abusive neglect' in relation to either 'crushed victim' or 'rebel'.

2. The presence of two or more partially dissociated RRPs (self-states), commonly including 'ideally caring' to 'ideally cared for' and 'emotionally blank' in relation to 'threat' (see Golynkina and Ryle, 2000). These originate in dissociation in the face of unmanageable emotional experiences and lead to the formation of distinct contrasting self-states, between which abrupt, evidently unprovoked switches occur.

3. Deficient self-reflection due:
    (a) to the absence of concerned attention from caretakers whose internalization might have provided a basis for self-concern; and
    (b) to the disruption of self-reflection resulting from state switches.

Reformulation with borderline patients

Diagrams of borderline patients are built up through four stages:

1. Identifying the different states experienced and characterizing these through careful history taking, patient homework and observation.
2. Identifying the other pole of the role expressed by the state. States represent the subjective experience of playing a role and are commonly recognized by the dominant mood but it is important to record the accompanying beliefs and behaviours. It is also crucial to identify the implicit reciprocating role, that is to say to describe the other who has provoked the state or towards whom it is directed. This other may be another person or an aspect of the self. For example, a patient in the abused role and preoccupied with misery or revenge will implicitly or explicitly be responding to perceived or actual abuse. Recognizing 'reciprocals' alerts the therapist to possible transference-countertransference involvement and to possible role reversals.
3. Monitoring the triggers, which provoke state switches, can be done once the states are clearly located on the diagram. It is particularly important to identify the procedures and the events which precede switches to damaging procedures such as self-harm. An example of a diagram of a borderline patient is given in Figure 9.2.

'X' in Figure 9.2 indicates the point at which cues, memories, the acts of others or associated events evoke the unmanageable feelings first experienced in childhood of disappointment, rejection, abuse etc. This may provoke rage, directed against self or others, or it may provoke a switch to a different, partially dissociated self-state – in this case to the emotionally numb zombie state. Such switches may be accompanied by dissociative symptoms such as depersonalization or perceptual disturbances.

Borderline features are present in a considerable proportion of patients who fail to respond to therapy; failure is the result of their tendency to elicit unhelpful reciprocations from their therapists. Recognizing the presence of dissociated self-states is therefore very important. It can be aided by the use of a simple 8-item screening questionnaire – the Personality Structure Questionnaire (Pollock et al., 2001) – the replies to which indicate the patient's experience of discontinuity in the experience of self and are a good starting point for exploring the features of the different states.

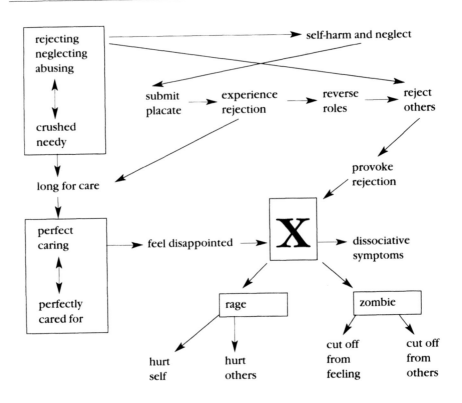

Figure 9.2. Example of a borderline patient's diagram

Research evidence

CAT grew from outcome research, and its development has been accompanied and fuelled by continuing research activity into both process and outcome. This has comprised case studies, naturalistic studies, small randomized controlled trials and detailed process research. This research, which remains inadequate in extent and permanently underfunded, is summarized in Ryle (1995) and in a new introductory text (Ryle and Kerr, 2002). A detailed naturalistic study of borderline patients treated with this model is presented in Ryle and Golynkina (1999). It remains difficult to design research into the complexities of dynamic therapy, where the aims are to modify self-processes rather than behaviours or beliefs, but the conceptual revisions offered by CAT make some aspects of the task more accessible. In the meantime the accumulation of imperfect data and the growing numbers of professional therapists committed to the model provide at least as strong a claim for clinical and cost effectiveness as can be made for most dynamic therapy models.

Conclusion

So where does CAT stand in relation to other object relations models? While addressing many of the same issues and while sharing a conviction that, in the end, it is the therapeutic relationship which determines the effect of therapy, CAT proceeds on a number of different assumptions and uses a number of different techniques. The major differences are as follows:

1. CAT practice is built on the collaborative creation and use of jointly created written and drawn tools, used to enhance self-reflection by the patient and to avoid or correct collusion from the therapist.
2. The unconscious conflicts and ego defences described in classical psychoanalysis are reconceptualized in terms of the internalization of actually experienced depriving, critical or harsh parental 'voices'. But the central concern is with the problematic procedures acquired during early life which are not dynamically repressed and which, once described, can be recognized and become open to change.
3. Discontinuities and poor integration due to partial dissociation in the face of trauma and deprivation are seen as key factors in many more disturbed patients.
4. Projective identification is understood to be an extreme form of the universal processes whereby others are invited or induced to reciprocate the patient's extreme, segregated role enactments (see Ryle, 1994).
5. Countertransference may involve both a reciprocating response to pressures to collude and an empathic identification with a role and affect of which the patient may not be fully aware.
6. The creation of concrete reformulation tools is emphasized; their development and use are examples of sign mediation in Vygotskian terms, assisting internalization. In particular, accurate mapping of procedures and self-states is considered essential in the treatment of borderline patients where, as a result of shifts between partially dissociated self-states, the form of transference may fluctuate rapidly through time and contrasting countertransference feelings may co-exist. The value of CAT is particularly clear in the treatment of more disturbed patients for, with such patients, the destruction of the therapeutic relationship is the most common cause of failure.
7. The various CAT concepts, tools and techniques, most of which are unfamiliar to traditional psychodynamic therapists, serve to enhance the patient's capacity for accurate self-reflection and to support the maintenance of a non-collusive relationship the internalization of which allows a more accurate and respecting sense of self.

References

Donald M (1991) Origins of the Modern Mind. Cambridge, MA: Harvard University Press.

Golynkina K, Ryle A (2000) The identification and characteristics of the partially dissociated states of patients with borderline personality disorder. British Journal of Medical Psychology 72: 429–45.

Kelly GA (1955) The Psychology of Personal Constructs. New York: Norton.

Leiman M (1992) The concept of sign in the work of Vygotsky, Winnicott and Bakhtin: further integration of object relations theory and activity theory. British Journal of Medical Psychology 65: 209–21.

Leiman M (1994) Projective identification as early joint action sequences; a Vygotskian addendum to the procedural sequence object relations' model. British Journal of Medical Psychology 67: 97–106.

Leiman M (1997) Procedures as dialogic sequences: a revised version of the fundamental concept in Cognitive Analytic Therapy. British Journal of Medical Psychology 70: 193–207.

Mann J (1973) Time-limited Psychotherapy. Cambridge, MA: Harvard University Press.

Pollock PH, Broadbent M, Clarke S et al. (2001) The Personality Structure Questionnaire (PSQ): a measure of the multiple self-states model of identity disturbance in Cognitive Analytic Therapy. Clinical Psychology and Psychotherapy 8: 59–72.

Ryle A (1975) Frames and Cages. London: Sussex University Press.

Ryle A (1982) Psychotherapy: A Cognitive Integration of Theory and Practice. London: Academic Press.

Ryle A (1985) Cognitive theory, object relations and the self. British Journal of Medical Psychology 58: 1–7.

Ryle A (1990) Cognitive Analytic Therapy: Active Participation in Change. Chichester: J Wiley & Sons.

Ryle A (1992) Critique of a Kleinian case presentation. British Journal of Medical Psychology 65: 309–17.

Ryle A (1993) Addiction to the death instinct? a critical review of Joseph's paper 'Addiction to near death'. British Journal of Psychotherapy 10(I): 88–92.

Ryle A (1994) Projective identification; a particular form of reciprocal role procedure. British Journal of Medical Psychology 67: 107–14.

Ryle A (ed) (1995) Cognitive Analytic Therapy; Developments in Theory and Practice. Chichester: J Wiley & Sons.

Ryle A (1997a) Cognitive Analytic Therapy and Borderline Personality Disorder: The Model and the Method. Chichester: J Wiley & Sons.

Ryle A (1997b) The structure and development of borderline personality disorder; a proposed model. British Journal of Psychiatry 170: 82–7.

Ryle A, Golynkina K (1999) Effectiveness of time-limited Cognitive Analytic Therapy of borderline personality disorder: factors associated with outcome. British Journal of Medical Psychology 73: 197–210.

Ryle A, Kerr IB (2002) Introducing Cognitive Analytic Therapy; Principles and Practice. Chichester: J Wiley & Sons.

Stern DN (1985) The Interpersonal World of the Infant: A View from Psychoanalysis and Developmental Psychology. New York: Basic Books.

CHAPTER 10

Sexual abuse, post-traumatic stress and object relations: an integrative way of working

DEIRDRE MANNION

Introduction

It is now recognized beyond question that sexual abuse has a deep and profound impact on people's lives. While children emerge from childhood with a defence structure in place that allows them to move into adulthood, the pervasive wound of abuse lies buried within the psyche. The expression of this wounding manifests in emotional, behavioural, cognitive, physical and relational disturbances. Feelings of anxiety, guilt, anger, shame, depression, deep and profound mistrust and a fragmented and torn inner self are common.

Therapists have been cautious and reluctant about working with sexually abused clients for many reasons: the horror that abuse tends to evoke, the emotional intensity of the work and the fear of 'doing more harm than good'. The lack of a cohesive road map to negotiate the aftermath of abuse has been a source of anxiety and concern to therapists. The feminist and humanist schools emphasize safety to enable disclosure, and containment and support for the retrieval and expression of deeply painful memories. Cognitive and behavioural schools have helped clients understand how they construct the world internally and how to alter and actively change thinking and behavioural patterns that are maladaptive and unhelpful. Psychoanalytic theory has helped us to understand how abuse is both met and internalized within the unconscious and how the defensive strategies are put in place to help the child cope with such a painful event. In the late 1980s Gelinas (1983), Herman and van der Kolk (1987) and Rieker and Carmen (1986) made major contributions to an emerging understanding of incest related symptoms in terms of a delayed post-traumatic stress disorder (PTSD). They focused on abuse as a fearful and emotionally overwhelming experience leading to a traumatic neurosis. In 1990 Meiselman elaborated the PTSD model and proposed a Reintegration model of psychotherapy for clients who had been abused. She reconceptualized incest related disturbances as representing a delayed or chronic post-traumatic stress disorder, causing affects and memories to be shut off from consciousness. These models have helped to inform our understanding of the impact of sexual abuse, but have been insufficient to describe some core elements of its legacy. Why is trust so damaged? Why is self-esteem and sense of self so distorted and pained? Why is the guilt and shame of abuse so severe? Why do abuse victims feel so split and divided? What of the relationship context within which abuse happens?

Sexual abuse is not just a deeply traumatic event or series of events. It happens within a relational structure. The child who is being abused both lives within a family system and their own internal world, conscious and unconscious. Object relations theory deepens our understanding of how the abuse is internalized and how the burden of the badness of the abuse is introjected, leading to the most profound sense of shame, guilt and loss. In placing the need for relationship as primary, object relations helps us to understand the relational context within which abuse happens and how these relationships are internalized. If the deepest human need is for contact, but love itself is destructive, the internal world becomes fraught with anguish and is carried on into adulthood. The dovetailing of object relations theory with the Reintegration model provides a rich and diverse integrative approach that has within its contours a respectful wisdom for working with the aftermath of abuse.

Understanding the impact of sexual abuse – a post-traumatic stress model

Gelinas (1983) saw sexual abuse as a traumatic event too large for a child to handle. The child, overwhelmed and frightened, quickly learns to disassociate, deny and repress both feelings and memories of the abuse (Figure 10.1). Rieker and Carmen (1986) saw abuse followed by a process of disconfirmation and transformation, which allows the child to defensively alter reality to accommodate the family system. Transforming the incest experience through denial, displacement and reinterpreting the meaning of events allows the child to survive, but results in an adult dependency on the mechanisms of repression and disassociation to isolate the affects and memories that threaten to be overwhelming. Moreover, 'the most enduring psychological legacy of these accommodations to abuse is a disordered and fragmented identity. This is observed clinically in the form of low self-esteem, self-hatred, affective instability ... and disturbed relationships, with an inability to trust and behave in self protective ways' (Rieker and Carmen, 1986). Herman and van der Kolk (1987) noted that chronic recurrent trauma in childhood resulted in identity diffusion, splitting of the good and bad self, and a relentless sense of inner badness. The adult legacy of abuse is a delicately balanced system where the abuse is defensively compartmentalized, yet leaks out, either in involuntary intrusions of the trauma or secondary elaborations (Figure 10.1). It may only take a small trigger to cause the collapse of this defensive organization, often propelling the person to seek help. The PTSD model began to allow therapists to conceptualize the way in which the abuse was originally experienced and transformed within the child and the consequential effects in adulthood. It also made sense of the wide variety of symptomatology in clinical presentation of sexually abused adults.

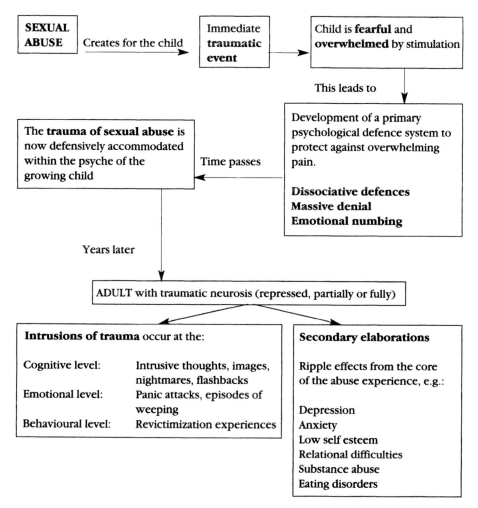

Figure 10.1. Psychological effects of abuse from childhood to adulthood: a post-traumatic stress model.

Reintegration therapy (Meiselman, 1990) was born out of the PTSD model and provided a more useful road map to therapists working with sexual abuse. It holds that the essential goal of therapy is to provide a safe and secure environment within which clients can gradually recall and retrieve the painful memories that were split off from consciousness. Drawing on the humanistic, cognitive/behavioural and psychoanalytical schools, therapy is seen as a 'healing process that will gradually reunite these elements into a self structure that can resume the growth that was stopped or distorted when the trauma occurred' (Meiselman, 1990, p. 94).

Limitations of the post-traumatic stress model

The limitations of the PTSD model and reintegration therapy are that they only provide a road map for the first phase of the therapeutic work with clients who have been abused. While it is without doubt that breaking the secrecy and working through the traumatic recall and emotional pain of abuse brings overwhelming relief for clients, it is only part of the story and the healing process is not complete. This is only the initial meeting of the abuse; a 'swap' during which the non-judgemental accepting and holding presence of the therapist is internalized as a 'good object', allowing an 'emptying out' of the black painful feelings and memories lying within the client. However, if the therapy ends here, albeit in hope and renewal, the client can gradually sink back into a nameless, unfulfilling, unhappy place. Because the new found hope has now eroded, there is a 'second wounding', confirming the deepest fear that the pain of abuse does not go away.

Once the initial trauma of abuse has been acknowledged and worked on therapeutically, slowly and painfully other bad inner objects rise like silent dinosaurs from the depths. Silent in that they are not easily detected, and slowly take shape as they are brought to consciousness. Like dinosaurs in that they come from another era and contain a powerful energetic force. The introjected abuse and the split, internalized family still rule from within: the relentless pernicious guilt, the fractured sense of self, the non-protective abandoning parent, the sadistic parent. It is in these deeper layers of the psyche that the abuse is truly buried and it is in this meeting place that the deepest hope for healing and resolution lie. It is the slow, painstaking identification of inner destructive forces and their taming together with the internalization of good objects, sufficient for a meaningful and better life.

Object relations and sexual abuse

If object relations has taught us that a close relationship is a vital and necessary context for human development and an essential part of a satisfying life, what then of the sexually abused person where trust is wounded, love distorted and closeness dangerous? What happens to the psychological and emotional development of that person? How does a child navigate the developmental stages when weighed with the burden of abuse? Object relations helps us to understand how abuse forms a person, how the external reality reaches into and changes the internal world in the deepest possible ways. The conscious and unconscious internal world is altered both between different aspects of the self, in the relational system that is laid down internally, and in relationships in the external world. It throws light on how they become divided within themselves and against themselves. The splits and fractures that clients know in themselves are built on compliance to ensure survival and lead to the inevitable development of a 'false self'.

Developmental aspects affecting the impact of sexual abuse

It is now widely accepted that the successful negotiation of the first years of development, with its oral, anal and oedipal issues, is what provides a basic stock of trust and goodness in oneself and an ability to relate easily and productively to others. Each stage presents its own central issues, challenges and possibilities for resolutions. When these are fraught with problems, life becomes inevitably troubled and difficult. Moreover, 'any stage in development is reached and lost and reached and lost over and over again' (Winnicott, 1988, p. 37). Sexual abuse, because of the profound demands it puts on a child, and its emotional difficulties, reawakens the primary anxieties and may provoke a regression to earlier stages of life.

The predominant issue in infancy is how much trust can be established that the world will care and provide. This forms 'the basis in the child for a sense of identity ... a sense of being "all right", of being oneself' (Erikson, 1995, p. 224). In the sexual abuse experience, essential boundaries are violated, both emotionally and physically. The child is then overwhelmed and engulfed by the abuse. This results in a sense of loss of integrity of the self and a deep wounding of trust. This then throws the child back into the paranoid-schizoid anxieties (Klein, 1946). In an attempt to manage these anxieties, the child resorts to the primitive defences of splitting, projecting, introjecting and denying. The abuser, like the parents, is sometimes experienced as either entirely good or bad. Persecutory anxiety abounds, and not alone may the child feel unloved by the abusing parent, but the non-protective parent can also be internalized as a persecutory figure, deepening the child's fear that they are unlovable. The badness of the abuse is introjected by the child: 'I am unlovable, therefore I get abused'. This primitive attempt to manage and control the abuse is somehow easier than facing the terrifying reality of the cruelty and destructiveness in the abusing adult. 'By taking the burden of badness within we can continue to see the needed external person as good enough ... so continuing to relate to them. We maintain an outward sense of security at the price of inward security and conflict' (Gomez, 1997, p. 65). Fairbairn (1943) named this relocation of badness 'the moral defence'. The introjection of the burden of the badness of the abuse can leave an enduring legacy of an inner sense of profound shame, guilt and inherent badness. Long after the initial trauma of the abuse has been worked through, these deep and silent anxieties prowl around in the depths of the unconscious or eventually become voiced in the quietness of the therapy room.

Splitting also leads to projections, which are often extreme and unrealistic. The child projects their own intense rage, hate and anxieties. Goodness is also projected, partly to have something good to rely on, and partly to protect it from the badness within. Denial is obviously the other way children may cope with abuse, either pretending it is not happening or, in the face of continuous abuse, denying the emotional reality of it. The whole context of 'secrecy' within which abuse happens, and the subtle ways in which abusers try to blame the child, further exacerbates the sense of badness.

By now we might well ask what is happening to the child's dependency needs? It may be that the child has now inverted their dependency needs into a pseudo self-sufficiency and indifference to other people. Thus her feelings of neediness are disowned and ridiculed. As the world's goodness becomes more tainted, so too does the child's. Their anger and rage must now be managed. In the depressive position (Klein, 1935), anger is internalized so as not to destroy the other. The fear of the loss of the internalized good object (person) is a direct threat to the child's very survival, so rage is forfeited for need. This creates an undermining of the self deep down which manifests itself as lack of confidence, low-grade feelings of guilt, despair and resentment. What may now be developing within the child is a split between a pleasant, placatory, compliant self on the one hand and repressed feelings of rage, disappointment and need which seem unacceptable or disastrously destructive, on the other. Thus a false self develops, on top of unbearable anxiety. This false self 'develops on a compliance basis ... and becomes organised to keep the world at bay' (Winnicott, 1988, p. 108). The true self is hidden away and therefore protected.

Following on the issues of building trust in the relationship, the next challenge developmentally may be to negotiate a sense of power, control and self-worth: 'Who controls who? How worthwhile am I to other people?' Whether coerced or bullied, abuse is always a power issue. The child is stripped of self-determination and autonomy and is used as part object by the abuser. Defiance and refusal to cooperate are rare. Passive resistance is by far the most common reaction on the part of the child. This 'giving in' to accommodate the abuse is the child's way of surviving an overwhelming power imbalance. Boundaries previously established are now destroyed. The enduring adult legacy can be a rigid wish to over-control, or a compulsive lack of boundaries. If the child has internalized a sadistic controlling relationship, they may become masochistically attached to being treated badly, only feeling safe when under the control of a powerful other. Thus the childhood script is repeated in adulthood, often with great tenacity. The major defences of this stage are repression and reaction formation, and again both are widely employed to deal with the abuse.

When oedipal issues are successfully resolved, usually before the age of five or six, the child is on the way to becoming a social being, a little 'junior citizen' closely identified with peers. During these years the inner oedipal drama and conflicts are resolved with the child relinquishing the omnipotent desire to possess one or other parent. It learns to identify with the same sex parent and becomes able to come to terms with the fact that she can still cope even though she is not the centre of the universe. It is long recognized that the exclusion of overt adult sexuality from the parent–child relationship is an important precondition to the healthy psychological development of the child. Overt sexual gratification by the adult confuses and traumatizes the inner world of the child and destabilizes the nurturing bond. The child is not free to resolve her oedipal instincts and impulses when forced to gratify sexual needs at such a tender age. Moreover the secrecy, shame and burden of the abuse and the emotional toll of coping with it can leave a child feeling different, bad and alienated from peers. Spontaneous fun and play are hard to engage in and the sense of goodness and trust in self is deeply compromised. Thus the child tries to join life, but with a deep sense of difference and hollowness. This again can endure through adulthood, the person playing an 'as if' role but inside perhaps marginalized and exiled.

Legacy of child sexual abuse: impact on the formation of a 'relational self'

The patterns of a child's relationships are deeply imprinted in the inner representation of her relational world, and this carries on into adulthood. The internal model is a reflection of the kind of care she has received and the sense of self that is born out of it. The secure, loved child has an inner sense of a lovable self together with a responsive, caring internalized 'other'. The insecure, ambivalent child has an inner sense of being unlovable in relation to an internalized other who is unpredictable and has to be manipulated or coerced. In a childhood where there is a lot of disturbance and abuse, it generally results in an insecure, avoidant child who has a sense of self, which is unworthy of care, and an internalized other, who does not care (Bowlby,

1988b). In this latter template, the child represses her longing and anger and need in order not to drive the other even further away. It is not at all unusual for the sexually abused child to feel that the stability and survival of the entire family system is dependent on her silence.

If, as Fairbairn suggests, our deepest motivation is for contact, then separation anxiety is our deepest fear, the dread of the loss of the other on whom our psychological and physical survival depends (Fairbairn, 1952). A child will do anything possible to ensure the continuation of the relationship system. When parents, through fragility, insensitivity or cruelty, deny a child's reality and fail to support their emotional truth, the child then accommodates to the family system. The price of this is that the contradictions of reality can only be resolved by excluding feelings and perceptions by containing and repressing them. In this way they may form part of an internal sense of a 'bad self'. So the child denies her own truth to survive but is left deeply confused. This 'defensive exclusion' born out of acute emotional shock and unbearable pain results in dissociated 'frozen' blocks of cognitions and feelings and a distorted and fragmented internal model of relationships which endures into adulthood and forms the template for future experiences. The extent of wounding varies greatly from person to person and no two adults emerge the same from the experience of sexual abuse. The degree to which the child has been able to take in goodness, experience the trust and feel the care and concern of a significant other changes the inner world.

On the other hand people may carry the wound of abuse in unbearably painful ways. The conscious wish is for wholesome, creative possibilities, but the unconscious internalizations have a power of their own and go on to be re-enacted. Thus it is not just childhood that is lost, but adulthood as well. Whether the wounds of abuse are lived out close to the surface or buried deep, the contents of the internalized abuse world are very similar. The badness of the abuse has been introjected, leading to deep feelings of shame, guilt and badness. The sense of self is distorted, incoherent and damaged. Trust is deeply compromised, needs are disowned, anger and rage are repressed and projected. It is these deeper unconscious internalizations that form the silent dinosaurs underneath the abuse and it is these that must be met in the therapy room if the abuse is to be healed.

The therapeutic endeavour: accompanying the client

The function of therapy is twofold. On the one hand it is to help facilitate a healing catharsis of the trauma of abuse, to provide safety and containment for feelings and memories that can be overwhelmingly painful. On the other hand it is to venture into the inner world to make conscious the old, uncreative solutions, and the compulsion to repeat, so that the person 'can refuse the role of mere player ... manipulated by an uncontrollable destiny' (McDougall, 1986, p. 127).

The relationship between the client and therapist is the cornerstone of the work needed to heal abuse. The client can gradually learn a 'new way of object relating based on the repair of broken trust' (Gomez, 1997, p. 118). This takes time, dedication, patience and a deep understanding of the client's struggle. Within the containment of this ongoing relationship certain themes and issues may emerge at different phases in the therapy. I am now going to explore these in more detail.

The early phase of therapy: the unfolding of the story

By the time a person who has been sexually abused finds herself sitting in a therapist's room, much has already happened. There has been some kind of collapse of the defensive structure that contained the abuse. They may have been experiencing increased emotional pain, distress, anxiety, depression or a progressive intrusion of memories, flashbacks and dreams. The person is by this point often in deep internal conflict, grappling with inner chaos; things that don't make sense and a breakdown of the order that ensured survival. Moreover, because of the secrecy that has been internalized and the perception that the family's entire fragile survival is dependent on this secrecy, there can be intense conflict about breaking the secret. Once this happens the person has already broken a powerful internalized family rule and fear of its catastrophic consequences runs high. This can be the loneliest of times as the client begins the long journey into self, to discover and confirm the truth of their internal reality, often at the price of the family myth, for example a myth of normality or happiness. Implicit in this first step away from the 'myth' is the first step towards the therapist, who will be tested again and again for their trustworthiness, wisdom and strength. This early phase of therapy is full of disorder, of confusion, of pain, sometimes of shock as what has been repressed comes into consciousness. Because of the very way the abuse is defensively accommodated, its retrieval is also confused and fragmented. Clients can feel fearful of being overwhelmed or of breaking down altogether. How do they experience and express feelings that seem too unbearable to bear? How do they trust when life has taught that to trust is to be abused, abandoned or let down?

The therapist has to have a presence, sufficient enough ('good enough mother') to provide a safe and wise space. The client will sense unconsciously whether the therapist has worked through their own defensive reactions to the trauma of abuse, so that the therapist is not going to be repulsed or overwhelmed, either by the details of the story or its pain. The capacity for self-rejection is so deep in the abused person that they will consciously and unconsciously search for any signs in the therapist that they are 'too much', or that their inner contents are unbearable or repulsive. Clients need to tell the story, to wash out, purge, hand over the details to another human being, otherwise shame binds the abuse. In facilitating this, the therapist allows the client to go back in time and re-enter the abuse world of the child, but this time the burdens are shared.

As the ego defences ebb and flow, repressed and split off feelings are experienced with more and more intensity. By witnessing these feelings and containing the client, the therapist helps the client to bear the unbearable. Thus the client can slowly move towards the truth, confirming their own internal reality and dismantling the accommodations that led to the distortions in the first place.

This is a very difficult time for clients as memories and feelings can be experienced with shocking intensity or pain. The old order is gone and grief is everywhere. The client can often feel they are trying to stay afloat on a very fragile raft in very stormy waters. Conceptualizing what is happening to the person as a delayed post-traumatic stress disorder, not a breakdown into psychosis, can bring overwhelming relief to clients, and the beginning of a road map, solid enough to step onto. The first meeting of the story is happening, in all its traumatic aspects. Through this time the client has begun to experience a relationship with the therapist unlike anything that has been known before. This opens out the possibility of a deepening relationship with self.

The middle phase of therapy: experiential meeting of the story and first resolution

The client is now moving into a deeper experiential relationship to her own story. The relationship context of the abuse has been opened and is beginning to be explored more fully. The client may have learned that moving away from destructive relationships in the external world still leaves them at the mercy of their own inner demons. Abuse evokes revulsion. Its enduring legacy is an abiding sense of inner badness and self-repulsion. There are three aspects to this: the abuse itself as it was perpetrated physically, all the feelings that it generates and the inner objects that were formed out of the relationship system. Thus what is 'put into' the child is not just the abuse itself, but the attitudes, feelings and conflicts within the perpetrator and the family system.

Rejection and the unjustness of the abuse give rise to unbearable anger. The emotional demands of the therapy itself evoke anger and rage: 'Why me?', 'Why more?' Anger is a complex issue. Clients need to be helped to access repressed and split off rage on the one hand, yet be protected from destructive acting out experiences on the other. Anger can also be a powerfully healing and regenerative experience for the client. If in phase one of the therapy anger serves to effect a sense of separateness from the abuser in the external world, in the second phase of therapy it serves to create a much deeper sense of separateness from the abuse itself. Thus the client is no longer identified with the abuse, or defined by it. It is the combination of an increased sense of self-worth and a deep and legitimate rage that helps form the new self.

It is difficult for any of us to face our own destructive tendencies. It is perhaps more difficult for the sexually abused person because of their deep fear that they are essentially bad. In my experience these deep levels of rage can often not be negotiated until the client has internalized sufficient goodness in the therapy to be able to withstand their own destructive forces. Thus 'the internalized good' becomes the container. While the impulse to destroy is there, it can be experienced in its full intensity without actually destroying. In the reclaiming of split off rage lies the further possibility of an acceptance of self that is not sanitized or idealized, but deeply human.

In this phase of therapy a deeper meeting of feelings and introjections takes place. The internalized revulsion is experienced, as well as the repulsed parts of the self that are split off and un-integrated. This cannot happen any earlier: it is too painful and too dark. This aspect of the work can be the turning point in the healing process, an energetic release that reverberates in every aspect of the client's life. The overwhelming relief that 'I am not essentially bad.'

Running through the whole therapeutic experience is the issue of mourning and loss. But it is in this phase that it is felt at its deepest. The tension that is released when the severity of the introjected badness is softened does not always stay in relief, but can move into a period of loss and grief for all that has been lost – both in adulthood and childhood. This resembles closely Bowlby's description (1979) of the mourning process. It is deeply poignant to see clients yearning and searching for their lost childhood. If the client is supported to tolerate the pining, the restless searching, the endless questioning of why these losses occurred in their lives and their anger about it all, they can gradually 'recognise and accept that the loss is in truth permanent and life must be shaped anew' (Bowlby, 1988a, p. 93).

By now the pain of history can begin to recede for the client. They no longer feel ruled by the abuse experience. As the relationship with the therapist has been slowly deepening, so too has the relationship with self. This is a taut and difficult process with many storms along the way. The support and goodness of the therapist has been internalized sufficiently to provide a stock of goodness on the inside and heal self-esteem. There can be a sense of closure, of relief, of resolution. This can be followed by a period of quiet in the therapy or even an ending. Either way some kind of first resolution has been reached. There can be an energetic need to rest before the next phase can be negotiated. Clients don't want any more pain, therapists don't want any more pain. Both may have carried a deep fear of being overwhelmed by the abuse experiences. Both are grateful to have survived.

The later phase in therapy: silent dinosaurs and the deeper regression

Possibly the deepest fear of both the client and the therapist is that, after all the work, the abuse experience has left a legacy that is unchangeable. The wounds of the abuse can lie in very deep places. Introjects, like silent dinosaurs, prowl the depths of the unconscious, as do defensive modes of survival that compromise relatedness. In this latter deeper excavation of what lies within, rests the hope for the deepest resolution of the abuse.

Balint's 'Basic Fault' describes a sense of brokenness at the core of one's being. When anxiety is being felt by the client at this level it necessitates a much deeper regression in the therapy than the earlier work entailed. Thus, if the client's 'life long anxiety is to be reached, she has to enter into an exquisitely vulnerable dependency, living through the risk of disaster without any idea what the outcome will be' (Gomez, 1997, p. 118). This is Balint's 'New Beginning' (Balint, 1968). In it lies the potential for much greater possibilities around trust to emerge and for resolution of the deeper primitive anxieties. In this phase of therapy there is a more profound excavation of what lies within.

Dependency is fraught with terror for the sexually abused client. They may as children have split off their unbearable neediness in a withdrawal from the external relationship. The perceived intolerably depriving parent is frequently internalized as a 'rejecting object' giving rise to the 'internal saboteur' (Fairbairn, 1952). In the regression in therapy clients will inevitably oscillate between contemptuous rejection of their own neediness and raging against the therapist for daring to evoke it. Conversely, there can be periods of hysterical reaction to their experience of neediness. This can be a frightening time for clients as they struggle, yearn and search for a strong, gratifying figure to hold on to. It can be hard for the therapist not to be seduced by the endless suffering of the regressed client and when faced with such pain. However, to do so is a trap and the therapy quickly deteriorates. Balint warns us that, in this 'malignant regression', the client, contrary to what it seems, is not seeking a real relationship but gratification. The therapist is perceived as the all-powerful, holder of all that is good, offering either the possibility of extreme joy or of persecutory withholding. If the frame is firmly but sensitively held and the client is helped to experience her overwhelming dependency, a gradual ease begins to happen. Her ultimate need has not been for gratification, but for personal recognition.

Fairbairn (1943) felt that it is loyalty to our internal objects that provides that greatest resistance to change. To risk letting go of these can be terrifying, a dangerous step into totally new territory. It matters little if these internal objects are unsatisfactory, painful or destructive; they are familiar. Familiar is manageable because it is known. A client can only begin to abandon their internal objects when a secure trust in the therapist begins to grow. Being vulnerable does not mean having to lose autonomy. The genuine concern and understanding of the therapist allows the client to re-own her split off capacities for anger and need and reintegrate them. So how then does the therapist position herself to best facilitate the client at this stage? Winnicott (1988) and Balint (1968) both stress the need for a quiet sensitive alliance. Winnicott speaks of the 'good enough' quality in the therapist that allows the client to regress. Balint (1968) describes a fluid, ordinary, low key being together, to provide the intimate rapport of the 'New Beginning'. The client's ego structure will need support to withstand the tensions and conflicts of this period. Deep fears obstruct the way towards re-adaptation. The giving up of the old defensive positions, costly as they are, is an overwhelmingly frightening proposition. Emotions are primitive, intense and highly charged. It is a time during which the therapist must 'hold one's nerve' and be steadfast as the client struggles in the painful birth pangs of the new potentialities.

On the return journey the client begins to see the therapist as neither idealized nor demonized, but as an ordinary, imperfect human being. Thus the recognition of the good and the bad in the therapist allows a gradual acceptance of 'the good and the bad in the self, of the hopelessness and that which is hopeful, of the unreal with the real, all the contrasting extremes' (Winnicott, 1988, p. 142). Client and therapist sit awhile, allowing a resolution to the grief to happen and focusing on the realities, hopes and potentials of the life that now is. The journey is both complete and by its very nature will always be incomplete.

Conclusion

Working with sexual abuse is complex. It puts profound demands on the resources of both client and therapist. It is always a voyage into the dark and painful unknown. Different clients achieve different levels of resolution. The loss for clients is when these levels are dictated, not by their own unique needs, but by the limitations of the therapist. Abuse can evoke not just extreme horror but also deep sympathy. A therapeutic response that is well intentioned but misguided and limited is insufficient. It has the implicit danger of leaving the client in a more hopeless place. The complexity of abuse demands within the therapist a diversity of knowledge and skills that can only be encompassed by an integrative approach. Mastery of the therapist's own personal defensive reactions to abuse, a knowledge of the post-traumatic stress model and a grounding in object relations go a long way to providing what is needed. Once the traumatic discharge of the story has happened, the relational system and its internalizations, held deep in the unconscious, need to be unravelled. The steadfast relationship with the therapist can provide a unique opportunity for a transformation to occur in relatedness, both to self and others. The wound of abuse can never be erased, but the richness of life need no longer be eclipsed. As therapists, our continued dedication to an integrative way of working will ensure that the space that we invite clients into is an evolving tapestry of wisdom built on solid theoretical ground.

References

Balint M (1968) The Basic Fault: Therapeutic Aspects of Regression. London: Tavistock.

Bowlby J (1979) The Making and Breaking of Affectional Bonds. London: Tavistock.

Bowlby J (1988a) Attachment and Loss. Vol. 3. London: Pimlico.

Bowlby J (1988b) A Secure Base: Clinical Applications of Attachment Theory. London: Routledge

Erikson E (1995) Childhood and Society. London: Vintage.

Fairbairn R (1943) The Repression and Return of Bad Objects. Psycho-Analytic Studies of the Personality. London: Routledge.

Fairbairn W (1952) Psychoanalytic Studies of the Personality. London: Tavistock.

Gelinas D (1983) The persisting negative effects of incest. Psychiatry 46: 312-32.

Gomez L (1997) An Introduction to Object Relations. London: Free Association Books.

Herman JL, van der Kolk BA (1987) Traumatic antecedents of borderline personality disorder. In BA van der Kolk (ed), Psychological Trauma. American Psychiatric Press.

Klein M (1935) Love, Guilt and Reparation. London: Virago (1988).

Klein M (1946) Envy and Gratitude and Other Works. London: Virago (1988).

McDougall J (1986) Theatres of the Mind. London: Free Association Books.

Meiselman K (1990) Resolving the Trauma of Incest. London: Jossey-Bass.

Rieker PP, Carmen EH (1986) The victim-to-patient process: the disconfirmation and transformation of abuse. American Journal of Orthopsychiatry 56: 360-70.

van der Kolk BA (1987) The psychological consequences of overwhelming life experiences. In BA van der Kolk (ed), Psychological Trauma. American Psychiatric Press.

Winnicott D (1988) Human Nature. London: Free Association Books.

Chapter 11

An integrative approach to body oriented psychotherapy

Lennart Ramberg and Björn Wrangsjö

Body oriented psychotherapy and object relations – an introduction

Body oriented psychotherapy is an approach to working with psychological problems and symptoms within a verbal psychotherapeutic tradition, together with a focus on concomitant body processes and body interventions. An object relations theoretical perspective is one of the cornerstones of this approach.

In this chapter we will first give a short historical background before introducing some basic concepts such as body image, internal objects and affect motor schemes which are related to the experience and expression of emotions. Some neuro-physiological aspects, which would influence or govern these processes of body–mind functioning, will be outlined. We will then present a model to clarify different levels of experience. The use of opening and grounding techniques will be discussed in relation to the level of the intrapsychic structure of the client. A clinical example of working therapeutically with both verbal and bodily aspects will be presented before the chapter concludes with some remarks on the use of touch in body oriented psychotherapy.

Historical background

The concept of the internal object is central to object relations theory. Freud (1917) introduced this concept in *Mourning and Melancholia* with the famous description of how 'the shadow of the object falls upon the ego'.

Klein (1981) coined the concept of an inner world, in which part objects dwell together with whole objects. They reveal themselves through the handling of outer objects and by 'part-object like' verbalizations in the play of children in psychoanalysis. She also showed that part objects dominate the inner world of adults with severe mental disturbances.

Bion (1967) suggests that a child will experience dread if it meets an emotionally charged situation and has no adequate inner objects, which enable it to think about that situation. Therefore he or she cannot deal with the experience adequately. If the mother does not have the capacity to contain the situation or is absent, the child will create persecutory or hallucinatory inner objects.

Fairbairn (Fairbairn-Birtles and Scharff, 1994) abandoned Freud's drive theory and instead regarded the relationship to the object as more important than instinctual gratification, which follows the pleasure principle. He proposed that the first triangular conflict that the child experiences in its inner world, is between the 'central ego' and the split off 'exciting' and 'rejecting internal objects'. The central ego is conflict free, formed out of a real mother–child interaction, while the split-off objects are seen as the result of a dysfunctional mother–child interaction.

Focus on the body

Freud was never interested in working with the body, despite the fact that it was important in his theory. This was evident in his discussions of hysteria, the subconscious and the drives. However the psychoanalysts Groddek (1977) and Ferenczi (1980), who were close to Freud in periods, sometimes worked with the body therapeutically.

Reich (1949) was the first psychoanalyst to formulate a theory about how certain character traits, negative transference and certain body characteristics could constitute important defences affecting the development of the personality.

Even if in our opinion his later work is of less interest, Reich's pioneering work inspired many followers, the most important being Lowen (1975), who developed bioenergetics. George Downing (1996), a modern theoretician and clinician, combines object relations theory and body psychotherapy work with a special focus on how the transference–countertransference process unfolds when the body as well as the mind are worked with.

We will now examine modern knowledge and research about the mind–body and how the embodiment of the mind can be understood.

Mind–body aspects

A theory of how to work with the mind–body, not only through words but also through bodily contact, manipulation and other directive methods, requires a systems thinking in which both domains may be integrated. Neuroscience and research on the function of the brain appear to bridge this gap. However there is a controversy about the issue of discussing in an inter-changing way subjective experiences on the one hand, and positivistic and empirical data on the other.

In recent decades some well-founded theoretical propositions have evolved which suggest that the mind–body are seamlessly integrated, thereby mending the Western split between Mind and Body (Edelman, 1992; Damasio, 1994, 1999).

Motivational systems

In a development of Freud's concepts of libido and partial drives, Lichtenberg's (1989) motivational systems and Panksepp's (1998) social emotions and basic emotional processes, the following formulation outlines what humans share with all mammals:

- basic physiological needs
- a seeking system with qualities of anticipation and curiosity
- sexuality
- a need for belonging (attachment, motherly and other nurturing behaviour) as well as a capacity to handle separation
- ways of learning and unlearning through the mechanisms of play, and its corresponding emotion of joy, and dreaming, in which there is a selection of experiences to be stored in the long-term memory
- emotions, such as anger, fear and anxiety.

An example of how humans are able to handle separation is the capacity to be alone through the internalization of objects and through the mechanisms of mourning (Winnicott 1965).

The human symbolizing system, which is created in the process of learning and unlearning, is related to the list of emotions and needs presented above. The values which are thus created would overarch, and at the same time build upon the basic motivational systems (Ramberg 1992).

In addition to the emotions mentioned above, man has developed other category affects (Darwin 1965), such as disgust, sadness, distaste and shame as well as secondary affects like shyness and guilt feelings. For practical reasons, we will use the term 'emotion' in the following text for all emotional experiences related to the motivational system outlined above.

Emotions, inner objects and the brain

Emotions are intrinsically linked to inner objects. Also each emotion generates a definitive and primitive set of attitudes and action patterns of its own. Each one carries a specific conscious feeling tone, which has an important significance in helping us to decipher and evaluate the object relation which evoked the emotion. Thus, we can link it with other object relations which contain the same feeling tone. Furthermore, our mind can, through symbolizing activity, create an abstraction of some common qualities of these object relation units (Kernberg 1980) which can generate new inner objects.

Affect motor schemes

The concept 'affect motor scheme' of emotions is central to body psychotherapy. It implies a personally flavoured, idiosyncratic set of embodied emotional response patterns, which mainly would have been formed within the first years of life. Working bodily in therapy will highlight and influence the individual's particular set ways of perceiving and mis-perceiving, and also his or her emotional 'language'.

The affect motor schemes have a genetic origin, but each individual develops characteristic ways of perceiving and expressing himself. A person's mind finds its own ways to make conscious, thwart or inhibit the emotion and finally to modify the motor expression of it. In contrast to the comparatively inborn maps which animals have, people create much more personal maps of how to engage in the world. Based on his subconscious anticipation, a person organizes his perception of situations to evoke the emotions he expects.

This is the basic model of how for example projections, projective identifications, and transference–countertransference reactions are formed.

All these affect motor schemes are integrated into what we could call an unconscious body scheme (Schilder, 1950) that shows our way of perceiving, feeling and acting in life. This scheme is intrinsically linked to the person's inner objects and symbolizing self and is perceived by us as our body image.

Structures underlying empathy and projective identifications

The evolution of interlacing patterns of motivational affective and cognitive structures of the brain into verbal speech and 'silent speech' (or thoughts), has taken a long and complicated path. Langer (1972) suggests that speech has evolved from the need to communicate a way of dealing with the outer world. She explains that it has also developed out of the unintentional sounds that for example pigs emit when they feel good in their flock and is echoed by the other animals. This is similar to the way some apes utter a throat song, creating a singing dialogue with their partner to deepen their sense of belonging. It has also evolved out of the animals' non-intentional sounds when they perceive danger. These examples demonstrate the importance for animals of conveying their inner emotional states to others and simultaneously to themselves.

There are rich connections between the areas of abstract cognition and 'the emotional brain', which indicate that motives, cognition and affects are biologically interwoven (Barbas 1995). When certain experiences in life are cognitively reflected on, specific areas of the brain are 'turned on'. This induces concomitant feelings, which could be regarded as the conscious aspects of the emotions (Damasio, 1999). These sites of induction send signals through the autonomic nervous system to mediate a specific bodily expression for each category affect. This applies especially to the facial muscles, which, together with the expression of the eyes, convey the emotional state of the individual. This in turn is subconsciously perceived and coded by another person. This process is most often responsible for the excessive (Bion, 1962) and intrusive (Meltzer, 1986) projective identifications occurring when the therapist cannot consciously code a client's non-verbal and verbal communication. On the other hand it might also be consciously perceived and categorized by the conscious symbolic system in this person, for example a therapist.

The autonomic nervous system changes the state of the body, which in turn influences the state of the brain, inducing a new cognitive mode, which in turn influences the body and the thought process. When an emotion strikes a cord, there is an intricate self-reinforcing process going on between the body and different levels of the brain, which makes the emotion reverberate through the body–mind.

In the right hemisphere of the brain, there is a current preconscious registration of the emotional and bodily inner state of the person, which Damasio (1994) calls 'the somatic-marker hypothesis'. This capacity is necessary for the process of empathy, which could be understood as another person's emotional state being not only perceived but also taken in and simulated. The result of this simulation is integrated with the verbal content that is communicated. When a person is stressed or preoccupied by problems he has a tendency to be less empathic, because the capacity for simulation is impaired.

Through short-circuiting mechanisms our mind can bypass the body and engage the cortical areas of the brain. This speeds up thinking, but does not integrate the thoughts and emotions. Damasio (1994) calls this an 'as if' loop. The feeling is not felt but thought. A body oriented psychotherapy can ensure that this 'as if' loop is developed into a full body–mind experience, with an awareness of the affects inherent in motives and thoughts.

The body–mind unity: motive, affect and cognition

People can modulate or 'tame' the expressions of emotions through the influence of higher cognitive levels of the brain. The techniques in body oriented psychotherapy can help the client to gradually discover inhibited emotions and experience them so that he is not blinded by them. This formulation is not only a metaphor, but actually true in the sense that the dominance of an emotion hinders the brain from utilizing 'cognitive parts'. The lack of cognitive connections might be one reason why the client may feel frightened by these emotions.

Oliver Sacks (1991) proposes that when a part of the body is cut off, for example in spinal anaesthesia, the unconscious association to this part is also cut off which makes it hard to remember experiences linked to this part of the body. Thus, it is important that 'mind needs to experience its body' in every psychotherapy, even in verbal approaches to psychotherapy – the therapy needs to 'be embodied'.

We cannot have a thought without a concomitant feeling and motive. Motive, affect and cognition are all one even if some aspects are in the foreground and others in the background. Furthermore, if for psychological reasons an affect cannot be consciously felt, its concomitant motive and cognition cannot be fully reflected on. However, preconscious and subconscious thinking are always present (Shevrin et al., 1996) outside of focused awareness and the material can later be dealt with, for example in a dream.

Playing and dreaming

Playing (Winnicott, 1980) and dreaming (Levin, 1991) are the vehicles to genuine learning and thus central to the processing of new experiences as well as to the processes of change and development in psychotherapy. Play is one of the social emotions and has according to Panksepp (1998) its own inductor sites in the brain. Playing is a psychological state, which could be seen as one of the social emotions. Within the boundaries of play all other social emotions, like sex, nurturing and category affects, even the threatening ones, can be contained and played out in a way that feels safe. It seems that the social emotion of play and the activity during dreaming fulfil the task of learning from experience. The good solutions as well as the dangers are selected and stored in long-term memory, for future use (Winson, 1985).

Dreaming seems to be the conscious side effect of the brain's way to replenish itself, to rid itself of unfinished business and to replace less useful scripts with more constructive ones. In other words, it saves what is worth saving in the long-term memory. The dreaming state is similar to play in that all themes that are contained in the scripts are played out in the mind and not by motor actions. The neurological pathways for concrete actions are blocked by mechanisms in the brain while the dreaming is going on (Solms, 1997).

Clinical work with emotions and inner objects

Earlier, we suggested that the brain has inborn emotions, each with a specific conscious feeling which is expressed in a particular way. Through personal experiences a person will develop his own, unique modifications of his affect motor schemes. He modifies and integrates them with other schemes into more elaborate maps, which contain newly created complexes of motivation, drives, affects and cognition. Through this process inner objects are created. For example, the whole inner object 'father' would be an inner abstraction of a complex pattern of different object relations and affect motor schemes. This can be conceived of by his face or another image related to him.

In order to activate motives and affects in the object relation units, a therapist can let the client enact his inner world through gestalt and psychodrama techniques. Psychotherapy can be looked upon as a serious kind of play with its special rules – the setting. Under the impact of a deepening trust and positive transference, the client begins to remember more of his traumatic past. In so doing he will also be able to consider other ways of understanding and acting.

Most of this process will be symbolized subconsciously (Bion, 1962). The therapist helps the client to rejuvenate his inhibited ability to express emotions, or inhibited affect motor skills, in a new way. The clinical vignette outlined below is an example of this. Presumably, the client did not receive sufficient help from his parents in developing skills to handle and regulate strong emotions earlier in life. The therapy can facilitate the client in developing more constructive emotional and social capacities, to use both in his internal and social life. Ideally, the therapist is able to help the client to tolerate deep regressive states.

A severely disturbed client in therapy will not be capable of tolerating the reactivated inner situation, as he would easily feel flooded, and resort to his perhaps inadequate psychological defence system.

As part of this process, the client's dreams with their mix of wish fulfilment and genuine learning can increase the understanding of the client's internal situation. Work with imagery can also be used to deepen this awareness. However, it is essential that the client can understand his traumatic experience in the context of a new inclusive view of and attitude to his own life. This entails a working through on a higher level to form a still more comprehensive psychological 'map'.

The traumatic as well as the more constructive affect–cognitive complex that the client has worked through in his therapy are engraved on this new map. For example, in the course of psychotherapy one can observe that important inner objects, for example one's parents, gradually acquire positive qualities. The inner objects are thus developing and changing through the client's internal work in therapy.

Intrapsychic structure and psychotherapeutic process

We will now examine some general aspects of treatment. The client's level of intrapsychic structure (ego strength) is an important guide for the choice of treatment in body oriented psychotherapy. The term intrapsychic structure refers to the level of mental organization within the personality, which a person can rely on in psychologically stressful situations. For example the ability to wait in spite of strong needs, urges or feelings, or the ability to recover reasonably well when hurt or frightened.

Mental problems in clients can reflect intrapsychic under-structuring. For example some personality disorders are formed predominantly through a lack of fit between emotionally intense experiences, individual coping capacity and parental holding. This could create in the child unbearable inner experiences on the core self-level (Stern, 1985), which he coped with mainly by primitive psychological defences such as projective identification and splitting.

Clients with an adequate inner mental structure may present emotional problems on a more neurotic level. These problems involve the internalization of strong negative emotional attitudes to their own feelings, fantasies and behaviour. This could bring about unbearable inner conflicts in relation to self-image, which result in less primitive and severe neurotic defences such as rationalization and intellectualization.

In order to treat symptoms and other problems in psychotherapy, one needs to establish a trusting therapeutic relationship, which can facilitate a containing process. In mentally under-structured clients, unbearable experiences may be activated within the transference–countertransference, through memories originating from encounters with intrusive or neglecting significant others in the past. These experiences are addressed within a holding relationship (Winnicott, 1965) where they can gradually be shared with the therapist, and experienced and expressed in terms of feelings, body expressions, inner images and words.

Before this is possible it is necessary to introduce structure building interventions such as work with body awareness, affect differentiation and the capacity to tolerate feeling in 'small doses'. These interventions lead to structuring and restructuring of the body image, transformation and resymbolization in the inner world which signifies that the earlier unbearable experiences are assimilated and integrated.

Treatment of problems and symptoms related to unbearable inner conflicts, such as neurotic disturbances, also need a safe therapeutic context. However much less preparatory work is needed, since the person has enough inner structure (ego strength) to tolerate the underlying feelings and fantasies.

Defences reflected in the body

On the body level, muscular tension and regulation of breathing patterns regulate conscious access to emotions. Chronic muscular tensions and defensive breathing patterns indicating problems in handling inner emotional tension are sometimes reflected in the posture and body shape of the client. The observations of these aspects as well as of the way in which the client moves and talks might indicate a certain kind of inner mental dilemma. For example, thin legs in conjunction with a massive body, with muscular shoulders and an inflated chest, might suggest that the torso, on an unstable foundation, holds back intense feelings. At the same time he may also hold back a need to push away an imagined intrusive 'other', covering a deep longing for authentic recognition. However, deep-seated psychological dilemmas are not always reflected in the body structure.

Five levels of experience and functioning

Emotions seem to be the most powerful organizers of mental activity. Feelings are central in the developmental and process model used in body oriented psychotherapy. The model consists of five phenomenological domains in which the inner chaotic excitation from senses and inner organs turns into information on which more or less conscious choice of appropriate motor/verbal action can be made (Downing, 1996).

To constitute an actual experience, stimulus input comes from three different sources: sense organs reflecting outer reality, inner sensors reflecting the body and from association centres in the brain itself. These inputs create an excitation in the nervous system, which has to transform the excitation into information about the different components of the ongoing experience. This information is the basis for motor activity, behaviour and speech. The excitation is processed into information on the following *levels of experience and functioning*:

- *body sensations level*: what happens in the body and on the surface of the body?

- *level of feelings*: what feelings or mixture of feelings are activated?
- *image level*: what inner visual pictures or 'co-enestetic narratives' (a clear *sense* of what is going on without a visual image) emerge?
- *cognitive level*: what thoughts come to mind?
- *action level*: information from the other levels leads to action and the action itself gives information about how the situation is experienced.

One goal in body oriented psychotherapy is to support a full experience on each of the above levels. In neurotic states each level would be sufficiently well developed, but access may be blocked by emotional conflicts and the warding off of experiences which would feel alien to the ego. In the case of an under-structured personality, the basic problem may be an inability to tolerate emotional intensity, sometimes due to insufficient affect differentiation.

The symptoms can also come from an under-differentiated organization on the image level, containing fantasies and dreams. It may also arise from insufficiently differentiated body sensations or problems with sustaining thought processes. This leads to too much excitation, which may be directly expressed through acting out instead of dealing with this on a symbolic level.

In each session, the goal is to support shifting the focus from level to level while facilitating an increasing capacity in the client to tolerate the experience on each level. Often the client shifts levels as a defensive manoeuvre. For example, he may move into body sensations, thoughts or motor activity instead of staying with the feelings. Certain motor actions however, such as 'affect motor activity', are an integrated part of the expression of feelings, for example hitting with the fist when angry. The client can also defensively move from one feeling to another, for example from anger to escape feelings of grief or vice versa. During this process, defensive changes in breathing patterns and muscular tension can often be noticed.

Grounding and opening interventions

Opening techniques facilitate access to feelings and grounding techniques support inner psychological structuring. Normalizing breathing patterns is one way to open up and access the path of emotions to the inner world. Both learning to empty inflated lungs or to fill collapsed lungs, and learning to synchronize breathing in the chest with breathing in the stomach, give more access to actual feelings, inner conflicts, painful memories and frightening fantasies. This process often activates defensive muscular tensions in different parts of the body. Also, temporary and chronic muscular tensions seem to 'hold' feelings and motor activity impulses. Often by focusing on or mobilizing these tensions, parts of affect motor patterns, can allow access to the same emotions, images and thoughts as when the therapist works on facilitating a normalized breathing. Grounding refers to the stability and flexibility of the relationship of the body to the ground. Insufficient grounding is most clearly observed in a standing position. Work with grounding therefore often engages legs and feet. An example of a starting point for this type of work is to let the client stand on the floor with slightly bent knees being in contact with his breathing and to focus his awareness on the contact between his feet and the floor.

The building of inner regulating structures happens, as in all long-term psychotherapy, through both internalizing the relationship with the therapist, and through work with the body. Merely focusing on body sensations and where in the body feelings are felt, stimulates the development of the body image. This development is also promoted by affect differentiation and by learning to tolerate and gradually express feelings of increasing intensity.

Development of a more stable and continuous body image can also be stimulated by so-called stress positions (Lowen, 1975). This involves a series of postures aimed at intensifying muscular tensions, activating body sensations and stressed breathing. Some of these help to increase body awareness and to organize and strengthen the body image. Others, however, also open up the body, thereby facilitating access to feelings and the inner symbolic world.

Through well-timed interventions the client is supported to express feelings, together with finding meaningful words and non-verbal expressions, to the therapist in the transference, or to a parent in an activated memory. Technically this can be facilitated by gestalt techniques, such as 'the empty chair', or by psychodrama techniques. However, it is important not to work with directing the full expressions of feelings towards an important person from the past until the client is able to tolerate the intensity of these feelings. 'Expression of feelings' refers to emotionally charged monologues or dialogues with the important other person with whom there is an 'unfinished business' whether based on intrusiveness, neglect or both.

The session in body oriented psychotherapy is often longer than ordinary verbal sessions due to the necessity to verbally work through experiences activated in the body work. The session can start with the traditional verbal presentation from the client or with an almost immediate focus on what goes on in the body in terms of body sensations or feelings. The work can also begin with work on breathing, sitting or laying on a couch or mat, or with a stress position standing on the floor. The flexible use of postures gives the therapist a tool to work on different levels of regression.

Work with autonomy, for example, is often most effective in a standing position which may allow the client to feel the stable ground under his feet. Longing on a preverbal level, for example, is often more easy to evoke in a lying position.

The body techniques offer the therapist alternative paths to the inner world of the client and can complement an ordinary psychodynamic method by a direct restructuring work with the unconscious body scheme.

A case example

The client is a young woman called Doris, who has a depressed mother and a controlling father. She has problems in distinguishing her feelings from those of her mother, whom she has had difficulty in separating from. Doris rapidly understands the feelings of other people, in particular those of her mother, but rejects her own feelings. In relation to body experiences, she reports sensations in her left arm, which she often connects with thoughts and feelings associated with her mother.

During the first six months, the therapist avoids direct bodywork and only uses verbal psychodynamic techniques, to build a working alliance, and to learn more about Doris. The following sequence takes place in a session after several months:

> At the beginning of the session, while talking about her mother, Doris's left hand starts to twitch, and she begins to pinch the skin on her neck with the same hand. The therapist asks her to stand up and structures a gestalt dialogue, in which she talks to her mother. Standing may help her to experience more contact between her trunk and her feet, resulting in an improved sense of being grounded. When Doris criticizes her mother she again starts to pinch herself. In an effort to be more separate from her internalized image of her mother the therapist asks her to push her arms forward towards her imagined mother as if to drive her away. Doris' breathing deepens. Suddenly, she raises and pushes her shoulders forward, emits a choking sound, and reports an experience of dizziness.
>
> A week later Doris tells the following dream: 'A woman ties a necklace shaped as a beautiful golden snake around her neck. The string to a necklace made of glass beads that she wears breaks when the new necklace is put on. She becomes sad and tries in vain to remove the golden necklace.' Doris associates this necklace with one that her mother had got from her husband when they married, and the glass beads with one she had proudly made for herself at nursery school.
>
> The dream could perhaps be understood as a constellation of her inner objects: the mother has placed her in an incestuous situation symbolized by the heavy golden necklace. The necklace has the shape of a snake - perhaps a phallic symbol related to the triangular situation in which the mother had not supported her but permitted the father to intrude on her autonomy. Her own symbolizing self, the glass bead necklace, has no place - it falls off.

In this vignette we have shown how the therapist, while doing verbal psychodynamic work, can actively support the client's work with basic affect motor patterns: pushing at times in a standing position combined with a gestalt dialogue which elicits anger, guilt and sadness towards an externalized inner object. Gestalt dialogues can often be useful to help the client to externalize internalized object relations. These interventions were alternated with grounding work and with a focus on her breathing to help to facilitate a deepened sense of autonomy. In this way symbolic representations of early object relations, such as the image 'the snake around the neck' in the dream were worked with.

Indications and risks in using body oriented psychotherapy

Body oriented psychotherapy as a frame of reference can be applied to all cases in which psychodynamic psychotherapy is considered appropriate. On the methodological level it works especially well with clients who defend themselves through intellectualization and rationalization. Body oriented psychotherapy also works well with clients who suffer from psychosomatic problems or from certain personality disturbances, such as 'borderline personalities' provided that a working alliance can be established.

Touch may or may not be a part of body oriented psychotherapy. Touch is used for technical reasons, for example in work with breathing and muscular tensions. It is mostly experienced by the client as ritualized, as in a physical examination by a doctor. A certain minimal amount of well timed supporting and empathetic touch can help a client to increase her tolerance for more intense feelings of sadness, loneliness or fright.

There is a risk that touch can be felt as intrusive, particularly if the therapist is not sufficiently tuned into the client's needs or if the therapist is acting out because of his or her own countertransference. Inappropriate timing of touch can also interrupt necessary processing and thus impede the development of the new symbol formation of emotionally intense experiences that needs to happen in the process of becoming more autonomous. Contrary to what might be assumed, touch does not generally trigger erotic transference or regressive processes, even if the risk exists in clients who would be particularly prone to this.

Body oriented psychotherapy is enhanced by the access of some powerful therapeutic techniques. Opening techniques inappropriately applied may flood the client with anxiety. They may elicit primitive defences and more symptoms. This is particularly precarious for clients who are intrapsychically under-structured, or suffering from an impaired capacity of their ego to cope with strong emotions and stress.

For these clients access to strong feelings early in the therapy may be destructive, since their difficulty in regulating emotional states is at the core of their problem. This flooding may be due to exaggerated work with breathing and stress positions that open up more than they can handle and integrate. It can also come about because of wrongly timed work with the motor expressions of affects.

Effects of opening body interventions often take time to be experienced. An inexperienced therapist can be tempted to intensify opening interventions, which seem to give little effect. This may eventually lead to a sudden activation of anxiety, due to excessive stimulation.

The method of adding a body perspective and body interventions to the verbal work, gives the therapist a broader range of tools to understand and treat clients. The therapist must be sensitive to the reaction of the client and to consider the effects of body interventions and touch as important aspects of the transference–countertransference interplay.

References

Barbas H (1995) Anatomic basis of cognitive-emotional interactions in the primate prefrontal cortex. Neuroscience and Biobehavioural Reviews 19(3): 499–510.

Bion WR (1962) Learning from Experience. London: Maresfield Reprints.

Bion WR (1967) Second Thoughts. London: Maresfield Reprints.

Damasio A (1994) Descartes Error. New York: Putnam.

Damasio A (1999) The Feeling of What Happens. New York: Harcourt Brace & Co.

Darwin C (1965) The Expression of the Emotions in Man and Animals. Chicago: University of Chicago Press.

Deacon T (1997) The Symbolic Species. London: Penguin Books.

Downing G (1996) Körper und Wort in der Psychotherapie. Munchen: Kösel.

Edelman GM (1992) Brilliant Air. Brilliant Fire. London: Allen Lane/Penguin Press.

Fairbairn-Birtles E, Scharff DE (1994) (eds) From Instinct to Self: Selected Papers of WRD Fairbairn. Vol. 1. London: Jason Aronson Inc.

Ferenczi S (1980) Final Contributions to the Problems and Methods of Psychoanalysis. London: Hogarth Press.

Freud S (1917) Mourning and Melancholia. Standard Edition 14: 237–58. London: Hogarth Press.

Groddek G (1977) The Meaning of Illness: Selected Psychoanalytic Writings. London: Hogarth Press.

Kernberg O (1980) Internal World and External Reality: Object Relations Theory Applied. New York: Jason Aronson Inc.

Klein M (1981) Love, Guilt and Reparation. London: The Hogarth Press.

Langer S (1972) Mind: An Essay on Human Feeling, Vol. 2. London: John Hopkins Press.

Levin FM (1991) Mapping the Mind. New York: The Analytic Press.

Lichtenberg JD (1989) Psychoanalysis and Motivation. Hillsdale, NJ: The Analytic Press.

Lowen A (1975) Bioenergetics. London: Penguin Books.

Meltzer D (1986) Studies in Extended Metapsychology. Reading: Clunie Press.

Panksepp J (1998) Affective Neuroscience: The Foundations of Human and Animal Emotions. Oxford: Oxford University Press.

Ramachandran VS, Blakeslee S (1999) Phantoms in the Brain. London: Fourth Estate.

Ramberg L (1987) Kroppens roll i personlighetsutvecklingen. In B Wrangsjö (ed), Kroppsorienterad psykoterapi. Stockholm: Natur och Kultur.

Ramberg L (1992) Tänkbart – om individuation och tillhörighet. Stockholm: Mareld.

Reich W (1949) Character Analysis. New York: Orgone Institute Press.

Sacks O (1991) A Leg to Stand On. London: Macmillan Books.

Schilder P (1950) The Image and Appearance of the Human Body. New York: International University Press.

Shevrin H et al. (1996) Conscious and Unconscious Processes: Psychodynamic, Cognitive and Neurophysiological Convergences. New York: The Guilford Press.

Solms M (1997) The Neuro Psychology of Dreams. New Jersey: Erlbaum Publishers.

Stern D (1985) The Interpersonal World of the Infant. New York: Basic Books.

Winnicott DW (1965) The Maturational Processes and Facilitating Environment. London: Hogarth Press.

Winnicott DW (1980) Playing and Reality. New York: Penguin Books.

Winson J (1985) Brain and Psyche. Garden City, New York: Auchor Press.

Wrangsjö B (ed) Kroppsorienterad psykoterapi. Stockholm: Natur och Kultur.

CHAPTER 12

Supervision from an object relations and integrative perspective: a learning from experience

GERTRUD MANDER

Supervision has been defined as an activity that is 'more than teaching and less than therapy'. In fact, it draws on learning theory as well as on object relations and psychodynamic theory for an understanding of its complex task. It has become an essential ingredient of the training of counsellors and psychotherapists, contributing to their ongoing development and to their maintenance of a professional identity. As such it includes constant assessment of their suitability for and competence in the therapeutic work and constitutes a professional quality control, which ensures that the patients' welfare is carefully safeguarded and held in focus.

My understanding of supervision as a formative and restorative activity devoted to training and supporting therapists in their difficult task of listening to people in distress is based on the knowledge that it consists of many layers of relating, facilitating, holding and reflecting, on the complex dynamic processes of human interaction which together constitute the therapeutic endeavour and which demand constant attention, considerable knowledge, and continuous careful monitoring.

Holding and attachment

There is a great multiplicity of ways in which supervision is given and received, but it carries similar emotional burdens as teaching and therapy, as it is an activity that always happens in a relationship. This relationship is further deepened by the invisible presence of the client who adds a third dimension to the twosome of supervisor and supervisee, and it is also complicated by issues of authority, dependence, identification, and resistance, as well as by the unspoken expectations and demands made by the participants on each other. In order for supervision to become creative it needs to be informed by rigorous thinking and sensitive attunement (Stern, 1985) based on good rapport and communication in the dyad of supervisor and supervisee to allow for the exploration and application of theory to clinical practice which is necessary for the establishment of a well-functioning learning climate. This is well defined by Winnicott's (1971) concept of the 'potential space' and by Bowlby's (1988) use of the term 'secure base', both of which indicate a safe place where holding and attachment occur, ensuring the growth and well-being of the person.

I have already used a number of clinical concepts by various thinkers (Winnicott, Bowlby and Stern) to characterize my understanding of supervision, and I have become aware of the way I consistently draw on different theories about the environment in which supervisory learning is facilitated and where the supervisory task can happen. In this instance, I have used ideas from object relations and self psychology, but I have also hinted at the oedipal dimension of supervision when I mentioned the triangular supervisory relationship which always includes the client. Furthermore I have defined supervision as formative and restorative in the manner of some of my person-centred supervisory colleagues (Proctor, undated; Foskett and Lyall, 1988) and have mentioned developmental and didactic aspects of the supervisory activity which would be particularly stressed by humanistic practitioners of supervision (Carroll and Holloway, 1998).

The integrative basis of supervision

The practice of supervision requires an integrative basis combining a plethora of theories to do with learning, relating, training, reflecting and monitoring which are the essential ingredients of all supervisory activity. This means drawing on a diversity of concepts about object relating and human development which can be used alongside each other without contradiction, and it also implies encouraging trainees if necessary to use more than one theory or their practice as long as they can construct and knit these into a coherent argument in order to explain the dynamics of complicated situations. According to Karl Popper (1967) all theorizing is hypothetical and hence provisional until falsified, and it is pragmatic to keep asking oneself the question: 'does this work?' rather than: 'is it true?'

The learning environment of supervision

A good working alliance is necessary to do supervision and to be supervised. In this the supervisor assists the supervisee's 'learning from experience', i.e. the application of their theoretical knowledge and their technical skill to the practice of helping another understand and deal with their difficulties of living. He/she tries to provide the optimal learning environment in which supervisees can identify, understand and eliminate their 'blind' spots and their 'dumb' spots, i.e. their 'problems about learning' (Ekstein and Wallerstein, 1958), be they lack of self-awareness or lack of knowledge. This learning environment needs to be a containing, reflective space in which anxieties and defences are carefully monitored in order to help the supervisee manage them creatively, either by identifying their transference-countertransference reactions or by interpreting the unconscious parallel processes which operate in the interpersonal field, in the form of projective and introjective communication between all the participants of the activity.

Adapting to the difference in supervisees' styles of learning

It is essential that the supervisor observes the supervisees' different styles of learning and thinking (Jacobs, David and Meyer, 1995), can allow for and adapt to a diversity of therapeutic attitudes and recognizes the particular developmental level supervisees have reached, as each of them require different supervisory input – firm parental holding, facilitating, exploring, dialoguing or mentoring. Another important factor is to take into account the contexts, backgrounds and organizational settings in which the supervision takes place, and there is a decisive difference if it concerns trainees, beginners or experienced practitioners each of whom require different amounts of support, of challenge, assessment, and teaching input.

Learning theorists distinguish 'assimilative' from 'mutative' learning (Szecsödy, 1990) and emphasize the emotional component next to the cognitive component in learning. Like good teachers the wise supervisor would refrain from becoming didactic in order not to overwhelm or overteach the learner, who is making discoveries of his or her own on the job and managing cases on their own. The supervisor accompanies rather than directs the supervisee while learning from the patient (Casement, 1985) and is intent on helping him or her develop an 'internal supervisor' by trial and error. By unconsciously modelling him/herself on their therapist and their external supervisor their analytic attitude, therapeutic style, and ongoing self-reflective stance will become an example and a prototype for their own practice.

Attunement

Much knowledge and expertise is required from the supervisor and in particular the persistently empathic and attentive attunement (Stern, 1985), which respects difference, diversity of personality, awareness and temperament in the supervisee. It is usual that the supervisee puts up a measure of resistance to learning and change, and this has to be expected and put to good use, as it indicates the learner's idiosyncratic way of absorbing and processing material, of relating to another who is in authority, and of protecting themselves from infringement, domination, and merger by and with another. Object relations theories of transference and countertransference need to be applied and observed in the supervisory relationship as much as in the therapeutic relationship which is the subject of supervision. Equally, the supervision will need to focus on the complex interaction of psychodynamic processes in the whole supervisory field which includes the patient in order to sharpen the supervisee's understanding of their therapeutic work.

Ethics and integration

An integral part of supervision is constant assessment of supervisory effectiveness, of the therapist's competence and effectiveness, and of the patient's response to the treatment, which is at the centre of all supervisory endeavour. It will have to be anchored in an ethical climate that facilitates processes of growth, understanding, integration and mutual respect and that supports tolerance of difference, pluralism and diversity. Supervision hence is 'ensuring and enabling' (Proctor, undated), a 'formative, normative and restorative' experience for the supervisee, which works best when a balance of support and challenge is offered.

Supervision was developed as a training tool in the early years of analysis and it has since become an absolute imperative in the training of all counsellors and psychotherapists. More recently, however, it has also established itself as a professional service for qualified practitioners and it is now recommended in most professional associations' Code of Ethics and Practice as an ongoing necessity for all practising therapists. As such it functions as a valuable consultative resource which offers the practitioner expert advice, comment and dialogue and, in many instances, a second opinion from a more experienced practitioner in the field. It also constitutes a form of emotional containment and facilitation of complex processes and has therefore aptly been called 'thinking about thinking', which constitutes invaluable help with the exploration of and reflection on clinical material.

The development of and stages in the supervisory relationship

It is useful to look at supervision from a developmental perspective and establish the stages and levels a supervisee undergoes in the course of acquiring a professional therapeutic identity (Hogan, 1964; Stoltenberg and Delworth, 1987; Erikson, 1950).

The purpose of supervision in this model is to foster the growth of the trainee toward independent functioning based on acquired skills, an insight into the client and the trainee's own person. The roles of the trainee and the supervisor change over time as development occurs. The trainee moves from student to colleague and the supervisor from expert to consultant (Stoltenberg and Delworth, 1987, p. 20).

1. The process starts with the trainee as beginner, who, like the young child, needs parenting and guidance in the context of a 'facilitating' holding environment where learning and experimenting by trial and error can be attempted. The supervisor's first role is that of parent and teacher, and the trainee's task is the acquisition of basic trust, while he/she overcomes beginner's anxiety and allows him/herself to be dependent and imitative. As in a game of chess one could speak of this phase as the 'opening game' in which the players establish a creative working relationship, and in which the trainee is allowed to be self-centred, while the supervisor is facilitative and containing.

2. The next stage is like adolescence. The trainee enters an apprenticeship in which the supervisor figures as tutor and apprentice master who enables the supervisee to learn the necessary skills and techniques on the job. The aim is to achieve professional autonomy, which involves the experience of ambivalence, shame and confusion on the trainee's part, and requires the supervisor to use his/her authority and experience, supporting and confronting the supervisee appropriately. One could call this the Middle Game, a rich phase of learning the craft and its principles.

3. Early adulthood follows, in which there is consolidation of professional identity, intimacy with equals and concern for others. The supervisor's role becomes one of mentoring and sponsoring his/her charge, in order to get him or her ready to enter the external world and to take the risk of working independently, though still needing and being provided with consultancy and further teaching, perhaps in the form of master classes.

4. Last, maturity, and the End Game phase. The supervisor offers him/herself as expert, colleague and consultant, while the supervisee's task is to reach the Eriksonian attributes of ego integrity, generativity and reciprocity by way of creative dialogue and exchange of ideas in the supervisory encounter.

Every transition to the next stage, as described by Erikson, could produce a crisis, which brings with it the possibility of regression or dropout, and is the opportunity for progress and forward movement. The therapist's professional identity will become firmly established and stabilized, he or she has had to connect to him/herself, has been developing a feeling for the right timing of interventions and has been encouraged and enabled to find their own personal style.

In this process the supervisor has been a model, which, if the experience was good, will have become internalized, and this will amount to the establishment of an internal supervisor.

If, however, the trainee has failed to prosper and to develop the necessary competence, emotional maturity and reliability for working in the field the supervisor will have to prevent their moving to professional status and is forced to withhold their accreditation, though only after careful ongoing assessment and consultation with the training institute. Not everybody makes it to the final state.

The internal supervisor

In his book, *On Learning from the Patient*, the psychoanalyst Patrick Casement (1985) elaborates Hogan's ideas about the supervisee's professional development in supervision as follows:

> During the course of being supervised, therapists need to acquire their own capacity for spontaneous reflection within the session, alongside the internalized supervisor. They can thus learn to watch themselves as well as the patient, using the 'island of intellectual contemplation' as the mental space within which the internal supervisor can begin to operate ... (p. 32)

It is not just the patient who needs to develop the capacity for a therapeutic dissociation within his ego, which Sterba (1934) describes. The therapist also has to be able to maintain this benign split within himself, whereby his experiencing ego is free to move between himself and the patient, between thinking and feeling. Kris refers to this as 'regression in the service of the ego' (Kris, 1950). The analyst uses a controlled regression within himself in order to cross the boundary between his conscious (rational) thinking and his unconscious (primary process/irrational) thinking. Allowing himself to enter a state of listening reverie, alongside the patient, he can monitor what it may feel like to be the patient' (p. 34). Casement thus describes the capacity for putting oneself into the patient's shoes by practising unfocused listening, of balancing different potential meanings, playing with material and practising with material in the form of 'trial identification'. His definition of supervision as 'a dialogue between the external and the internal supervisor' is inspired, as it emphasizes the supervisor's modelling function as well as the supervisee's gradual 'internalizing' of the supervisor in the supervisory relationship.

> Towards the end of training, I believe that the process of supervision should develop into a dialogue between the external supervisor and the internal supervisor. It is through this that therapists develop the more autonomous functioning that is expected of them upon qualification ... The shift from an initial dependence

on the external supervisor, via the internalised supervisor, to a more autonomous internal supervision is a slow process – and at times it will not be steady. (p. 49)

In effect this amounts to a recommendation for continued supervision, as an ongoing support of the internal supervisor beyond training and as a practitioner resource for joint reflection on ethical dilemmas and therapeutic impasses.

Dyads, triads and the clinical rhombus

In supervision the therapeutic dyad is augmented into the supervisory triad.

> There are two people present in the room during the supervisory session, yet these two people are there because of a third person, the patient, who influences what they are doing and thinking together. Hence the potential space of supervision always includes the therapeutic couple, and it is constantly concerned with problems arising in their relationship, otherwise it becomes therapy or teaching. (Mander, 1998a, p. 57).

The pull of unconscious forces in the three-person field of supervision is as powerful as in the two-person field of therapy, but the issues are complicated by oedipal anxieties to do with inclusion and exclusion, jealousy, rivalry and competition. In her book *The Reflection Process in Casework Supervision*, Janet Mattinson (1975), who coined the phrase 'oedipal tangling', emphasizes the importance of distance and difference as imperative to good supervision, as is the supervisor's capacity to survive oedipal tangling. The task is to be flexible about the process of getting involved with the therapeutic couple, and of relinquishing involvement, which is an experience of constantly getting drawn into twos or intruding into twosomes, becoming an active participant of a 'tangle' while trying to retain the position of an observer. 'The art of supervision is to go in and to come out again and to achieve and sustain an "object relationship of the third kind" (after twosomes of love and hate) in which one can allow oneself to be a witness and relinquish the need to be a participant'. 'Given this', states Britton (1989), 'one can also be observed.' This stance requires an ability in the supervisor to make quick choices as to where to focus during the presentation of clinical material. It requires an ability to choose between being active or sitting back, trusting the therapist's work with the patient and waiting for the moment when an intervention is necessary and will be tolerated.

> In supervision the model of object relations which is based on the dyad has to be augmented by a form of object relating which involves triads and multi-personal constellations and in which distinctive problems and anxieties arise. It could be said with Klein that it is essential for the supervisor to have mastered the tasks of

the oedipal phase, to have reached the depressive position and developed the ability to identify and overcome instinctive stirrings of jealousy, envy and sadism in order to be objective and effective. (Mander, 1998a, p. 63)

There is a fourth requirement: vigilance. Closely linked to concentration and attentiveness this follows and facilitates the constant reflective processing of clinical material, which constitutes the living process of supervision.

Contexts and contracts of supervision

When clinicians began to conceptualize the task of supervision in the teaching and training of therapists they realized that they had to take note of the contexts in which supervision is given and received. Invented to support and challenge the analytic trainee who was preparing to work in private practice, supervision acquires another dimension when it is practised within an organization where managers and administrators are responsible for the running of therapeutic services. To the supervisory triad a fourth angle gets added and this complex professional situation can be diagrammatically expressed as a 'clinical rhombus' (Ekstein and Wallerstein, 1958).

The supervisor has a contract with all three persons, as he/she is accountable to A for T and P. The therapist also has a contract with three persons, as he/she is accountable to A and S for P, but may resist authority, collude with the patient or with the supervisor and get caught in the complex dynamics of an organization which is dependent on the administration's managerial style. The patient relates to A and T, while S is observing, guiding and influencing T in his/her therapeutic work.

Chaos is possible at any corner, inevitably there are issues of exclusion, collusion, power and difficulties of communication, conflicts of training and staffing needs, sibling rivalries, and overall the complex dynamics of the large group obtains. When the supervisor is incompetent he/she may seek help from the administrator and the therapist may be blamed or sacked. The patient who has a contract with T and A may complain or leave. The precarious

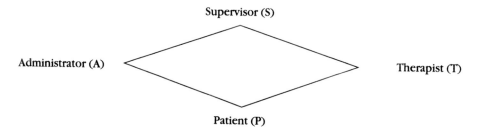

Figure 12.1. The clinical rhombus.

balance in the clinical rhombus is liable to shift and collapse, when the lines of communication become blocked, if the administrator is unable to keep them going and to remain objectively supportive.

Supervision always has a role to play in an organization's efforts to manage its own internal processes and to monitor the task of achieving its goals. A supervisor will often need to mediate between the demands of the administration and the need to protect the sanctuary of the consulting room. Providers of counselling and psychotherapy in organizations have to contain a great deal of anxiety by the very nature of their task. Part of the supervisory role is that such anxiety can be held without resort to excessively defensive mechanisms by either the therapist or the administrator. Failure to do so can result in a service to fall victim, in its own functioning, to the most prevalent presenting problems of its clientele (Menzies-Lyth, 1959).

Supervisors can be internal or external to organizations – whether these are training institutes, medical or educational settings, the corporate sector, or voluntary organizations, to name only the most important employers of counsellors and psychotherapists nowadays. They are thus directly or indirectly accountable to managements, may or may not have clinical responsibility for the therapeutic work and can become involved in the assessment of therapists and clients, depending on the individual context of their work. In an age in which short-term therapy is on the increase and its provision has become largely free, the supervisor's role as the holder of boundaries, anxieties and responsibilities is significant and crucial. The relative freedom of private practice has become rarer. Employment contracts and job descriptions, qualifications and accreditations are 'de rigueur' and even supervisors are now required to undergo specific training for their work. On top of this, there is a new prescription for the supervision of supervision, at least in the counselling camp, in order to protect therapists and clients, and to open up supervisory relationships to inspection and monitoring, too.

It is important to be aware that with every organizational context the supervisor's task changes, as particular environmental issues influence therapeutic styles and requirements. When it is training, ongoing assessment and eventual accreditation fall within the remit of the supervisor. When it is primary care provision or GP practice work, the supervisor will need to look out for the inevitable split transferences between medical staff and counsellors, which will have to be addressed so as not to have negative therapeutic effects. In this setting, too, there are specific patient groups like 'somatizers', patients suffering from serious illnesses or from long-term mental health problems and supervision will have to focus on different pathologies. In educational settings, whether primary, secondary or tertiary, the age range of the clientele is usually limited and issues specific to this are uppermost – such as parent involvement in schools where learning is the primary task, age-appropriate separation from the family in secondary and university education, and themes specific to adolescent functioning. The security of the frame, so important in effective brief work, will often be more difficult to maintain in organizational settings than in the private practice and so will confidentiality when patients are shared by different practitioners. The large-group dynamics of organizations which creates primitive and paranoid anxieties (and defences against these) is always influenced and complicated by the patients' pathologies.

As for counselling at the workplace, which is mostly handled by providers of employment assistance programmes (EAPs), this is a different ball-game altogether, as the purchasers and the providers of these services create an even more complex organizational conundrum for counsellor and supervisor, with the former usually remaining invisible, while the latter mediates between the purchaser, the clinician and the customer, aiming to manage, satisfy and contain all three.

Supervising brief and time-limited work

The supervisor has to be sufficiently familiar with and knowledgeable of the structures, expectations and functioning of each individual context in order to adapt his or her strategies to the particular requirements and ground rules of the service. While they all nowadays practice brief or time-limited counselling, their understanding of what this amounts to in terms of duration or style may vary drastically and in particular their procedures of assessment, contracting, and referral-on which are central ingredients of this way of working. It is not enough to have extensive supervisory experience of generic counselling, it is equally essential to understand the specific techniques, the selective and limited aims, and the possible and desirable outcomes of time-limited work in order to guide and facilitate the supervisee. Doing brief work he/she is often very anxious about the severe time constraints one has to work under. Brief counsellors usually work integratively using one or other of the various models developed for doing brief work. An integrative model has been shown to work best in time-limited and brief counselling. This requires the supervisor to be flexible and well-versed in the diverse techniques which move on brief work quickly, while remaining well-grounded in their own core orientation, in mainstream theory and in their experience of doing long-term work.

For the supervisor it is essential to adapt to the specific requirements of work that is done briefly, actively, and fast and that may not offer the opportunity for much supervisory input between beginning and ending, assessing and wrapping up a case. While the clock is ticking, it is imperative to think fast and formulate one's supervisory input carefully, to rely on intuition and countertransference responses in order to contain the supervisee's anxiety and to model a particular stance of working that is active, decisive and confident enough to fulfil the basic tasks of assessing, focusing, structuring and being mindful of the ending. Apart from assisting with the assessment hypothesis, the finding and guarding of the dynamic focus, the modelling of a particular relationship and of the active style of working, there is the ongoing assessment of the counsellor's ability to implement the model and if necessary the ability to tell a counsellor that they haven't got it in them to do brief work. Not every client benefits from brief work, and equally, not every counsellor is able to work in this mode. It follows that not every supervisor can or wants to supervise it.

Finally and most importantly the supervisee needs assistance with endings, with the ensuing mourning and grief work and with any other finishing business, clearing the ground and the memory for the next beginning, attending to issues of referral, follow-up and feedback.

Other supervisory dimensions

So far I have concentrated on individual supervision which is practised most widely, and is easiest to set up, though there are training situations and settings in which group supervision has become the preferred model, as it is economical, enables supervisees to learn from each other and to supervise each other, and can cover a variety of cases and problems. The group supervisor needs to be mindful of the group dynamics, of the reflection and projection processes in the multi-personal field, of issues of sibling rivalry, competition and envy, and has to consider the optimal number of group members, in terms of presentation time, frequency and personality matching. When it is a group of peers, the supervisory leadership may rotate and the boundaries need careful watching, as these groups tend to fall short on commitment and clinical rigour. As for supervisory consultation, this may be periodic or a one-off, and it usually requires special expertise, wide professional experience and a professional status that attracts supervisees from a wide spectrum of clinical experience. It can also be a form of crisis management, a second opinion or a specialized enquiry relating to unusual pathologies, like eating disorders, sexual abuse, HIV/AIDS, forensic problems or psychopathy.

I believe that supervision is a discipline which can integrate different theoretical orientations and is essential to different practitioners in the helping professions, from social work to telephone counselling, old-age psychiatry, befriending, bereavement and victim support work. In order to function in these diverse scenarios the supervisor needs to possess the core conditions of genuineness, objectivity and authenticity. At the same time he or she has to have the ability to function as a participant observer who provides a vigilant 'third eye', guards the professional boundaries, watches the practitioner's ethical stance, assesses competence in their particular model, and alerts them to acting out or acting in, when the strict principle of abstinence is infringed. While basing myself firmly on the theoretical model of object relations which postulates attention to the interactive and intersubjective dynamics of relationships, including the bedrock of the therapeutic and the supervisory relationship, I am always open to a pluralistic perspective which works with and recognizes the spectrum of approaches from cognitive behavioural to person-centred and existential psychotherapy, including problem-solving and solution-focused work.

Supervision is an indispensable form of quality control, which ensures that codes of ethics and practice are implemented in the profession, and that standards of quality and performance are maintained. As such it operates as a holding environment and as a safety-net that prevents the clinician from falling off the tightrope.

The stance of a supervisor – qualities and cautions

Objectivity, sustained observation and clear-headedness (not to be confused with intellectualization or cleverness) are necessary qualities of the good supervisor. Something achieved naturally in their emotional development or, more likely with the help of a thorough personal therapy, it is akin to selflessness in the sense of not wanting something for oneself, not wanting the patient, not wanting to have all the insights, not making all the interpretations. It is a gift of seeing straight through the veils of projections, identifications, defences and resistance to the interactive processes reported by the supervisee. It is an ability of being inside and outside simultaneously, of participating and observing, at one remove from the therapeutic couple and yet being a participant in the supervisory relationship.

It happens all too easily that a supervisor is tempted to take over, to get drawn into giving advice and being all-knowing. The temptations of power are all-pervasive in these oedipal situations where the partners are of different quality and weight, are more or less experienced, intelligent, knowledgeable. The powerful supervisor comes in many guises: stern judge, strict parent, admired guru, laissez-faire friend, all of which can do damage or impair objectivity. Unless the supervisor remains on constant alert, examining his or her own emotional responses, this activity can become counter-productive, useless, or abusive, and then it will infect rather than elucidate the therapeutic activity which it is intended to benefit.

References

Bollas C (1999) The goals of analysis? In The Mystery of Things. London/New York: Routledge.

Bowlby J (1988) A Secure Base: Clinical Applications of Attachment Theory. London: Routledge.

Britton R (1989) The missing link: parental sexuality in the Oedipus situation. In R Britton, M Feldman, EO Shaughnessy (eds), The Oedipus Complex Today (83-102). London: Karnac Books.

Carroll M, Holloway E (1998) Counselling Supervision in Context. London: Sage.

Casement P (1985) On Learning from the Patient. London: Tavistock.

Ekstein R, Wallerstein R (1958) The Teaching and Learning of Psychotherapy. New York: Basic Books.

Erikson E (1950) Childhood and Society. Harmondsworth: Penguin.

Foskett F, Lyall D (1988) Helping the Helpers: Supervision and Pastoral Care. London: SPCK.

Grawe K, Donati R, Bernauer F (1997) Psychotherapy in Transition, from Speculation to Science. Gottingen: Hogrefe & Huber.

Hawkins P, Shohet R (1989) Supervision in the Helping Professions. Milton Keynes/Philadelphia: Open University Press.

Hogan R (1964) Issues and approaches in supervision. Psychotherapy, Theory, Research and Practice I: 139-41

Houston G (1990) Supervision and Counselling. The Rochester Foundation.

Jacobs D, David P, Meyer DJ (1995) The Supervisory Encounter. New Haven/London: Yale University Press.

Kris E (1950) On pre-conscious mental processes. Psychoanalytic Quarterly 19: 540-60.

Kuhn T (1962) The Structure of Scientific Revolutions. Chicago: University of Chicago Press.

Langs R (1994) Doing Supervision and Being Supervised. London: Karnac Books.

Mander G (1998a) Dyads and triads: some thoughts on therapy supervision. In P Clarkson (ed), Supervision, Psychoanalytic and Jungian Perspectives. London: Whurr.

Mander G (1998b) Supervising short-term psychodynamic work. Counselling 9(4): 301-5.

Mattinson J (1975) The Reflection Process in Casework Supervision. London: TIMS.

Menzies-Lyth I (1959) The functioning of social systems as a defence against anxiety. In Containing Anxieties in Institutions: Selected Essays, Vol. 1. London: Free Association Books.

Page S, Woskett V (1994) Supervising the Counsellor: A Cyclical Model. London: Routledge.

Popper K (1967) Conjectures and Refutations: The Structure of Scientific Enquiry. London: Routledge.

Proctor B (undated) Supervision: a co-operative exercise in accountability. In M Marken, M Paynes (eds), Enabling and Ensuring, Supervision in Practice. Leicester: National Youth Bureau.

Salzberger-Wittenberg I (1983) The Emotional Experience of Learning and Teaching. London: Routledge.

Samuels A (1989) The Plural Psyche, Personality, Morality and the Father. London/New York: Routledge; London: Free Associations Books.

Slunecko TT (1999) On harvesting diversity into a dynamic directedness. International Journal of Psychotherapy 4(2): 127-43.

Sterba R (1934) The fate of the ego in analytic therapy. International Journal of Psychoanalysis 15: 117-26.

Stern D (1985) The Interpersonal World of the Child: A View from Psychoanalysis and Developmental Psychology. New York: Basic Books.

Stoltenberg CD, Delworth U (1987) Supervising Counsellors and Therapists. San Francisco/London: Jossey-Bass.

Szecsödy I (1990) Supervision: a didactic or mutative situation. Psychoanalytic Psychotherapy 4(3): 245-61.

Wilkinson H (1999) Pluralism as scientific method in psychotherapy. International Journal of Psychotherapy 4(3): 313-28.

Winnicott DW (1971) The use of an object and relating through identification. In Playing and Reality. Harmondsworth: Penguin.

CHAPTER 13

The strengths and limitations of a psychodynamic perspective in organizational consultancy

ERIC MILLER[1]

Aim

This chapter explores the proposition that a psychodynamic perspective is a necessary but not sufficient condition for effective organizational consultancy. It describes the set of conceptual frameworks that the Tavistock Institute inherited, articulated and began to use when it was set up immediately after World War II and their further development and application by the author and colleagues at the Institute. The specific aim is to identify the elements of psychoanalytic theory in these frameworks and their place in current consultancy on organizational design, development and change (cf. Miller, 1993, 1999b; Trist and Murray, 1990, 1993).

Origins and early development of the Tavistock Institute

The parent body of the Institute was the Tavistock Clinic which was itself formed in the aftermath of World War I as a voluntary outpatient clinic for adults and children with neurotic disorders. Most of the founders had been involved in treating soldiers with neuroses labelled as 'shell-shock' and they wanted to learn from and build on this experience. Among them were psychiatrists, neurologists and general physicians, some with training in psychology and anthropology. That culture of disciplinary inclusiveness continued. Approaches to psychoanalytical psychotherapy were influenced mainly by Freud but also by Jung and Adler. There was also an interest in studying social factors in neurosis – an interest that was reactivated by experience of the Depression in the early 1930s (Dicks, 1970).

---

[1]Eric Miller died in April 2002. He was one of the leading figures in the field of organizational consultancy in Europe. This chapter was his final publication.

By then the Clinic had grown substantially. Training in psychotherapy had become an important function, bringing in social workers and psychologists as well as doctors. Teaching in medical schools and research publications had enhanced the Clinic's reputation nationally and also internationally, especially in the United States, though it was dismissed as not quite kosher by the psychoanalytic establishment in the UK. Also at that time the Clinic departed from orthodoxy by abandoning the traditional medical governance of senior consultants in favour of a multidisciplinary democracy with elected leadership. This released the creativity of younger staff such as Wilfred Bion, Henry Dicks, Ronald Hargreaves and A.T.M. Wilson, all of whom made innovative contributions during and after World War II and became eminent in their fields. Wilson was the first chairman of the Tavistock Institute.

Evidence of the Clinic's wider influence was the appointment in 1938, when the war clouds were gathering, of the elected director, J.R. Rees, as Consulting Psychiatrist to the Army (later chief of the Army's psychiatric service). Subsequently about 30 Clinic staff – half the total – joined the forces, mostly under him. He appointed a senior psychiatrist to each of the five army commands in the UK. 'Command Psychiatry' extended beyond the treatment of individual casualties. The concept built on the experience in the Clinic of World War I veterans and the recommendations of a 1922 report on shell-shock. These included, for example: assessment of new recruits; instillation of esprit de corps during training and attention to possible misfits; early intervention and treatment for soldiers showing signs of breakdown; rapid return of such soldiers to, preferably, their original units; and providing alternative placements where necessary (Harrison, 1999). The broadly defined task of the command psychiatrist was to identify pressing problems and to devise ways of tackling the underlying factors. One example might be a unit with low morale among the troops. A social psychiatry approach would define the unit as the 'patient' and the 'treatment' might involve working with officers and men in groups.

Other interventions went way beyond any ordinary definition of psychiatry. One example was recruitment of the tens of thousands of officers needed in the expanding army, candidates from the traditional 'officer class' were too few and about half failed during training. The 'Tavistock group' pushed for a broadening of the nomination process (including a very successful experiment in which the rank and file put forward candidates with officer potential) and for a radical transformation of the War Office Selection Boards (WOSBs). The new procedure included more systematic interviews, psychometric tests and, most importantly, group tests, in which candidates were observed in a series of unstructured interactions, including a free discussion, a challenging practical task that required collaboration, and an intergroup transaction.

> No lead was given about organization or leadership: these were left to emerge and it was the duty of the observing officers [the selectors] to watch how any given

man was reconciling his personal ambitions, hopes and fears with the requirements exacted by the group for its success. (Bion, 1946, pp. 77–8)

The effectiveness of this process was demonstrated by a pass rate rising from
50 to over 80 per cent and, after the war, by applications of the selection
procedure in the other armed services, the civil service and industrial organizations such as Unilever.

Bion was heavily involved in the transformation of the WOSBs and it was
he, with John Rickman, who applied the idea of the leaderless group in developing the first therapeutic community (Bion and Rickman, 1943). This was in
1942 at Northfield Military Hospital in Birmingham, where far too many
neurotic casualties were being discharged from the army instead of being
returned to military duties. Taking charge of the training wing, he introduced
an approach in which power, traditionally monopolized by doctors, was
redistributed among patients and other staff. The approach was successful in
re-engaging alienated individuals and enabling them to go back to their units,
but the attendant chaos antagonized the military and medical hierarchies and
the experiment was abruptly terminated. Learning from this, a year later
Bridger (who was to be another of the founders of the Tavistock Institute)
tried again, this time mobilizing the power-holders in the process, and the
outcome was remarkably effective (Bridger, 1990).

The closing year of the war brought another enterprise of the Tavistock
group: establishment of Civil Resettlement Units (CRUs) for repatriated
prisoners. For some the transition was unproblematic: they collected a
civilian suit and a ration book and went home. Others stayed for days, weeks
and even months, being helped to recover from the physical and psychological traumas of the prison camps and perhaps to adjust to a new unfamiliar
world in which loved ones had died or abandoned them. So the CRUs were
another version of therapeutic communities.

There were other interesting examples of army psychiatry in action
(Harrison, 1999). Tom Main (who was later to develop the Cassel Hospital as
a leading therapeutic community) was psychiatric adviser to the Army Battle
Schools on approaches to training most likely to inoculate troops against the
noise, confusion and fear of the battlefield. He also investigated and helped to
resolve a major mutiny in Italy. Henry Dicks, founder of cultural psychiatry,
was a 'minder' of Rudolf Hess after his unexpected arrival in UK in 1941 and
was then seconded to Military Intelligence. He used depth interviews with
German prisoners to study the structure, morale and cohesion of the German
Wehrmacht and more generally to analyse personality traits in National
Socialist ideology (Dicks, 1950, 1970).

Those Tavistock Clinic staff who had maintained the base in London were
of course aware of all this – there were frequent visits – but were only half

prepared for the consequences. When the war ended, their army colleagues came back (with a few associates from the WOSBs and CRUs) filled with enthusiasm for applying their experience to the postwar reconstruction of British society. There was still a commitment to clinical work with individuals linked with research and with training of other professionals. To this was added the beginning of group psychotherapy: study by the group itself of the tensions within it. (Bion ran a weekly therapy group for staff during the painful transition that followed.) Beyond that, however, was the determination to provide sociatric services for 'sick' organizations. The outcome in 1946 was a decision to create within the matrix of the psychotherapeutic Clinic a new division, the Tavistock Institute of Human Relations, to focus on the social and preventive tasks, while maintaining the Clinic's action research philosophy: 'no research without therapy; no therapy without research'. It then became clear that the Clinic would be moving into the National Health Service, which would take in only the clinical activities. Accordingly the Institute was separately incorporated in 1947 to pursue the new mission: 'the study of human relations in conditions of well-being, conflict and change, in the community, the work group and the larger organisation, and the promotion of the effectiveness of individuals and organisations'. At the same time it launched the journal *Human Relations*, carrying a subtitle reflecting part of that mission: 'Towards the integration of the social sciences'. And the founding group certainly included a range of disciplines: anthropology, clinical psychology, economics, education, educational psychology, mathematics, medicine, psychiatry and social psychology.

The influences of psychoanalysis

Readers of that account of wartime developments and of the emergence of the new Institute might well doubt that psychoanalysis had any contribution at all. That would be quite wrong. The 'Young Turks' who became influential in the Clinic in the late 1930s valued the psychoanalytically oriented work being done but were unhappy about the split from the psychoanalytic establishment. They began to go into analysis themselves. Thus in 1938–39 Bion was in analysis with John Rickman who had been in therapy with Melanie Klein. Gradually there was a rapprochement with the British Psycho-Analytical Society (which, with its 'controversial discussions', was itself undergoing an identity crisis during the war years). By 1946 this was complete. It was agreed that all staff of the Clinic and Institute would undergo personal analysis if they had not already done so. For new Institute staff this was mandatory until 1957 and after that voluntary. 'The Society agreed to provide training analysts for acceptable candidates, whether they were going to become full-time analysts, mix psychoanalytic practice with broader endeavours in the health field or use psychoanalytic understanding outside the health area in organisational and social projects. The Society, therefore, recognized the relevance for psychoanalysis of work in the social field, while the Institute affirmed the importance of psychoanalysis for psycho-social studies' (Trist and Murray, 1990, p. 6). Two of the founding staff of the Institute became analysts and were followed by others later. In addition a number of Clinic staff, some of them analysts, had part-time attachments to the Institute.

A key factor in this shift was Klein's formulation of object relations theory (e.g. Klein, 1932, 1949, 1952, 1959) and its development and dissemination by Fairbairn and Rickman. Fairbairn's 1940 paper on 'Schizoid factors in the personality' (Fairbairn, 1952) anticipated Klein's definitive formulation of the paranoid-schizoid position (Klein 1946) and Rickman was also building on her theory and applying it to the behaviour of groups and larger social systems (Harrison, 1999, pp. 44ff, 302-8). Both had links with the army Tavistock group – Fairbairn with Jock Sutherland, his ex-analysand (who became medical director of the Clinic in 1947), and Rickman not only with Bion but many others – and Harrison argues that Rickman's influence on the significant wartime projects has been underestimated. Those projects involved drawing together the psychological and social fields in a multidisciplinary approach and the experience 'had shown that psychoanalytic object relations theory could unify [those] fields in a way that no other could' (Trist and Murray, 1990, p. 30).

The new Tavistock Institute presented itself as a 'social therapeutic organisation' (Jaques, 1947) practising 'social psychiatry' or 'social therapy'. It quickly became involved in a number of projects, small and large, mainly in industry and mainly related to issues of morale, productivity and communications. The emphasis was on identifying and teasing out unconscious factors, for which awareness of transference and countertransference was obviously pivotal. A common method of working was interpretive group discussion (Jaques, 1948a): the group was the 'client' and the purpose of interpretation was to enable the group to solve its own problems. In this work they were interacting with and influenced by Bion, who was adopting a similar role of quasi-analyst in his therapy groups and in groups run for Tavistock colleagues and who was developing and publishing his emerging theories of group behaviour. His key proposition was that a group is always functioning at two levels: as a work group it engages rationally in its task; at an unconscious level it is enacting one of three basic assumptions: dependency, fight–flight and pairing (Bion, 1948-51, 1952, 1961). Initially he believed assumption behaviour to be instinctive, but later described it as an early post-natal defence in line with the thinking of Klein, who had been his training analyst (Miller, 1998).

Jaques (1953, 1955a) took the application of psychoanalytic theory to organization a step further by putting forward the proposition that 'one of the primary dynamic forces pulling individuals into institutionalized human association is that of defence against persecutory and depressive anxiety; and, conversely, that all institutions are unconsciously used by their members as mechanisms of defence against these psychotic anxieties' (1953, p. 25). Resistance to change has always been a preoccupation of organizational consultants, but he was probably the first to assert that 'effective social change is likely to require analysis of the common anxieties and unconscious collusions underlying the social defences which determine phantasy social relationships' (ibid., p. 26). (Later he was to retract that proposition: see below.) Menzies (1960) followed this with her well-known study of a nursing service, and there have been many other accounts of unconscious defences against anxiety in organizations ranging from airlines and dry-cleaning businesses (Miller and Rice, 1967) to residential care (Miller and Gwynne, 1972).

Social psychology, socio-technical systems and open system theory

Alongside, and amplified by, the psychodynamic perspective, social psychology was a significant discipline from the early war years onwards. Particularly influential was the work of Kurt Lewin, who saw social psychology as needing to be multi-disciplinary, embracing the perspectives of cultural anthropology, sociology, individual psychology, physiology and even physics (Lewin, 1939). He developed and applied a *gestalt* perspective with two basic propositions: first, that in any system, including a social system, the whole is greater than the sum of its parts; and, second, that a part within a whole is something other than that part in isolation or within another whole. The place and function of a part is defined by the 'structural property' of the whole, and this derives from the relations between the parts rather than the characteristics of the elements themselves. His argument that one can best understand how a system works through changing it was one often repeated in the early days of the Institute. Related to this was Lewin's field theory (Lewin, 1936, 1939), which was seen as a significant tool in social therapy (Jaques, 1947, 1948b). Put briefly, a system could be seen as being in a state of 'quasi-stationary equilibrium', with forces towards change counterbalanced by forces towards maintaining the status quo.

> The introduction of incentives without reference to the total setting does not necessarily produce desired changes which last for any effective period of time ... A field theoretical approach leads to abandonment of the search for incentives in favour of consideration of conditions which allow for maximum co-operation and morale in groups. (Jaques, 1947, p. 67)

Also reflected in that approach was the influence of the American human relations school of management, from which the Institute derived its journal's name. This had emerged in the early 1920s as a reaction against technologically focused scientific management – Taylorism – with its mechanistic models of work organization and the breaking down of jobs into their component activities. The seminal work of Elton Mayo, including the well-known Hawthorne experiment in General Electric, showed that employee involvement could have positive effects on morale, commitment and productivity. The need to meet the psychosocial needs of employees was both ideologically consistent with the democratic values of the founders of the Institute and also made practical sense. Studies in coal-mining (Trist and Bamforth, 1951; Trist et al., 1963) and experiments in cotton-weaving (Miller, 1975; Rice, 1953, 1958) led to the concept of work organization as a 'socio-technical' system. Whereas Taylorism gave ascendancy to the technical system and the human relations school to the social, the socio-technical system was seen as a product of the joint optimization of the activities of both systems (Emery and Trist, 1960). This work opened up the possibility of organizational choice – for a given technical system there could be alternative work organizations – and showed that technical systems were not, as commonly assumed, immutable: they could be modified in the service of joint optimization. Self-managing or 'semi-autonomous' work groups based on this principle showed significant gains in performance and job satisfaction and the concept of the socio-technical system gained wide international influence.

A further perspective, added from the beginning of the 1950s, was that of the 'open system theory', derived from Bertalanffy (1950a, 1950b). Originally formulated in studies of biological systems, it offered a way of analysing a human system, such as an enterprise, as an organism relating to its environment through a continuing cycle of taking in resources – raw materials, equipment, supplies, people – across the boundary, processing them in some way, and exporting the outputs. Any work organization is engaged in multiple tasks, some conscious, some unconscious, but Rice's proposition was that 'each system or sub-system has ... at any given time, one task which may be defined as its *primary task, the task which it is created to perform*' (Rice, 1958, p. 32, emphasis in original). Examples would be, in a business enterprise, to make profits or, for a public utility, to provide services. (Later he slightly reformulated it as 'the task that it must perform if it is to survive' (Rice, 1963, p. 13).) Within his open system framework, management, whether at system or sub-system level, can be seen as a *boundary* function, equivalent to the ego function of the individual, mediating between the inner world and the external environment.

Current theory and practice

By the mid-1960s, therefore, a set of four theoretical frameworks – psychodynamic, psychosocial, socio-technical, and systemic – was available and being used in the Institute's action research and consultancy with organizations. They have since been developed, built on and found serviceable in a wide variety of types of organizations, ranging from small community groups to nationalized industries and multinational businesses (see for example: Hirschhorn, 1988; Hirschhorn and Barnett, 1993; Miller, 1976, 1993, 1999b; Obholzer and Roberts, 1994). The experienced consultant, working with organizational design, development and change, determines, almost intuitively, which elements of this portfolio to use in different settings and in different phases of an intervention.

The psychodynamic perspective is never irrelevant. Initially it was taken for granted that the consultant/client relationship was analogous to the therapist/patient relationship. Today that feels less comfortable. The consultant is often interacting differently with different individuals in various roles and accountability becomes complex. Nevertheless the transference and countertransference are always there and can yield a rich source of data. The questions are whether, how and when to use it. Rice describes the professional judgement that has to be made:

> In responding to the contradictory demands made on him the consultant can behave in four ways: take up the overt problem only; deal with the overt problem but take account of what he believes to be the underlying difficulties without referring to them; take up both directly; or ignore the overt problem and take up directly only what is underlying. Which of these courses he takes will depend on his insight into the total situation; on his judgement of the real, as distinct from the expressed, needs of his client; on the relationship he has already built with his client; and on his belief in his ability to cope with whatever develops in the situation he helps to create. (Rice, 1963, p. 6)

In a long-term relationship the consultant may 'educate' the client system to pay attention to unconscious group and organizational dynamics; some clients are more sophisticated than others in this respect. Psychotherapists accustomed to working with individuals often find it difficult to shift their focus to the processes of the group as a group. However, even when these processes are identified, experience suggests that the psychodynamic interpretation is rarely effective on its own. While it may help a malfunctioning work group, it is not appropriate to operate as if it were a therapy group: it is also necessary to pay attention to the task and roles that the members bring to it. Indeed the focus of such a consultancy is better seen not just as the group itself but as the group in relation to its task and environment. Insight into unconscious processes will not produce useful change if, for example, structures are inappropriate. This was the point picked up by Jaques when, as mentioned earlier, he recanted his earlier proposition that all social institutions are used by their members as defences against anxiety: he now argues that rational organizational design eliminates the intrusion of dysfunctional unconscious processes (Jaques, 1955b). This is partly true: clarification or redrawing of organizational boundaries, for example, can 'design out' some of the ambiguities and discrepancies that cause unnecessary stress and conflict (Miller, 1999a). However, so long as the workplace remains a significant part of the individual's overall life-space it will continue to be a receptacle for shared unconscious projections.

This raises the wider question of how far this set of four theoretical frameworks remains relevant in light of the changes over the last 30 years. People have been withdrawing their psychological investment in the work organization; their dependency on it is less. Distance working is increasing and in some cases 'organizations' resemble networks rather than open systems. Given the rate of change, consultants may need to add complexity theory to their repertoire. Other organizational theories have proliferated and some can be useful. Nevertheless, when we look at the steps typically involved in a collaborative approach to organizational consultation, in which one is helping a client system to clarify and engage with its problems, it is evident that the four frameworks continue to be central.

Diagnosis is likely to require addressing the following set of questions:

- What are the throughputs of the system?
- What is being imported from the environment?
- How are these inputs being processed, and what are the outputs? The processing, which may be of raw materials in a manufacturing company or of people in a service, requires importing and mobilizing human and physical resources in a socio-technical system, and the perceived quality of the outputs – for example, the products of a factory or the graduates of a university – must be such as to generate the ongoing financial resources to sustain the cycle.
- What task(s) is the client engaged in? Developing Rice's notion of the primary task, Lawrence (1979) distinguished three types of tasks: normative, existential and phenomenal. The normative task is what the enterprise is set up to do: thus for a hospital it is treating patients. Existential tasks include other activities that people are aware of engaging in, such as: meeting performance indicators (which in the British National Health Service, for example, means that shortening waiting lists may take priority over treating patients); maintaining the 'informal organization' of interper-

sonal relationships; and increasing the power and influence of one's own sub-group. Awareness of political processes is essential, since any significant organizational change almost always involves a redistribution of power (Miller, 1979). Finally, the phenomenal tasks are those in which the members of an organization are unconsciously engaged, such as the collective defences against anxiety described by Jaques and Menzies.

- Where are the boundaries between sub-systems and between individual roles?
- Are they in the right place?
- Are they clearly defined or fuzzy?
- If fuzzy, is that helping or hindering performance of the normative task? A common problem is delegation of responsibility for a task without the requisite authority.
- What are the processes of transference and countertransference experienced by the consultant? Here the experienced psychotherapist has an advantage over many consultants in being able to recognize these processes and gain insights from them.

Plainly not all these questions can be asked outright – answers often have to be inferred – but these are the kinds of data that the consultant needs to collect, from interviews, discussions and available documentation, in order to arrive at a preliminary diagnosis. From these one can develop working hypotheses about why things are the way they are, what changes might be needed and where and how to start.

This last point is vital. As indicated earlier, one may have the most brilliant hypothesis, but if the client system cannot hear it nothing will happen. In collaborative consultancy, unless the client group is small enough for face-to-face work, it is often useful to prepare a 'working note' as a basis for dialogue with the people involved. This is not a report of the kind often used by management consultants but a more tentative document which presents, perhaps selectively (there may be constraints of confidentiality), the data collected so far, acknowledges that this may be incomplete and that there may be errors, puts forward a hypothesis, and suggests next steps that the client might take. The recommendations of a conventional report often lead to defensiveness and confrontation. By contrast, a working note, because its conclusions are avowedly tentative and the consultant is not over-identified with the content, provides for more genuine dialogues and makes it more possible for the client to take ownership of the decisions and actions that follow (Miller, 1995). In a limited consultancy contract the intervention may end there. Preferably, however, after action comes evaluation, which may lead to a reformulation of the hypothesis, further action, and so on. (In one case the author produced a series of 15 working notes over a period of three years of substantial change.)

What is being described here, therefore, is a macro-version of the ongoing cycle in which the psychotherapist is engaged while working with the individual patient. The difference is in the wider range of variables – social, systemic, technological, economic, and political – with which the effective organizational consultant needs to engage.

References

Bertalanffy L von (1950a) The theory of open systems in physics and biology. Science 3: 23-9.

Bertalanffy L von (1950b) An outline of general system theory. British Journal of the Philosophy of Science 1: 134-65.

Bion WR (1946) The leaderless group project. Menninger Clinic Bulletin 10: 77-81.

Bion WR (1948-51) Experiences in groups, I-VII. Human Relations 1-4.

Bion WR (1952) Group dynamics: a review. International Journal of Psycho-Analysis 33: 235-47.

Bion WR (1961) Experiences in Groups and Other Papers. London: Tavistock.

Bion WR, Rickman J (1943) Intra-group tensions in therapy. Lancet 2: 678-81.

Bridger H (1990) The discovery of the therapeutic community: the Northfield experiments. In EL Trist, H Murray (eds), The Social Engagement of Social Science: A Tavistock Anthology vol. I: The Socio-Psychological Perspective (68-87). Philadelphia: University of Pennsylvania Press; London: Free Association Books.

Dicks HV (1950) Personality traits and national socialist ideology: a war-time study of German prisoners-of-war. Human Relations 3: 111-54.

Dicks HV (1970) Fifty Years of the Tavistock Clinic. London: Routledge & Kegan Paul.

Emery FE, Trist EL (1960) Socio-technical systems. In CW Churchman, M Verhulst (eds), Management Sciences, Models and Techniques vol 2 (83-97). Oxford: Pergamon.

Fairbairn WRD (1952) Psychoanalytic Studies of the Personality. London: Tavistock.

Harrison T (1999) Bion, Rickman, Foulkes and the Northfield Experiments: Advancing on a Different Front. London: Jessica Kingsley.

Hirschhorn L (1988) The Workplace Within: Psychodynamics of Everyday Life. Cambridge, MA: MIT Press.

Hirschhorn L, Barnett CK (eds) (1993) The Psychodynamics of Organization. Philadelphia, PA: Temple University Press.

Jaques E (1947) Social diagnosis and social therapy. Journal of Social Issues 3(2).

Jaques E (1948a) Interpretative group discussions as a method of facilitating social change. Human Relations 1: 533-49.

Jaques E (1948b) Field theory and industrial psychology. Occupational Psychology 22: 126-33.

Jaques E (1953) On the dynamics of social structure: a contribution to the psychoanalytical study of social phenomena. Human Relations 6: 3-23.

Jaques E (1955a) Social systems as a defence against persecutory and depressive anxiety. In M Klein, P Heimann, RE Money-Kyrle (eds), New Directions in Psycho-Analysis (478-98). London: Tavistock.

Jaques E (1955b) Why the psychoanalytical approach to understanding organizations is dysfunctional. Human Relations 48: 343-9.

Klein M (1932) The Psychoanalysis of Children. London: Hogarth Press.

Klein M (1946) Notes on some schizoid mechanisms. International Journal of Psychoanalysis 27: 99–110.

Klein M (1949) Contributions to Psychoanalysis. London: Hogarth Press.

Klein M (1952) Some theoretical conclusions regarding the emotional life of the infant. In M Klein, P Heimann, S Isaacs, J Riviere (eds), Developments in Psychoanalysis (198–236). London: Hogarth.

Klein M (1959) Our adult world and its roots in infancy. Human Relations 12: 291–303.

Lawrence WG (1979) A concept for today: management of oneself in role. In WG Lawrence (ed), Exploring Individual and Organizational Boundaries (235–49). Chichester: Wiley.

Lewin K (1936) Principles of Topological Psychology. New York: McGraw-Hill.

Lewin K (1939) Field theory and experiment in social psychology: concepts and methods. American Journal of Sociology 44: 868–97.

Menzies IEP (1960) A case-study in the functioning of social systems as a defence against anxiety. Human Relations 13: 95–121.

Miller EJ (1975) Socio-technical systems in weaving, 1953–1970: a follow-up study. Human Relations 28: 349–86.

Miller EJ (ed) (1976) Task and Organization. Chichester: Wiley.

Miller EJ (1979) Open systems revisited: a proposition about development and change. In WG Lawrence (ed), Exploring Individual and Organizational Boundaries: A Tavistock Open Systems Approach (217–33). Chichester: Wiley.

Miller EJ (1993) From Dependency to Autonomy: Studies in Organization and Change. London: Free Association Books.

Miller EJ (1995) Dialogue with the client system: use of the 'working note' in organisational consultancy. Journal of Managerial Psychology 10(6): 27–30.

Miller EJ (1998) A note on the proto-mental system and 'groupishness': Bion's basic assumptions revisited. Human Relations 51: 1495–1508.

Miller EJ (1999a) Dependency, alienation or partnership? The changing relationship of the individual to the enterprise. In R French, R Vince (eds), Group Relations, Management, and Organization. Oxford: Oxford University Press.

Miller EJ (ed) (1999b) The Tavistock Institute Contribution to Job and Organizational Design (2 vols). Aldershot: Ashgate.

Miller EJ, Gwynne GV (1972) A Life Apart: A Pilot Study of Residential Institutions for the Physically Handicapped and the Young Chronic Sick. London: Tavistock.

Miller EJ, Rice AK (1967) Systems of Organisation: Task and Sentient Systems and Their Boundary Control. London: Tavistock.

Obholzer A, Roberts VZ (eds) (1994) The Unconscious at Work: Individual and Organisational Stress in the Human Services. London: Routledge.

Rice AK (1953) Productivity and social organisation in an Indian weaving shed. Human Relations 6: 297–329.

Rice AK (1958) Productivity and Social Organisation: The Ahmedabad Experiment. London: Tavistock.

Rice AK (1963) The Enterprise and its Environment: A System Theory of Management Organization. London: Tavistock.

Trist EL, Bamforth KW (1951) Some social and psychological consequences of the long-wall method of coal-getting. Human Relations 4: 3–38.

Trist EL, Murray H (eds) (1990) The Social Engagement of Social Science: A Tavistock Anthology, vol. I. The Socio-Psychological Perspective. Philadelphia, PA: University of Pennsylvania Press; London: Free Association Books.

Trist EL, Murray H (eds) (1993) The Social Engagement of Social Science: A Tavistock Anthology, vol. 2. The Socio-Technical Perspective. Philadelphia, PA: University of Pennsylvania Press.

Trist EL, Higgin GW, Murray H, Pollock AB (1963) Organizational Choice: Capabilities of Groups at the Coal Face under Changing Technologies. London: Tavistock.

CHAPTER 14

Tribal processes in psychotherapy: the stand off between psychoanalytic and systemic schools

SEBASTIAN KRAEMER

Introduction

Throughout its history family therapy has tended to disclaim any connection with psychoanalysis. Unlike the cold and unyielding analyst, the family systems therapist sees herself as much more equal and friendly. This posture has its origins at the beginning of family therapy, when it seemed necessary to overthrow the prevailing methods of psychiatry and psychoanalysis. As in the Russian revolution existing authorities were simply obliterated, as if they had never been. Even psychology was removed, and replaced with philosophy and engineering.

The conflict between psychoanalysis and systems therapy was historically necessary, but there is no continuing need for mistrust. Because each has a different task, both approaches will continue to develop in their own ways, but this will be greatly enriched if they can acknowledge each other's unique contributions to psychotherapy. Systems therapists cannot pretend that there was no useful therapy before they came along. Psychoanalysts, especially when their work is applied in mental health settings besides the consulting room, can learn from the strategic innovations of systems therapy. This is not a recommendation for integration, but for mutual recognition. Object relations psychoanalysis,[1] in particular, has many areas of overlap with systems theory, even though the languages are different.[2]

Patient or agent

Family therapy began in the 1950s, mainly in the United States. In the USA at that time psychoanalysis was a patriarchal profession. Only physicians could practise it. Transference interpretations would be given to a horizontal patient as if they were injections of the truth. Apart from 'material', patients

199

probably felt that they contributed little to the process. Family therapists wanted to engage more actively with their patients, and found the transference a constraint. In family therapy

> the therapist is less authoritarian. The traditional status differences of patient and therapist are downgraded, and there is a greater sense of mutual respect. The therapist is more humble, more open, more human and spontaneous. He takes the patient as a partner in the healing process ... (Ackerman, 1966)

Yet the transference, the fostering of which leads to so much mystification and misunderstanding, is not something that was invented by psychoanalysts. They were the first to describe it in any detail, and made it an analytic tool that brings experience to life in the room. But it is a naturally occurring phenomenon. When you go into a shop, for example, you have certain expectations of service, which are carried over from previous encounters of asking something for yourself. Children at school from time to time call their teachers 'mum'. Whether it is used or not, the transference is always at work in any kind of therapy.

The proper technique of psychoanalysis involves sitting out of sight behind the patient but this does not have to render the relationship distant or unfriendly. While therapists should not become friends with their patients there must always be opportunities for closeness, whether hostile or friendly, which may lead to change. Systemic therapists emphasize the conversation that takes place between client and therapist. This is in contrast with the more hierarchical ('expert/dummy' (Hoffman, 1985)) interaction that is supposed to take place in psychoanalysis. The use of the word conversation to describe warmer therapeutic encounters is also evident in modern work derived from object relations analytic practice, such as Robert Hobson's (1985). It is a useful term for the process of therapy in that it shows that some kind of exchange of views is taking place. But it also leaves out a lot. In day-to-day work with families most of us have also to make sense of more obviously emotional data, both in ourselves and our clients – movements, muscle tone, gestures, play, jokes, facial colour and expressions, clothing and manner, even smell. Most therapists would accept this list, but the language used to describe systemic work filters out these stressful or exciting bodily phenomena, so that only perceptions, thoughts and meanings are left. It tended, until relatively recently, to leave out the exchange of *experiences*, as if the therapy as described in its learned texts were really conducted over the phone or by email.

There is a richer use of the term 'conversation'. The interaction between infant and mother (or other caregiver) has been described in this way (Stern, 1985; Trevarthen, 1984), yet it is clearly not one that could be reduced to verbal exchange. Imagine trying to converse with a baby on the phone. The original 'system' is the mother–baby couple. 'There is no such thing as an infant', said the paediatrician/psychoanalyst Donald Winnicott in 1940.[3] Postwar psychoanalysis in the object relations tradition became increasingly interested in the way babies and mothers converse.[4] All psychoanalytic trainees now have to undertake infant observation for at least a year before starting clinical work. This combines theoretical and experiential data in a powerful way. Long before they can speak babies reach deep into our own minds by drawing us to them in an intense association, the prototype of all relationships (Murray and Andrews, 2000).

Alongside any more adult and reasonable requests they might make, people in distress will also have quite primitive assumptions about what we are going to do with them. The person seeking help always has two parts – the 'agent' who has to ensure the possibility of cooperation with the therapist (such as turning up for an appointment) and the 'patient' who brings more infantile expectations to the relationship (the transference). Therapy will be limited if either of these aspects is minimized. Classical psychoanalysis risked neglecting the agent, while systemic therapies may have neglected the patient.

The political impasse of psychoanalysis

Psychoanalysis inspires fear because analysts might read your mind. In spite of their best and most thoughtful efforts, the august psychoanalytic organizations have had considerable difficulty in showing to their critics that they have understood why they create such terror. The transference is, after all, always there and provokes a very primitive awe. Critics of psychoanalysis are wary of its power, particularly as it can be so easily abused. Systemic therapists, meanwhile, have grown up with the ghastly revelations of child sexual abuse, which we now know took place on a far greater scale than could have been believed in the past.[5] While psychoanalysis developed in spite of sexual abuse, the newer therapies have rightly tried to include an understanding of all abuses of power, both between genders and generations, into their methods. This, alongside embracing postmodernism, has been the decisive shift in systems therapy since the 1980s. By contrast the psychoanalytic institutions have until very recently seemed to be out of touch with social abuses such as racism, sexism and homophobia. This is partly due to the nature of psychoanalysis itself. Important social change does not necessarily impact on analytic ideas about early infant experience. For example, however much fathers may increase their participation in child care, for almost all infants the mother is usually still the primary psychological object, with whom the child wishes to have an exclusive relationship (Steiner, 1996). Psychoanalytic theory of mind does not seem to owe much to events in the external world. And psychoanalysts *were* slow to acknowledge real external events in the lives of their patients:

> What is true is that psychoanalysis for a long time tended to close its eyes and ears to psychic trauma. This includes the abuse of power, for example by adults against children, as well as social terror and violence. The complaints of survivors who suffered persecution and were threatened with extermination were for too long attributed to neurotic mechanisms dating from childhood ... Ill-treatment of children, sexual abuse and incest were frequently overlooked. (Halberstadt-Freud, 1996, p. 988)

Revolutions

Real and necessary differences between psychoanalysis and systems therapy have been polarized to such an extent that each denies the value of the other's work. In the beginning of family therapy psychoanalysts were simply too horrified at the upstarts to take them seriously. (Harold Searles (1965) is an exception.) The paradoxical interventions of the Mental Research Institute in California, for example (e.g. Watzlawick et al., 1967), seemed truly 'wild'. Later, the use of video and one way screens were regarded as unethical and intrusive, as they sometimes are. But they also create a new kind of openness between colleagues, and a guard against retrospective adornment of therapeutic bravado. While psychoanalysis has evolved greatly in the past fifty years, few analysts have acknowledged that any of this could have been due to the innovations of systemic therapy (see Dare, 1988; Larner, 2000; Luepnitz, 1988; McFadyen, 1997; Roberts, 1996).

Family therapists tended to see their own beginnings as a revolution rather than as any kind of development. By ignoring their roots, systems therapy wrote off the previous generation, with persecutory results. The ruthless suppression of the past led systemic therapists to a shared unconscious fantasy of an autocratic and insensitive person who cannot understand anything about racism, sexism and homophobia, or indeed about modern families. This figure is the ghost of Sigmund Freud. A brief survey (in a specialist bookshop) of the lists of references in around a dozen texts in psychoanalysis and systems therapy showed no evidence of mutual recognition. The vast majority of the texts cited by systems writers were published after 1956.

In that year, the centenary of Freud's birth, a brilliant quartet at Stanford University in California produced the first theoretical masterpiece of systems therapy - 'Towards a theory of schizophrenia' (Bateson et al., 1956). This - the proposal of the double bind hypothesis - was a challenge not only to the prevailing practices of psychiatry, but also to classical psychoanalysis, which was far more influential in mainstream psychiatry than it is today. Bateson, Jackson, Haley and Weakland offered a radically different way of looking at the workings of minds in severe pain. They identified chronic and perverse misunderstandings in an intense relationship as a condition of thought disorder.[6]

New voices were being heard in many places. This was at a time of postwar stirrings against imperial power in the Western world (decolonization of the British and French empires, Suez, Hungary etc.; and even revisionism in the East: in 1956 Khrushchev denounced Stalin at the 20th Soviet Party Conference), the very beginnings of anti-nuclear and anti-racist protest, and the first expressions of adolescent moods in theatre, literature and music. In the mental health field in Britain the psychoanalyst John Bowlby found himself isolated as he began to introduce ethology to the study of childhood development (Holmes, 1993). He was also seeing whole families in therapy, which no one had done before (Bowlby, 1949). While Bowlby was undertaking a radical revision of psychoanalysis, the Palo Alto researchers overthrew it entirely. They dispensed with psychology, and in its place put a theory of communication based on the early mathematical work of Bertrand Russell and Alfred North Whitehead (and to a lesser extent on the theory of self-governing systems – cybernetics – derived originally from engineering). Though brilliant, this was a significant step which left family systems therapy without a developmental and psychological base. It is significant that much of the most original systems work was based on the Palo Alto studies and on the work of Gregory Bateson, who was an anthropologist with no claim to clinical competence.

On the other hand the actual clinicians, such as Salvador Minuchin, Don Jackson, Carl Whitaker and Virginia Satir were superb, and charismatic, therapists. One of the crucial influences on the practice, as opposed to the theory, of family therapy was the work of Milton Erickson, a physician with a remarkable gift of hypnosis. He could entrance whole audiences. Gregory Bateson and Jay Haley (Haley, 1973) had observed his work closely, and strategic and structural techniques of family therapy, derived from Erickson's work, dominated the field until the Milan therapists took over in the 1980s. Making people change was the simple goal, and the methods were far from analytic. It is a curious irony that Freud himself started as a hypnotist.

While family therapy is approaching its half-century, psychoanalysis has already passed its centenary. *Studies on Hysteria*, by Josef Breuer and Sigmund Freud, was published in 1895, the *Interpretation of Dreams* in 1900. Here are the conditions for a classical oedipal contest between the old master and the young upstart, in which gratitude is stifled by anger and rivalry, and the fear of therapeutic impotence is routinely projected by one into the other. Although, or perhaps because, many of the first family therapists had been trained as analysts they had to obliterate the record, but in so doing replicated some of the patriarchal attitudes they had tried to escape from. This continued until it was pointed out to the young masters by the next generation, the first to be led by women therapists (Goldner, 1985; Hare-Mustin, 1994).

And while systems therapies were being conceived, psychoanalysis moved in new directions, particularly in its focus on the mind of the analyst. The countertransference, through which the therapist attends to his or her own fantasies and reactions to the patient (Heimann, 1950), was recognized as a technical development of Freud's 'evenly suspended attention' (see below). These developments were lost to systems therapy until much later, when rediscovered under different names, and graciously recognized by the exceptional Flaskas and Perlesz (1996).

New skills and convictions

Psychotherapy is potentially very demanding on all participants. Not much work can be done without some anxiety and some courage to deal with it. This is true of both therapists and patients, whatever kind of work they are doing, but the pressures on family therapists are of a different kind. Pure psychoanalytical technique is limited in effectiveness in the presence of an active, restless group of people like a family in trouble. A family is a more primitive organization than an individual. This is an ethological, not a moral, statement. Humans are, like many other group living mammals, intensely social creatures under constant pressures both towards conformity and rivalry. Family and systems therapists have had to devise new maps to guide them through the chaos. Most of these depend on the understanding that, unlike the individual mind, a family is an organization with little capacity for thought. Although we use words in interviews and hope to reach the ears and minds of each person in the room, the context and process of the meeting – who attends, and for what purpose – has as great an effect on the outcome as any reflections made during it. Salvador Minuchin (1974) and his colleagues demonstrated this in brilliant consultations at the Philadelphia Child Guidance Clinic in the 1970s. Minuchin made a simple and enduring point about families: that whatever the underlying condition or symptom children tend to improve when the parents can collaborate in looking after them.

A particular application of the structural model is in dealing with families where the parents are separated and continue to fight over their children. I and a colleague were asked to see a child who was said to be desperate about visiting his father. His mother sent us a tape recording of him shouting after a weekend with father. It was at once clear that the parents were in a poisonous and continuing dispute, involving lawyers, school teachers, family therapists and many more. With enormous difficulty we managed to get the parents together, without the child, and saw for ourselves how they could only argue. Yet there were tiny opportunities for compromise, and after 35 minutes I told them we had finished, that this was the best they could expect to achieve. I explained that they risked harming their child's emotional development if they continued to fight, and that he would gain nothing if one or other of them were to 'win'. With the parents' permission I put this in writing with a copy to the head teacher of the boy's school, whom mother had been particularly keen that I should contact. The child, whom I saw some months later on his own, seemed satisfied.

During the brief session with the couple I found myself filled with magisterial power. There was very little opportunity for conversation or discussion. The parents were squabbling children and I responded by being a bossy parent. Had I not held in my mind a basic assumption about how families function this would quite possibly have been abusive therapy. But I was confident that if parents can reduce their disagreements, their children will benefit. Together with the parents' urgent demand for help, this conviction gave me the authority to do what I did.

This intervention seems to owe nothing whatever to psychoanalytic wisdom or practice. The active instructive therapist is certainly not an analytic creature (he more closely resembles the chairman of a TV political debate). Haley and Minuchin, though steeped in the new theories, also knew that promoting change required powerful methods, and they were not afraid to charm and challenge families in equal measure. But they were also working in parallel with the object relations tradition that sees symptoms as bearers of meaning (Home, 1966; Rycroft, 1966), and not merely as the result of linear causes. Rather than ask what made this happen, the question is 'What is the function of this behaviour or complaint?' In this case the shouting, and the mother's bringing it to me, demanded a joint parental response.

Neutrality

The family therapists who followed Minuchin and his colleagues were increasingly preoccupied with families who seemed stubbornly unable to change. Their adolescent children suffered from appalling problems: eating disorders and other bizarre symptoms. Where parents were clearly helpless and apparently at the mercy of their disturbed offspring a new strategy was required. Rather than pressing families to change, the Milan team[7] saw that in these resistant cases it was far more effective not to try. The 'positive connotation' contained elements of the paradoxical techniques of the Mental

Research Institute and of the hypnotic methods of Milton Erickson, but the state of mind of the therapists was different (Kraemer, 1994). It was much closer to that of a psychoanalyst. The family were told that they should not expect, nor even try, to change. They learned, with some amazement, that the symptom which had so far baffled every therapist and psychiatrist who tried to shift it was actually necessary for the family's functioning. No doubt a better arrangement could be found in due course but 'for the time being' it had to be accepted. The therapeutic attitude required to work this way is one of heroic neutrality. An obligation to understand the present state of the family in all its complexity has to take precedence over the wish to get rid of the offending symptom. The Milan therapists made much of neutrality, and how one must be trained to achieve it – 'to see the system, to be interested in it, to appreciate this kind of system without wanting to change it' (Boscolo et al., 1987, p. 152). But it is not a new idea. Almost eighty years ago Freud wrote of the analyst's obligation to have 'evenly suspended attention' in the presence of the patient,

> to avoid so far as is possible reflection and the construction of conscious expectations, not to try to fix anything that he heard particularly in his memory, and by these means to catch the drift of the patient's unconscious with his own unconscious. (Freud, 1922)

No one in Western medicine or psychology had ever before suggested anything so radical. The conventional attitude of a healing practitioner was, and usually still is, to try to work out what is wrong with the patient and then try to change it. Freud's instructions still read like a message from another culture, from the East rather than the West. The British psychoanalyst Wilfred Bion took up the theme with his dictum that the analyst should 'inhibit dwelling on memories and desires' (1970, p. 41). Later (1987) he spoke of the effort required to get to therapy, and advised analysts to be impressed by the very fact of the patient's attendance. There is a clear continuity between this approach and the later developments of Milan systemic therapy. Gianfranco Cecchin's reflections (1987) on the mental state of systems therapists – 'an invitation to curiosity' – have become a classic in the family therapy literature. But neither neutrality nor curiosity can exist without a secure base of theory.

Of course Freud was a nineteenth-century man, and even Bion, though he died in 1979, could be regarded as a creature of a lost age. He had, after all, fought in World War I. In contrast, modern systems therapists are proud of their acute consciousness of the effects of culture on judgement, but this does not mean that we are free from such influences. Indeed it may even become a restraint if you try to censor your observations for fear of being derogatory or prejudicial. What is curiosity? If you are curious about something you want to know more about it. Cecchin, demonstrating his approach in a 1992 conference discussion, emphasized the urgency and compulsiveness of this state. Presenting work with a couple who are in a violent relationship, he asks them 'Why do you do this to each other?' This seems to be just the sort of question that anyone might ask. How is this different from the similar-sounding comments made by the couple's friends and relatives? One important difference is that the therapist is actually struggling to be more interested in finding an answer than in stopping the offending behaviour. The usual reason for asking such a question is less out of curiosity and more a way of saying 'Why do I have to put up with this?', which is not the same question at all.

Though neutrality is a goal to be aimed at, it is not achieved by ignoring one's prejudices. It is necessary to have some very ordinary emotions as a therapist, including rather innocent ones – as a small child might wonder about why people do what they do. Curiosity in a therapist requires an active exploration of one's own states of mind. Much of the material presented to us in clinical settings is quite upsetting, sometimes disgusting. The activity of seeking to answer the simple question 'why?' must entail some kind of self-analysis. How else is it possible to know what to ask? One would not get very far, in Cecchin's case, if one had not oneself been in a potentially violent situation with a loved person.

The innovations of the Milan group were themselves superseded by yet another revolution. The view that all perceptions, even of one's innermost feelings and thoughts, are socially constructed appears to have distanced family therapists even further from their psychoanalytical past. Gergen (1991) argues that looking for a deep structure is impossible. Instead understanding evolves by co-construction between people. Yet as a definition of an object relations psychotherapy this can hardly be bettered! The postmodern therapist eschews 'psychic reality', but a successful consultation with such a person might well be experienced by the client as an exploration of something very real and immediate, whatever language the therapist uses in her discussions with colleagues and in learned articles. Although social constructionism finally buried any traces of the objective in the systemic approach it did not – could not – remove the subjective. The hoped-for readiness of both therapist and client to accept what they find is a common feature, separated only by tribal definitions.

Our effectiveness as therapists depends ultimately on the fact that we are suffering humans too, with the advantage that we have been thinking about mental pain and have a language in which to talk about it. None of this is novel or surprising, yet there was until recently little evidence in systemic literature that therapists are willing to say where their questions come from.

Of course they come from our own minds, but these are minds that have been practising for years to think, and talk about love and hate, about mental and physical pain, grief and gratitude, dreams, desire, anxiety, envy, anger, jealousy, powerlessness, guilt and shame, masochism, sadism and revenge, dishonesty and betrayal, and so on. Countertransference fantasies require disciplined review during therapy. In the sense that our most basic experiences are shaped in the earliest relationships, all judgements about mental states are socially constructed, but 'social' usually refers to the wider culture. If thoughts and feelings are seen only as cultural constructions they will not survive as useful information for therapy.

Common ground: triangular relationships

In any human predicament there is always a story to tell about attachments and origins. Two people, a man and a woman, create a third, and a new chapter of the story begins. The earlier chapters are of course the stories from the previous generation, and these exert a powerful influence on what comes next. The triangles of family relationships are the stuff of psychotherapy, from the Oedipus complex to circular questioning, and beyond. Whatever form the family takes – lone parent, adoptive, step, extended – it will be made up of interlinking triangular relationships, even when these are not evident to outsiders. This is common knowledge among the therapeutic child and adolescent mental health professions, but it is also implicit in the observation that one of the primary functions of ordinary conversations is to talk about 'third parties', that is, to gossip (Dunbar, 1996). Dunbar argues that, while apes cement social relationships by grooming, humans, who live in larger groupings (and have not enough body hair), use gossip for the same purpose. In our conversations we are almost always busy with observations about others, but it is the original triangle, so elegantly described in a much-quoted paragraph by Ronald Britton, that we are all born into:

> If the link between the parents perceived in love and hate can be tolerated in the child's mind it provides him with a prototype for an object relationship of a third kind in which he is a witness and not a participant. A third position then comes into existence from which object relationships can be observed. Given this, we can also envisage being observed. This provides us with a capacity for seeing ourselves in interaction with others and for entertaining another point of view while retaining our own, for reflecting on ourselves while being ourselves. (1989, p. 87)

Though they speak in different languages[8] the theories that explore this process most fully are modern psychoanalysis and family therapy.

The conversation that is just beginning

At no time since the beginning of psychoanalysis has it, or any psychotherapy related to it, had a secure scientific or political base. The most powerful authorities in science, medicine and mental health are not generally friendly to therapy, because 'there is no evidence that it works' (even though there is: see Leff et al., 2000; Richardson and Hobson, 2000; Roth and Fonagy, 1996; Vetere, 2000). Meanwhile psychotherapists argue among themselves, yet from Mars, or even from the offices of any newspaper or TV station, the differences between systems therapy and psychoanalysis are virtually undetectable. Our disagreements can be ascribed to 'the narcissism of minor differences' – to use Freud's (1930) apt phrase – but they are, like sectarian religious or tribal ones, necessary anthropological processes. These are disputes not only about therapy but about human nature itself.

If therapy were only a social activity then we would all do it very differently! Unlike social intercourse, which is casual, therapists depend upon people coming for help, one by one, or family by family. This is a necessary condition of therapy and our only chance of being effective. You cannot offer therapy to people who do not ask for it. But when they do, they bring the power of the transference with them: the primitive hope (or fear) that something can be done by someone more powerful than themselves. Therapeutic work begins with the request for help and the task is defined by the naming of the problem. If that turns out only to be a social problem no therapy is possible, nor is it ethical to attempt it. It is interesting how clearly and intuitively people understand this. They do not come to us to change the injustices of the political world, but in personal pain. And these pains are powerfully determined by the intimate spirals that entwine members of families to one another, both past and present and, indeed, the inevitable injustices of such relationships. All this takes place in a social context (including one that aims to protect dependent people from abuse) but it is not a social process. Even when it seems friendly, it is not a task that real friends can properly perform. While personal relationships can be profoundly therapeutic, that is a side-effect, not an end in itself.

Change in therapy can be quite unexpected, to both therapist and patient. Unlike friends we deliberately set out to be surprising. The moments of transformation that we look for in therapy depend on our taking considerable risks, which would not be ethical without a firm base in good practice and good theory. Yet patients are not interested in theory. They are interested in therapists. Like boxers, they will push their partner to the ropes to see what they are made of. Psychotherapy is intensely personal, after all. Besides sympathy and understanding, bullying and seduction are also ingredients in an intimate relationship, whether social or therapeutic. An explicit commitment to avoid these undesirables is necessary in any therapy training, but it is not on its own sufficient to prevent it. In any case we need to use our prejudices in a conscious and active way. Clinical hypotheses are generated from half-formed thoughts and feelings that are not always polite.

In the end the tale is a moral one. Moments of change in therapy depend on making connections, primarily between experience and thought, but the quality that makes the difference is authenticity. This is an aesthetic sense of rightness that (almost) everyone can recognize. It is what makes the difference between good and bad drama, novels, poems and so on. Whatever else it involves, our craft is a literary one, with all the possibilities and pitfalls that that entails. The greatest crime that the therapist, or the client, can commit is lying. We do not have to have a theory of 'truth' to accept that dishonesty undermines therapy. The experience of connectedness between therapist and client is, as every research study invariably concludes, one of the strongest predictors of effectiveness. Honesty and courage are the most highly valued qualities in therapy.

For and against integration

Integration of therapies should not be a goal in itself. It is a good idea to be acquainted with the range of therapies available. The monotherapist, who sees every problem in terms of one theory, is going to be helpful only to those patients that fit the theory. No theory fits all patients, so some will be mistreated by this approach. Therapy trainings must, and usually do, ensure that students know the limitations of the method they are learning. On the other hand an integrative or eclectic approach, though superficially attractive and inclusive, risks leaving the practitioners with no convictions at all, except an exaggerated belief in their own capacity to help everyone. A certain fundamentalism, based on principles to which one returns at points of crisis, is required to do therapy well. This is quite different from slavish adherence to dogma, so anathema to the theme of this book. Good theories always require exploration afresh at every new turn; they don't generate answers, only questions. True eclecticism has to weigh the relative merits of different methods to suit the skills, tasks and personality of the therapist. That is what patients want, and need: a person who understands the theories ('knows his stuff') and can at the same time note carefully just how and where the patient doesn't quite fit any of them. The patient will discover that such a person, when up against the ropes, will talk straight, and not take refuge in mystification.

The purpose of this chapter is not to propose an integration of psychoanalytic and systems techniques but to encourage the putting together of the fractured story of therapy. No doubt it was necessary to make the break in the 1950s and '60s. The gravitational pull of the prevailing theories was just too strong to allow for radical change. But now that the revolution is over an appreciation of the past is necessary, and evolution can take its place.

Acknowledgements

This chapter is a much revised version of 'What Narrative?', published in Renos Papadopoulos and John Byng-Hall (eds) (1997), *Multiple Voices - A Richer Story: Contributions to Systemic Family Psychotherapy from the Tavistock Clinic, London: Duckworth. Reproduced with permission.*

I am grateful to Jeremy Holmes, Peter Loader, Anne McFadyen and Justin Schlicht for helpful comments on the original chapter.

Notes

[1] Unless otherwise qualified, 'psychoanalysis' will refer to the object relations tradition in its broadest meaning, incorporating the work of Melanie Klein and her successors, and the Independent ('British') school, Donald Winnicott, W.D. Fairbairn, John Bowlby, Michael Balint and their successors.

[2] For instance, the state of mind attained by thinking systemically has something in common with the depressive position which acknowledges conflict within oneself, while 'linear thinking' is more preoccupied with an external cause and with blame, the paranoid position.

[3] This statement was never published, but Winnicott recalls that he said it in a scientific meeting of the British Psycho-analytical Society in about 1940.

[4] Attachment theory grew out of this preoccupation, and has led to new insights into underlying biological processes: 'a conversation between brains' (Schore, 1997).

[5] One of the reasons, perhaps, why Freud changed his mind about the origins of hysteria; his earlier post-traumatic theory of neuroses was abandoned in favour of what was to become psychoanalysis proper. The trauma was sexual abuse.

[6] See Jacobsen, Hibbs and Ziegenhain (2000) for a modern reworking of this desperate entanglement. The study of attachment disorganization (Solomon and George, 1999) promises to be a major step in the systematic understanding of pathogenic relationships.

[7] As reported in *Paradox and Counterparadox*, the second masterpiece in systems therapy (Selvini Palazzoli et al., 1978).

[8] It is a fundamental tenet of family systems theory that a quality or experience may be passed around from one person to another, so that one individual may carry an anxiety or symptom on behalf of others, or of the family as a whole. The mechanism of this is, however, dependent on processes such as projective identification - an entirely psychoanalytic concept - which was explored and developed in parallel with family therapy during the post-war years (Hinshelwood, 1991)

References

Ackerman NW (1966) Treating the Troubled Family. New York: Basic Books, p. 54.
Bateson G, Jackson D, Haley J, Weakland J (1956) Towards a theory of schizophrenia. Behavioral Science 1(4). Reprinted in G. Bateson (1973) Steps to an Ecology of Mind. St Albans: Paladin, p. 195.

Bion W (1970) Attention and Interpretation. London: Tavistock, p. 42.

Bion W (1987) Clinical Seminars, Brasilia and São Paulo, and Four Papers. Abingdon: Fleetwood Press.

Boscolo L, Cecchin G, Hoffman L, Penn P (1987) Milan Systemic Family Therapy: Conversations in Theory and Practice. New York: Basic Books, p. 152.

Bowlby J (1949) The study and reduction of group tensions in the family. Human Relations 2: 123-8. Reprinted in E Trist, H Murray (eds) (1990) The Social Engagement of Social Science: A Tavistock Anthology, Vol. 1: the Socio-Psychological Perspective. Philadelphia: University of Pennsylvania Press, 291-8.

Britton R (1989) The missing link: parental sexuality in the Oedipus situation. In R Britton, M Feldman, E O'Shaughnessy (eds), The Oedipus Complex Today: Clinical Implications. London: Karnac.

Cecchin G (1987) Hypothesizing, circularity, neutrality revisited: an invitation to curiosity. Family Process 26: 405-13.

Dare C (1998) Psychoanalysis and family systems revisited: the old, old story? Journal of Family Therapy 20: 165-76.

Dunbar R (1996) Grooming, Gossip and the Evolution of Language. London: Faber & Faber.

Flaskas C, Perlesz A (1996) The Therapeutic Relationship in Systemic Therapy. London: Karnac.

Freud S (1922) Two encyclopaedia articles, (A) Psycho-analysis. In The Standard Edition of the Complete Psychological Works of Sigmund Freud (trans J Strachey) (1955) vol. XVIII. London: The Hogarth Press, p. 239.

Freud S (1930) Civilization and its discontents. In The Standard Edition of the Complete Psychological Works of Sigmund Freud (trans J Strachey) (1961) vol. XXI. London: The Hogarth Press, p. 114.

Gergen K (1991) Exchanging Voices. London: Karnac.

Goldner V (1985) Feminism and family therapy. Family Process 24: 31-45.

Halberstadt-Freud HC (1996) Studies on hysteria one hundred years on: a century of psychoanalysis. International Journal of Psycho-Analysis 77: 983-96.

Haley J (1973) Uncommon Therapy: The Psychiatric Techniques of Milton Erickson MD. New York: Norton.

Hare-Mustin R (1994) Discourses in a mirrored room: a post-modern analysis of therapy. Family Process 33(19-35): 22.

Heimann P (1950) On countertransference. International Journal of Psycho-Analysis 31: 81-4.

Hinshelwood R (1991) A Dictionary of Kleinian Thought. London: Free Association Books, pp. 179-208.

Hobson RF (1985) Forms of Feeling. London: Tavistock.

Hoffman L (1985) Beyond power and control: towards a 'second order' family systems therapy. Family Systems Medicine 3: 381-96.

Holmes J (1993) John Bowlby and Attachment Theory. London: Routledge.

Home HJ (1966) The concept of mind. International Journal of Psychoanalysis 47: 43-9.

Jacobsen T, Hibbs E, Ziegenhain U (2000) Maternal expressed emotion related to attachment disorganisation in early childhood: a preliminary report. Journal of Child Psychology and Psychiatry 41: 899-906.

Kraemer S (1994) The promise of family therapy. British Journal of Psychotherapy 11: 32–45.

Larner G (2000) Towards a common ground in psychoanalysis and family therapy – on knowing not to know. Journal of Family Therapy 22: 61–82.

Leff J, Vearnals S, Wolff G et al. (2000) The London Depression Intervention Trial: randomised controlled trial of antidepressants v. couple therapy in the treatment and maintenance of people with depression living with a partner: clinical outcome and costs. British Journal of Psychiatry 177: 95–100.

Luepnitz D (1988) The Family Interpreted. New York: Basic Books.

McFadyen A (1997) Rapprochement in sight? post-modern family therapy and psychoanalysis. Journal of Family Therapy 19: 241–62.

Minuchin S (1974) Families and Family Therapy. London: Tavistock Publications.

Murray L, Andrews L (2000) The Social Baby. Richmond, Surrey: CP Publishing.

Richardson PH, Hobson RP (2000) In defence of NHS psychotherapy. Psychoanalytic Psychotherapy 14: 63–74.

Roberts J (1996) Perceptions of the significant other of the effects of psychodynamic psychotherapy: implications for thinking about psychodynamic and systemic approaches. British Journal of Psychiatry 168: 87–93.

Roth A, Fonagy P (1996) What Works for Whom? New York: Guilford Press.

Rycroft C (1966) Causes and Meaning. Reprinted in Psychoanalysis and Beyond (1991) London: Hogarth Press.

Schore A (1997) Interdisciplinary developmental research as a source of clinical models. In M Moskowitz, C Monk, C Kaye, S Ellman (eds), The Neurobiological and Developmental Basis for Psychotherapeutic Intervention. Northvale, NJ: Aronson.

Searles HF (1965) The contributions of family treatment to the psychotherapy of schizophrenia. In I Boszormenyi-Nagy, JL Framo (eds), Intensive Family Therapy. Hagerston, MD: Harper & Row.

Selvini Palazzoli M, Boscolo L, Cecchin G, Prata G (1978) Paradox and Counterparadox. New York: Jason Aronson.

Solomon J, George C (1999) Attachment Disorganization. London: Guilford Press.

Steiner J (1996) The aim of psychoanalysis in theory and in practice. International Journal of Psycho-Analysis 77: 1073–83.

Stern D (1985) The Interpersonal World of the Infant. New York: Basic Books.

Trevarthen C (1984) Emotions in infancy: regulators of contacts and relationships with persons. In K Scherer, P Ekman (eds), Approaches to Emotion. Hillsdale NJ: Erlbaum.

Vetere A (2000) On the effectiveness of family, marital and systemic therapies. In S McPherson, P Richardson (eds), Clinical Audit and Clinical Effectiveness: Resource Pack for Clinicians. London: Tavistock & Portman NHS Trust.

Watzlawick P, Beavin JH, Jackson DD (1967) Pragmatics of Human Communication. New York: WW Norton.

Index

Lightning Source UK Ltd.
Milton Keynes UK
UKOW04f0807260116

267096UK00002B/380/P